WHAT PEOPLE ARE SA[...]

BEING BRI[...]

This is a sane, witty and shrewd picture of British identity—neither cynical nor paranoid, which is quite an achievement. Chris Parish sketches very skilfully the history and habits that make up this many-layered identity and gives us some essential tools for working out what we can properly celebrate, what we should properly regret and what we might reasonably hope for—what a mature sense of national self-esteem might look like.
Dr Rowan Williams, Former Archbishop of Canterbury, theologian, Master of Magdalene College Cambridge

Enjoyed its breadth and ambition—and optimism
David Goodhart, Founder of Prospect magazine, former Director of Demos think tank, author of *The British Dream*

Chris Parish has written a comprehensive, provocative and deeply thoughtful exploration of what it means to be British today. He skilfully integrates a wide range of perspectives and approaches to provide a much needed and refreshing synthesis of the positive potential of British identity, understanding and belonging. He is fearless in his honesty and in addressing all the arenas which he believes are vital to a rearticulation of the 'British Journey' and a powerfully constructive and important role for Britain into the future. As a British citizen I felt inspired, challenged and expanded by the book, but most of all, a powerful pride, delight and enhanced positivity about being British. A must read for anyone interested in the nature of Britishness and a much needed contribution to this field.
Dr Lynne Sedgmore CBE, Previously Chief Executive of three organisations in the UK Further Education sector, currently organisational consultant.

Thought provoking, humbling, inspiring—a veritable tour de force. Concerned that our postcolonial guilt has left no metanarrative or clear sense of who we are, Parish steps lightly, yet studiously, through our shared story. He encourages us to be in touch with the creative thread of this country, to know the past, warts and all, so that we might rediscover our connection, continuity and rootedness and remain a major player in the postmodern world. I am left with strengthened pride in being British.

Prof Julia Hausermann MBE, Founder and President, Rights and Humanity

Chris Parish provides a welcome reasoned statement for moderation and integration in approaching major issues and Britain's place in the world. Parish calls for taking a long-term approach to these issues, one that incorporates a more positive view of Britain's past while integrating that history into British identity and Britain's approach to current problems.

Dr George L Bernstein, Professor of History, Tulane University. Author of *The Myth of Decline: The Rise of Britain since 1945*

Being
British

Our Once and Future Selves

For Joshua

With warm wishes
& thanks !

Chris Parish

Being British

Our Once and Future Selves

Chris Parish

Winchester, UK
Washington, USA

First published by Chronos Books, 2016
Chronos Books is an imprint of John Hunt Publishing Ltd., Laurel House, Station Approach,
Alresford, Hants, SO24 9JH, UK
office1@jhpbooks.net
www.johnhuntpublishing.com

For distributor details and how to order please visit the 'Ordering' section on our website.

ISBN: 978 1 78535 328 4
Library of Congress Control Number: 2015956007

A CIP catalogue record for this book is available from the British Library.

Design: Stuart Davies

Printed and bound by CPI Group (UK) Ltd, Croydon, CR0 4YY, UK

We operate a distinctive and ethical publishing philosophy in all
areas of our business, from our global network of authors to
production and worldwide distribution.

CONTENTS

Introduction

Why another book about the British, you may well ask? There's already, after all, quite a few of them out on the market. Is this some nostalgic journey back to an imagined rosy past, or its opposite twin, one more postmodern deconstruction of our history? And, in addition, there seems to be a rich seam to be mined in the genre of witty examinations of the peculiarities and eccentricities of this island race, such as Jeremy Paxman's *The English*. Well, this book is genuinely none of the above, which I hope by the end of this introduction, will be clear. I feel there is a genuine need to present a revised view of the British which is more inclusive and fluid in its approach and one that reconnects us to our national story: a story through time which is living and which could also help shape our future. A way to rediscover a lost sense of belonging and of feeling at home, which perhaps paradoxically, is at once both less traditional and more traditional.

Before going any further though, I'd like to address one obvious question. I'm saying us British. Why aren't I saying us English, you might ask? It's as confusing and contentious to natives as it is to everyone else, with the UK, Great Britain, the British Isles, Britain and England, all in common use. The 2013 Social Attitudes Survey of the UK found that only 43 per cent of people in England see their primary identity as being British, and that percentage goes down further in the other constituent countries of the UK. People in the UK are now more likely to see themselves as Scottish, Welsh, or English or Northern Irish. We also can't even think of identifying Britain as only a single island off the coast of continental Europe since it, obviously enough, includes many islands and part of the island of Ireland too. British 'Isles' is an attempt to include all of them; amazingly, some 6000, mostly tiny islets in total, though the people of Eire

1

understandably wouldn't want to be lumped in like this. Interestingly, the only section of the population in this country where a majority pick 'British' as their preferred identity, are those who are more recent immigrants.

I was at a fundraising dinner in London for a charity involved in Third World Aid and the keynote speech was by the then Labour MP for Glasgow Central, Anas Sarwar. This was before the SNP rout of Labour in 2015. The young speaker was impressively bright and inspiring to listen to. He said that his background was Pakistani and stated that he was 100 per cent British and Scottish too. Speaking in a broad Scottish accent, he talked of serving this great country of ours. Somehow it would have been very unusual to hear a similar spirit being expressed by a Briton *not* from an immigrant background.

Billy Bragg, the well-known singer/songwriter, is a great advocate for the English identity and has spoken strongly of the need to retire the term 'British' as long past its sell-by date. Yet there were ancient Britons (i.e. the British) long before the Anglo-Saxon invasions which followed the departure of the Romans in the fifth century AD, and the source, of course, of the name 'English'. So a good case could also be made that 'British' is not just an embarrassing colonial concoction to be abandoned. Yet, even so, it has to be said, it's a complex picture, especially since historians now dispute how much the Anglo-Saxon immigrants actually did displace the original inhabitants in order to lay down the foundations of Englishness. It seems we are a real mix, as comedian Eddie Izzard amusingly illustrated in his informative film on our identity, *Mongrel Nation*.

There's also the big question of whether it is a *united* kingdom at all, with the call for ever increasing devolution, if not full independence for Scotland. The September 2014 referendum on Scottish independence came far closer than most people expected to the Scots choosing to leave the union. This has shaken up any cosy and unquestioning notions of an unchanging Great Britain.

And also Wales, to a lesser extent, has increasingly chosen to devolve, though not to seek independence. Then there are people like me who use the terms British and English interchangeably to describe who I am, and feel that both apply at different moments. So I'm not going to attempt to settle this debate and will use both terms here. I am, in fact, half Scottish, half English, my mother coming from the Scottish western Isle of Bute, though I was born and brought up in England.

Now the subject of devolution for England and what it means to be English has taken on new life following the Scottish referendum. The terms English and British are particularly hazy for English people. It's worthy of a whole book in itself, yet in this study here, I am deliberately largely leaving aside a fuller investigation of that particular subject, because I want to focus on other issues. Similarly the subject of social class naturally comes up when the British are discussed, and this is a very valid subject in itself as to its origins, effects and seemingly particular persistence in this country. Yet I am deliberately also leaving class aside in this study in order to focus on aspects of our nation and ourselves which have in my opinion not been given sufficient attention.

From a twenty-first century perspective, a significant reality for us on this small rainy island with its myriad accompanying tiny islets, whatever name we give ourselves, seems to be that we are part of the EU; that is unless the current anti-European sentiment intensifies and in the planned referendum, we do decide to 'leave Europe', as if we could somehow tow the country a further distance off the coast of the continental mainland to emphasise our independence. We live in a de facto globalised world, where, like it or not, historical lines of demarcation on a map, or the small ribbon of water called 'The Channel' mean very little to the internet, to global markets, to the IMF, to multinational corporations; and mean nothing at all to climate change and the wind currents of carbon dioxide levels, or to the complex cycle of water currents which drive the Gulf Stream and thankfully, up to this point at least, prevent us from being an Arctic country, Britain being on the same latitude as Canada's Hudson Bay, where polar bears roam.

Then again, aren't many of us post-traditional individuals who have left behind antiquated fixations on nationality, which by their very focus on such labelling are inherently divisive? In this view, surely I'm a person who thinks for him or herself; a human being, a member of our interconnected global village? And yes, well, technically I'm British, as it states in my passport. After all, we all have to be born somewhere, on some particular patch of earth on this delicate blue planet.

Well, this was my more sophisticated view of myself, when I became an adult complete with a liberal university education under my belt. Although I have to admit that this view never really explained the strong feelings that I would sometimes experience within myself and which I gradually came to realise motivate me more than I would have imagined. For example, on one hand I felt bad about the exploitative imperialism of my country's history, and in another moment I could well up with pride and emotion about great British military victories of the past. And in another moment I could feel an inarticulate pessimism that this country is sliding ever further down the slope of decline. We are all more complex human beings than my sophisticated but somewhat two-dimensional former post-national view tended to suggest.

We all physically live in the same world and yet when it comes to the interpretation of our own experience, we actually live in many different and only partially overlapping worlds. And when it comes to nationalities, similar differences apply too. I've spent several years living in the United States, on both East and West coasts, as well as in Australia, and in Holland and Germany. Those years helped open my eyes to the fact that different nationalities really do have some significantly different basic assumptions about reality, and that there are important differences between nationalities as well as important national commonalities. The difference between the prevailing attitude in the United States where a first-term Barack Obama could initially have been elected on the wings of the campaign slogan 'Yes, we can!', and the British attitude, is greater than the Grand Canyon. The British zeitgeist would be better captured by, 'Well, actually, no, we can't, thank you!' The difference between the easy life in Australia, where 'No problems' is a stock answer in a land where the majority of the population live around the fringes of the continent near the sun drenched beach, and a British sense of decline with still lingering notions of a 'Broken Britain', courtesy of the Conservative advertising campaign for the 2010 General Election, are similarly large.

Yet if you are like me, and have a liberal background, you will no doubt also instinctively be repelled by such crude sounding aggregating generalisations. I would have dismissed such generalities as the raw material for downmarket comedians, or reserved for the gift shop book series, *The Xenophobe's Guide to the French/Germans/Japanese*, etc., etc... But I've come in fact to think differently over time and if I may say, through quite a bit of experience and contemplation. On returning to live in England, I came to realise that we really do have a certain cultural predicament in this Sceptred Isle, this green and pleasant land of ours. To say it simply and crudely, we currently have a overly pronounced tendency towards cynicism and pessimism, feeling we are in decline as a nation, with no clear sense of national identity; no living national story to inspire us; and precious little connection to our collective past or aspirations as to our future. I will first attempt to explain the problem in this book while not dwelling on what's wrong. More importantly and more interestingly, I identify the cause as I see it, and throughout the book attempt a rebalancing of this heavily skewed view of ourselves: towards what I could call a healthy national psyche, rooted in our shared story and able to draw upon our long term rich national resources. I also suggest possible ways to help effect this change. Throughout I include myself as the first object of study. I offer pointers as to how we may face our shadows, develop beyond our current limitations and discover a more positive self-identity and sense of belonging, both as a nation and as individuals, assisted in part by recognising and aligning with a deeper creative thread in ourselves.

I'm writing here for people like myself; for progressive liberals with postmodern, post-traditional sensibilities. I am proud of being British. I know that's not politically correct, and having been left-leaning my entire adult life, just writing that phrase can feel almost like mouthing a profanity. And I certainly don't unthinkingly back everything our nation has done in the past or is doing currently. I'm talking about basically feeling positive about myself and my national sense of self, as opposed to being cynical or ashamed about who we are as a nation and who I am. I feel passionately about liberating our creative talents, and it's not my intention to heap on further disparagement, as I am aware that complaining seems to have become something of a national mantra. I'm an idealist, but I don't think that has to mean jettisoning my rational faculties. I mean a realistic idealism. And if the notion of a realistic idealism sounds hopelessly starry-eyed and naïve to you, or even dangerous, well, just maybe, perhaps this could be a symptom of the very national syndrome I am pointing to?

This book is my sincere attempt to communicate and bring together threads that many of us may feel we already know, but perhaps haven't deeply considered as a whole. It's serious stuff, but I don't think that has to mean overbearing or heavy. In fact I've learned from my experience of public speaking that we British are far more likely to listen and consider information (and trust the speaker, too), if it is also delivered with a touch of humour. The subject here may at times appear sociological and academic, but my approach throughout is not. Yes, I bring in elements of developmental theory, history and a sprinkling of philosophy, but it's also very much based on real people, real incidents, and most of all, on my own personal experience.

I am not an historian, sociologist or any other kind of academic. I think of myself as a generalist, by which I mean my interests are broad rather than being specialist. Ever increasing specialisation is the inexorable direction in our times in the professions and academia, and of course this has been and continues to be very important in the advancement of human knowledge. But less valued these days, in my opinion, is the generalist who may be able to recognise patterns and connections from across the spectrum of life, culture and human endeavour, which may not be visible to the specialist. Carter Phipps in his *Evolutionaries: Unlocking the Spiritual and Cultural Potential of Science's Greatest Idea*, identifies being a cross-disciplinary generalist as one of the important characteristics of the type of people he has termed 'evolutionaries': which means those, in often very different fields of endeavour, who are forging new pathways based on a reframing and widening of evolutionary understanding.

This brings me to another key thread which runs through this book and which is a helpful orienting lens through which I am looking at the question of what it means to be British today. And this is namely an evolutionary worldview or perspective. This view has afforded me a wider context to make better sense out of my experience. It's a fairly recently emerging perspective of the last few decades, although its origins go back quite a bit further. On first hearing, this view can appear a bit abstract, so please do bear with me as I attempt in the following chapters to bring to life what it means. I feel it can enable us to come to a better understanding of how culture and society develops, of our intrinsic place and continuity in this national story, and also of the creative process in ourselves and in the nation.

You may already be wondering if I'm just suggesting an extension of classical Darwinism or of Neo-Darwinism as it has now become. I was originally trained in biology and value the evolutionary view of biology as a giant step forward in human knowledge. But by developmental or evolutionary perspective, I am meaning much more than the very circumscribed biological interpretation of evolution in which all human development and culture is seen only as a result of Darwinian natural selection and the random mutation of genes. This view is quite in vogue these days as an expanding catch-all explanation of human culture and society. Researchers keep coming up with ever more ingenious explanations of how human behaviour or culture can plausibly be traced back to the adaptive advantage that this gave us in our prehistoric past. For example, offering the explanation that religious feelings were adopted because they created stronger bonds between people, thus conferring a selective advantage to our tribal ancestors.

I mean by developmental perspective, however, something much wider than this: a worldview which encompasses the evolution of culture, the development of values, of ideas and beliefs, of perspectives themselves, of meaning, of sense of self and identity, of consciousness, of spirituality and religion; and well, virtually anything else. This viewpoint can give us, I feel, an illuminating way to see patterns in our human development and also to see potential ways forward and also limiting pathologies. I will explain how this view is both wide and philosophical and yet simultaneously personal and pragmatic.

What I'm endeavouring to do in this book, to put it another way, at its very simplest, could be summed up as this: in order to understand how to approach the future, we need to understand what it means to be British now, and to do this, we need to understand where we have come from and what has shaped and formed us. We always have been part of a story, but today in Britain we have lost conscious touch with that thread, and we are in need of a new living story. As Simone Weil said,

> To be able to give, one has to possess; and we possess no other
> life, no other living sap, than the treasures stored up from the
> past and digested, assimilated and created afresh by us. Of all
> the human soul's needs, none is more vital than this one of the
> past.

My aim throughout this book is to focus not on what's wrong,
but on a healthy reappraisal of ourselves and to effect a rebalancing of our overly pessimistic national view of ourselves; to
assist in seeing how we might best go forward in these times of
great disruption. So I guess you could say that I lean towards the
'Yes, we can!' school of thought. In the light of the 2012 London
Olympics, which, if you remember, brought to the fore another
side of the British, perhaps this sentiment might not be so far
from the British mind-set as we are used to thinking.

Chapter 1

It's Getting Better All the Time...Or Is It?

The past is not dead, it is living in us, and will be alive in the future which we are now helping to make.
William Morris

It would be useless to turn one's back on the past in order to simply concentrate on the future. It is a dangerous illusion to believe that such a thing is even possible. The opposition of future to past or past to future is absurd. The future brings us nothing, gives us nothing; it is we who in order to build it have to give it everything, our very life.
Simone Weil

A British Dream

Recently I had a lucid dream. It was one of those dreams so vivid and tangible that it really felt like I was awake throughout the whole experience. It was so striking and meaningful I recorded it in my diary. Here's an excerpt:

I don't recognize the place where I am except it's clearly somewhere in Britain and there is a sense of vast space without any limitations at all. Everything is bright and spotlessly clean and it all feels enormously inviting. I'm walking across the open ground in the brilliant morning sunshine, and there is a clear path and I become aware that I'm not alone. I am accompanied by a great throng of people of all backgrounds, ethnicities, young and old. And this multitude of us is walking together and everyone is disarmingly friendly and effusive and caring. They mainly seem to be British as far as I can make out from hearing their voices. There are also people who seem to be there purely to greet us and help us, and apparently no trouble is too much for them. Yet it seems that they are not employees; it is only out of love that they offer this generosity of spirit.

As we march on, I see people sitting strangely high above us as if on stilts, and these people offer us uplifting thoughts and cheerful messages as we pass. We enter a beautiful park and there are meadows of wildflowers swaying in the gentle breeze, and huge wonderful buildings sparkle in the preternatural morning light. I feel a weight drop away from me that I hadn't realized that I was carrying. In the experience I somehow know that Life is overwhelming good in spite of everything, and it feels like a deeply healing salve for the soul.

An uplifting dream...a British Nirvana, no less. And yet it wasn't a dream. Believe it or not, it's a pretty accurate description of my experience of alighting from Stratford station in East London and walking to the Olympic Park in the summer of 2012.

Up to right before the opening ceremony, the talk in Britain had largely been of how the transport system would creak and collapse under the strain. It would be chaos, there would be unheard of delays, terminal gridlock and London would more or less implode. The media was overflowing with all manner of predictable British moaning and dwelling on what could possibly, and most likely—in fact certainly—would go wrong, because it's Britain and everything is expected to go wrong.

As we all know, the Olympics was spectacularly successful on every level and none of these calamities came to pass. Danny Boyle's opening ceremony set the tone and it was staggeringly inventive, bold, positive and interwoven with humour, such as only the British could pull off. I found myself drawn magneti-cally to the TV to watch every scrap of the Olympics I could, and when the Paralympics came, well, that was, if anything, even more inspiring and moving. We believed we could succeed and we did, and with success came more and more positivity. The

Union Jack flags, so long the more or less exclusive domain and symbol of the BNP and fellow extremist travellers, came to represent again, at least for the duration of the Games, all the people of these islands, as Britons of all ethnic backgrounds would drape themselves in the national flag on their victory laps. The message was reinforced again and again: Being British equals success, positivity; black, white, brown equals inclusivity. We were proud to be British, yet, at the same time, not at all narrowly nationalistic, for we graciously cheered the endeavours of athletes from all the other countries, too.

I realized afterwards how amazing and refreshing it was to hear not a trace of cynicism or carping from the media for a full six weeks. It's only when it's absent temporarily that I realised just how ubiquitous it normally is in our country. It was like going on a fast from negativity for six weeks. This was a unique rejuvenating experience for me and truly gave a taste of how we could be as a nation.

How much the spirit of the Olympics truly might mark the birth of a new sense of positivity and confidence in us British as a nation still remains to be seen over a longer period of time. Commentators are quick to point out that there's always an 'Olympic effect' in host cities and countries, which wears off over time. Undoubtedly so, and in many ways we British did slide back to our default state after 2012. And yet I sense that something deeper may be happening in our 'Isles of Wonder', as Danny Boyle called them, and that the country may be ready for, and perhaps even already starting to shift in its mood and values. About this, much more later.

How we Perceive our own Country

There are facts about a nation and then there are feelings, sentiment, general mood, confidence and cultural zeitgeist. How much correlation there is between the more objective facts and the general mood in a country at any given time or decade seems to be extremely variable, and no doubt always has been thus. It's rather like the sentiment in the financial markets, which often seem to be driven more by mood and sense of confidence or lack of it, than by any actual reliable data. And, of course, our mood and attitude has a large bearing on how we will interpret facts anyway. I've long since realized that we human beings make decisions far less on rational grounds than we imagine we do.

Even as small a mood inducer as the right music playing in a clothing store can tip the balance and lead me to impulse buy some ridiculous jacket which I afterwards will never wear and end up throwing out. And how much more so when it comes to broad currents in culture which have such an effect on our outlook? We can get fed up with governments and vote for the opposition sometimes just out of boredom with seeing the same old political faces on the TV, irrespective of what the government or opposition's policies may be, or whether they seem effective or not.

Britain's prevailing mood and sense of itself has been through some seismic changes during the recent decades since the end of the Second World War in 1945. Consider this global survey conducted in 2011 and what it says about us British in terms of the difference between facts and our sense of ourselves. It really made me stop and ponder. Called the *Global Prosperity Index*, the survey aimed to capture what social progress means. What seemed particularly interesting about this survey was that it did so through not just measuring, as is often the case, economic growth, but by using a wide range of diverse indicators, such as levels of safety and security, prevalence of corruption, optimism about job prospects, and suchlike. Even more unusually, it also included in the ranking of the country, people's *perceptions of their own country*. It compared a total of 110 countries and it was the data about good old Britain that naturally caught my attention most. All the more so, believing, as I mentioned in the intro-duction, that nationality is one important part of what has formed and conditioned our sense of identity and our worldview.

In terms of the overall world ranking Britain came in 13th. This was based on an averaging of all the various indicators. Some of the findings were salutary. This country, the survey found, has the fourth largest proportion of people who give to charity. It has 'high levels of safety and security', 'a highly effective government', a 'robust democracy' and 'low levels of corruption'. Britain ranks fourth in the world for entrepreneurship and opportunity and also excels in terms of innovation and it has the sixth largest consumer market in the world. The report says that 'the United Kingdom has shown a notable increase in prosperity'.

These are the objective facts. But as I said, in this survey people's perceptions of their country also affect its ranking. When it came to this area, a strikingly different view of Britain emerges. When asked about confidence in their own government, Britain comes 74th in the world. When asked about feeling safe walking home alone at night the UK comes 40th. And this in the face of objectively 'high levels of safety and security'. In fact, British people's perceptions of the UK were so at odds with the actual facts, that it led the Legatum Institute, the authors of the report, to say in their press release about the report,

> Of the 110 countries covered by the survey, Britain ranked a
> staggering 101st in public confidence in financial institutions,
> 98th in optimism about job prospects and 93rd in expectations
> of future economic performance, the kind of ratings usually
> found in the world's poorest countries.

Our view of ourselves puts us, in the *Global Prosperity Index* ratings, according to our own subjective perceptions of Britain, in some measures a little below Rwanda and on a par with countries like Sudan and Yemen, and only marginally ahead of Zimbabwe. Something doesn't add up, for sure. Could this indicate, perhaps, a slight lack of objectivity on our part? Yet perception is what counts and politicians know full well how to campaign on issues like law and order since it is the sense of fear of crime that constituents feel that matters; much more so than whether crime is actually increasing or decreasing, or how likely or remotely unlikely you are to be a victim of crime. We feel things are getting worse and in the end that's what sticks.

Our view of ourselves as a nation is not fixed and our sense of ourselves can change seismically over the time scale of decades, let alone through the time scale of centuries. What seemed obvious to people in the 1950s may very likely seem strange and foreign to people in the 1970s and far more so today. I want to get across a sense of how our national attitudes and outlook are always being formed, responding and reacting to the general and inevitable changes in life and fortunes of the times. And our feelings and outlook are not just ephemeral; they can have a very significant effect on our actual lives.

A Post WWII Personal Story

To illustrate the profound shifts in the British mood and sense of identity through time, let me take you very briefly through the recent decades of this country. I don't mean this as a detailed history, for I am certainly not an historian, but more to highlight how people generally felt then, which I'll partly illustrate by my own personal story, and to see how this overarching mood, this *perception* of the nation and the prevailing circumstances, has changed and is changing.

As a child growing up in 1950s Britain, times were, in many ways, tough and austere; tougher than they've ever been since then, at least in my experience. Food rationing had only recently ended and food was not exactly plentiful. I recall going to school in London at times wearing what was euphemistically called a 'smog mask': a crude tin contraption with layers of cotton wool held on by an elastic strap round your head, to protect against the impossibly thick fog caused by millions of heavily polluting coal fires, the only form of home heating most families had. I can still almost taste and feel the biting way that the smog burned your throat with each breath. This was smog so thick that you could almost cut it with a bread knife. It's funny how American friends still ask me if, on coming to London, they can expect to be enveloped in a blanket of fog, like a scene, I think they imagine, from a Jack the Ripper film, and I have to inform them that, no, it isn't actually foggy in London and hasn't been for more than half a century.

I grew up in north-eastern suburban London. There seemed to be, through those early years, an unrelenting grey quality to the city and much of the city centre was like a mouth with missing teeth, dotted with the rubble of buildings destroyed by German bombing from a war ended just a single decade earlier. Rows of ugly, temporary pre-fab houses replaced the bombed-out homes that people once had occupied and they also filled the playing fields well into the 1960s before more permanent housing could be built. Yet despite the hardship, there was, as I remember, a simple optimism at work, and although as a child I didn't know this then, it was a renewed optimism after the depression of the 1930s. We were the victors in WWII. And it was a simple, just war with no ambiguities—at least that was the sense back then as a child. Good had prevailed over evil and a New Jerusalem was promised. Our comics, boy's comics and early graphic novels such as *War Picture Library*, celebrated it ad infinitum. In the cinemas jaunty newsreels never failed to extol the essential goodness of being British. Being British was good and so was history. These were truths which from a young boy's point of view, were absorbed as being self-evident. Life was bright, full of hope, with universal health care for the first time, a new education system, and a rocketing birth rate, producing the bulge in the population graphs which later came to be known as the Baby Boomers, which was my generation. Objectively, living standards were, by today's standards, low; everything had to be repaired, clothes patched up, handed down, never thrown out. Buying new was way too extravagant, unless absolutely necessary. People took a pride in this very make-do and mend ethos. Hardly anyone had central heating. I remember our primary school teacher trying to explain to us in the late 1950s what central heating was. She obviously had never seen this fabled invention and imagined that it must be something similar to how the ancient Romans channelled water from hot springs, with heated water flowing under the floor.

The economy continued to get better, and for many, we started to have more disposable income as we moved into the 1960s. For me too, as I entered my teenage years, these were exciting times. Britain seemed to be the vanguard of a cultural revolution. Our small island nation seemed to be at the forefront of all that was new and thrillingly different. Led by an explosion in popular music, with bands such as the Beatles, the Stones, the Who and the Kinks taking the world by storm, and extending through fashion, art and design, London suddenly became the place to be, the epicentre of a seismic cultural shift. This was swinging London and the mood was soaring optimism; anything was possible. In the background, Britain was quietly and with surreptitious embarrassment divesting itself of all its former colonies and granting independence to these new countries. Yet life was positive and the future looked good and these shifts in our status as a nation were still shadows swirling in the background. At least this is how it felt to the younger generation, though many older people were no doubt much more aware of and concerned by the sense of Britain's shrinking status in the world as the Empire evaporated before their eyes.

As the 1960s progressed, I remember getting haul my headmaster at my Grammar school, told I l violent 'yob' and demanded of that I get my long ha 1967 and the Beatles had just released *All You I* performing it to hundreds of millions on the first-ever worldwide television satellite broadcast, and I was profoundly moved by this event. I endeavoured to explain to Dr Jones, my stern yet even-handed headmaster, that my long hair, far from being a symbol of violence, was actually an expression of a new movement that was ushering in a different order of human life, a world based on peace and a new spirit of 'coming together'. Dr Jones, in his dignified and rather intimidating black gown, was not impressed, and regarded me, I would imagine from his uncomprehending look, as slightly unhinged, if not actually stark, raving bonkers.

So there was this interesting switch from the sense of a loyal, dutiful and proud people to a new ethos of freedom of expression tinged with a strong element of rebelliousness, but the common thread was, as I experienced it, a sense of optimism and unbridled possibility and potential; that Britain mattered and was going somewhere. And for a time this was true of this new, reincarnated version of our country. Another key and integral aspect of this cultural shift in the 1960s was a new, liberating sense of the importance of the individual rather than rote conformity to a collective and preordained will. The excesses of this new subculture have since been parodied as the self-centredness of the 'Me' generation, yet, in my opinion, it has to be said that much that emerged from the 1960s has genuinely proved to be of lasting value, and which I will return to and explain in more depth later.

Of course, it needs to be added that not everyone in Britain necessarily enjoyed the same expansive mood, and conditions remained hard for many. Recently watching the film *Made in Dagenham* reminded me of this. For the women workers at Ford in Dagenham in 1968, as portrayed in the film, it was a bitter fight to gain equal pay, including encountering implacable resistance from their male co-workers. Their eventual success though, came absorbed in, indeed helped take forward, the tapestry of a new society with new values on a worldwide scale: equal rights, women's rights, civil rights, gay rights, multiculturalism, pluralism, environmental awareness and much more, which are all the legacy of this cataclysmic period of the 1960s. By any objective standards, this short period was an amazing one in the history of our nation, in terms of social and cultural change. And, as already mentioned, in so many ways Britain was at the forefront of a shift that was occurring throughout the Western world.

The Indelible Legacy of the 1970s

So, from those bright and optimistic times—and, if not always so 'bright', then radical and questioning—how did we arrive at where we are now? How did we get to the point where, regardless of the objective picture, people (and I mean we British) tend to feel a certain sense of dejection about our own opportunities and the prospects for the nation, as evidenced by the survey mentioned previously. Certainly the Olympics and Paralympics provided a refreshing temporary suspension of that mood, and hopefully even the beginning of a more lasting shift to a more balanced view of us. Why, though, do we so easily slip into our old comfortable slippers, feeling that we have no opportunities, little hope, when the bigger picture is quite otherwise? Is it just that we like to be miserable, and if so, where does that come from? Is there, in fact, a very different way of understanding all this?

But I'm jumping ahead of myself here; so, if I may, I'd like to return to our quick overview of the last few decades. Following the euphoric days of the 1960s (a period which I feel is more properly dated as starting in about 1963 and ending roughly in 1973, since this more accurately delineates the cultural upheaval which gets labelled 'the 60s'), came a time of intense social and political problems. The 1970s were a key period, in my view, in the formation of our current national self-sense. Just looking at a

BBC website on a people's history of the decades, it informs us of the character of the 1970s. 'It', we are told, 'was the decade of strikes, electricity shortages and piles of rotting rubbish on the street.' We remember, if we are old enough, the three-day working week, power cuts, ongoing industrial unrest and strife. Perhaps, too, we remember the nickname for Britain, 'the sick man of Europe', a term incidentally coined for the Ottoman Empire in the nineteenth century and which has since been trotted out, at one time or another over the last century or more, to almost every mid to large-size country in Europe.

Our sense of ourselves in the 1970s was of decline. We were in decline. Britain was going downhill and our memories of the 1960s became relegated to a hazy, heady fantasy. No longer could we ignore that our Empire was a thing of the past and nearly all our former colonies were now proud, independent nations. Our competitors in Europe, including the ones that lost the War, like Germany, were now outperforming us, the supposed victors. These undercurrents of doubt in ourselves had slipped into the background through the 1960s, but now they dominated our sense of who we were. No longer a great power and certainly not a superpower, that was very clear. A poignant quote from historian Dominic Sandbrook writing about the 1970s and the then Prime Minister Jim Callaghan is worth pondering for a moment to let it sink in.

Even Callaghan himself seemed to have little faith in his native land. In November 1974 he told his colleagues, "Our place in the world is shrinking: our economic comparisons grow worse, long-term political influence depends on economic strength - and that is running out." And, he went on, "If I were a young man, I should emigrate."

If even the Prime Minister himself had such a view of his own country, it shows just how deep the currents of negativity and cynicism had begun to run. The 1970s are also strongly associated with the 'Winter of Discontent', a Shakespearean turn of phrase adopted by the British media, referring to the winter of 1978–79 in Britain: a bitterly cold winter marked by widespread strikes by local authority trade unions for pay rises for their members. This term has somehow lingered ever since in our collective subconscious, along with the particularly macabre memory of dead bodies lying unburied as a result of the gravediggers' unofficial strike.

Undoubtedly the 70s were a difficult time for many of us and the British couldn't avoid the fact of our relative decline in the world. Yet there is more to the picture. Much of what occurred could not be put down solely to Britain's decline or to political incompetence or truculent unions. The West as a whole experienced the worst economic decade since the Great Depression and the oil crises of 1973 and 1979, caused by factors in the Middle East beyond the West's control, led to rationing of power and petrol across the Western world, not only in Britain. American historian George Bernstein, for example, in his book about Britain since WWII, *The Myth of Decline: The Rise of Britain Since 1945*, comes to a very different and counterbalancing analysis: 'Apart from the catastrophic decades of the 1920s and the 1970s, both linked to larger worldwide economic phenomena, the peacetime story (in Britain) has been one of growth and prosperity.' Andrew Marr in the prologue to his book, *A History of Modern Britain*, makes a revealing and interesting comparison between Britain's post-war story and the personal psychology of an individual:

> If one decides that the breakdown of the Seventies was the single most important thing to have happened to post-war Britain, which shadows everything before and since, then inevitably the story of the Forties, Fifties and Sixties becomes darker. All the things that went right, all the successful lives

21

that were lived during 30 crowded years, the triumphs of style and technology, the better health, the time of low inflation, the money in pockets, the holidays and the businesses that grew and thrived, are subtly surrounded with "yes, but" brackets... guess what's coming next. But this is a strange way of thinking. In personal terms it would be like defining the meaning of a life, with all its ups and downs, entirely by reference to a single bout of serious illness or marital break-up in middle age.

Popular music can be an interesting way to read the shifting sands of the times although one has to be careful since styles can be so infinitely fickle and changeable, and react to all manner of cues, especially the fashion or style which immediately preceded it. Nevertheless, no one could fail to recognise the enormous difference between the upbeat, creative, expansive, life positive music of the 1960s, in contrast to say Punk, the defining musical movement of the mid 1970s which, with its nihilism, anger, hopelessness and boredom, appears as the complete antithesis of the 1960s. And yet Punk, too, is undoubtedly creative; there's raw energy, fresh expression and an understandable reaction to the 1960s, and especially towards the increasing self-indulgence of late 1960s and early 1970s rock music.

The 1970s became, in many ways, the defining decade for the modern British outlook and character and has had, I believe, a disproportionate influence on us. The hope of the 1950s and the soaring optimism of the 1960s evaporated and have not seriously emerged again in the decades since. However the pessimism of the 1970s has remained and has been largely unchallenged except in brief moments like the Olympics. Yet I will return later to why this downbeat mood seems to be our default state, since it is my firm conviction that the events of the 1970s are more of a contributing and precipitating factor, rather than the deeper reason for it.

The 1980s until Now

The 1980s are inextricably associated with Margaret Thatcher in political office and her tenure undoubtedly brought huge change to Britain, as the country went from recession into growth with her radical brand of free market economics characterised by privatisation and deregulation like never before. It was also a period where the sense of division, of the haves and have-nots, was painfully accentuated and intense polarisation took place within our society. Many of us were better off, and a quarter of the population became instant shareholders through the privatisation initiatives, though many others, like the miners, suffered tremendously. Despite this, these were also the years when the great causes of the 1960s revolution were consolidated: women's rights, anti-racism, the gay movement, environmental concern and so on. In terms of anti-racism it was also the time of the anti-apartheid movement and the role played by Britain in providing a sanctuary and support for this cause is one deserving of more than a little pride on our part. It was, of course, in 1990 when the struggle came to its fruition with the release of Nelson Mandela from prison.

If the 1980s and early 1990s were a time marred by an intense sense of social inequality, the coming to office of Tony Blair in 1997 was, at least briefly, one of those moments of renewed optimism and sense of purpose. His athletic positivity and unveiling of what was called the Third Way, seemingly beyond the tired old divisions of Left or Right, swept him into office, making him a beacon of hope for so many who had become cynical about politics. It's my contention that the enormous mistrust and dislike with which he is now viewed, whilst, of course, to a large degree explicable by the very dubious looking manner of his getting the country into the Iraq War, is also an unconscious reaction to the sense of the unfulfilled promise of the possibilities and aspirations which accompanied his becoming Prime Minister. People dared to hope and believe again and then felt their hopes dashed. The reaction to Tony Blair in Britain is so extreme and vitriolic that he can hardly dare appear publicly in this country, although he is popular in other countries, particularly in the United States. Friends of mine—exclusively British ones, that is—tell me, in all sincerity, how Blair was worse than Saddam Hussein and one friend is working with tremendous dedication to bring him to court for war crimes. Archbishop Desmond Tutu has thrown his considerable moral authority behind this cause. And so, having entered the twenty-first century, we have been faced again with recession, struggling through the greatest global financial crisis since the 1930s, which we have only tentatively emerged from, coupled with a profound lack of trust in the banks and the whole financial sector and not a great deal of confidence left in the political establishment or the print media either.

While I find the history and development of our nation interesting *per se*, my particular interest, as already mentioned, is in the profound ways national attitudes and even identity are constantly changing and how it affects us as individuals. How this is actually part of our personal identity and worldview, though often largely unseen, operating below the waterline, as it were, without us realising why exactly we feel so strongly and believe in the things that we do, including when our position and belief is one of non-belief and mistrust. Hence the above short thumb nail sketch of the recent decades seen through my personal and somewhat idiosyncratic lens. Our individual personal sense of self is, to quite a degree, and much more than I previously would ever have imagined, formed and influenced by the culture and society and the times in which we are born and live in.

For much of my adult life I always considered as self-evident that I'm an *individual* who thinks for himself and comes to his own conclusions, and is relatively uninfluenced by trends or fashions in society. I make up my own mind and am not part of any group thinking, thank you. I really deeply and genuinely believed that by and large I formed my own independent opinions based on the available facts. It was a profound shock when I realized that this just isn't true. Some years ago, I was at a friend's house idly looking at the books on his shelves, passing the time before dinner. I happened to notice that his book collection was pretty similar to my own collection. This chance observation for some reason started a train of thought in me that widened and escalated to a revelation far beyond the contents of bookshelves. I literally was halted in my tracks. It dawned on me that there were perhaps millions of people just like me in Britain, who all felt broadly the same as me; who read the same liberal media, bought the same books; liked and disliked similar things; felt independent from nationality; cared about the environment; were left-leaning politically, though not of course party members; and who as young men would have refused conscription had it existed to rebel against. It was a kind of humbling experience to realize that I am a product of my times. To take my particular case as an example, if you came of age in a middle-class, relatively well-off family in Britain in the 1960s, the chances are reasonably high that you would turn out sharing many of the same views as myself. You would very likely be conditioned to have a high regard for emphasizing the individual and his or her own free expression. And, of course, to quite an extent we all are products of our own times, of our particular background and reflective of the national society around us.

Becoming more Objective about Britain

The sense of national identity is not static and never has been. It changes and develops over time and while there is a definite thread which runs through it, our national and cultural identity is also very different today, as I mentioned already, than 45 years ago, or a 100 or 500 years ago. George Orwell in his brilliant essay *The Lion and the Unicorn*, writing in 1940, with his typical economy of words and gift for a fresh use of the language, puts it thus: 'What can the England of 1940 have in common with the England of 1840? But then, what have you in common with the child of five whose photograph your mother keeps on the mantelpiece? Nothing, except that you happen to be the same person.'

The prevalent post-1960s mood of pessimism has influenced pretty much all of us. I can feel the same pessimism in myself. Even, though, I know that I really am very privileged and have the good fortune to live in an affluent, free, civilized country, I would often catch myself murmuring how this and that in Britain is falling apart. Or I would recognise that I was harbouring some vague sense that the country is sliding ever further into decline, when it's not actually true. The thing is, we fail to recognize the difference between relative decline and absolute decline, treating them as interchangeable when they're not. Yes, Britain has obviously declined relatively in its position in the world from having the largest empire in history, to now being a decidedly mid-sized country. At the same time, allowing for minor spikes and dips in the short term, the average person in Britain continues to be progressively better off throughout most of the years and decades than he or she has ever been before in all of recorded history. And when we go back to before recorded history, well I don't think any of us would really want to endure what life must have been like back then. It has been estimated that prehistoric human life expectancy on the African Savannah, where, quite probably, the earliest members of our species roamed, was only about 20 or maybe 25 years.

Again, just to sprinkle a few salient facts to counterbalance our national more pessimistic self-sense. Far from being an insignificant, rainy island that the world now passes by, the UK is actually the sixth largest economy in the world according to the IMF, measured by GDP, as of 2014. The famed business school INSEAD in its 2014 Global Innovation Index, ranks Britain as second in the world for innovation out of 143 countries surveyed, second in market sophistication and first in the rating of its universities. It may also surprise you to know that Britain has the perhaps dubious distinction of still being one of the world's biggest defence spenders, despite the recent swingeing military cuts. In the West African Ebola crisis in 2014, Britain was second only to the USA as the largest supplier of aid, and proportional to our size, Britain was by far the largest aid donor of any country in that crisis. When we let in such facts and figures, I hope it will start to become apparent why the distinction I am making between relative decline and absolute decline is so key. Just to add, contrary to our popular narrative of decline, the Legatum Institute's latest 2014 *Global Prosperity Index* survey, which I mentioned earlier, showed Britain actually rising in the rankings to become Europe's most prosperous (a combination of wealth and wellbeing) large country, having now overtaken Germany.

As I said at the beginning, my aim is not at all to add any more to a collective sense of woe about how bad things are. I hope instead to show you how the part played by our *perspective* on how things are, is a far bigger deal than we are used to thinking. I hope too, to take you on a journey that will convince you there is a different and more creative lens to view our experience through; one that is totally valid and which offers more scope for us to discover a greater fulfilment of our sense of self, together with a healthier national sense of self. I hope this will also convey how we can rediscover an important felt sense of being part of a living story and to experience a sorely needed sense of belonging, in these times of dislocation and alienation. But I'm getting ahead of myself here once again. I'd first like to turn our attention to examining some of the more visible downsides of our British attitudes before coming to a more balanced and integrated sense of ourselves.

Chapter 2

The Downside of British Culture

There's a joke among cosmologists that romantics are made of stardust, but cynics are made of the nuclear waste of worn-out stars
Joel Primack and Nancy Abrams

Perhaps the best way I can introduce what I am referring to as the downside of British culture is by relating the story of how I came to embark on this whole project about the British. When I lived abroad and periodically returned home on visits, I would often be struck by small incidents and observations which would lead me to ponder. Often these tended to be of a superficial nature and not worth mentioning in isolation. I likely would not have noticed them at all were it not for the contrast with the cultures I was living in then: variously, the USA, Australia, Holland and Germany. Then on returning to live in the UK, my cultural antenna already attuned to this aspect of Britain, I started noticing a certain pattern in British life whether I was at work, shopping, or reading newspaper and magazine articles; a kind of insidious undercurrent. Investigating this became a kind of strange fascination for me for a certain period, and friends, hearing of my peculiar hobby, would send me cuttings and web links in a similar vein.

Let me explain by sharing a few of these observations and experiences of mine, bearing in mind that some of the examples are on face value, of a pretty superficial nature and some certainly do have a humorous side as well. They are merely indicators and of value chiefly because of what they may point to, lying beneath the particular example. These small vignettes served for me as the starting point for a more serious and in depth investigation, which I will go on to explain, that opened up valuable insights into much deeper and significant cultural currents in present day Britain, which to my mind do need attention.

Curious and Unsettling British Vignettes

A project which I had followed with interest and growing incredulity over recent years was the one to create a handbook for British citizens. Successive governments have busied themselves with this task for years, done, presumably, because we literally had nothing of its kind up to that point. The task was to educate new citizens as to what it means to be British today. A manual was eventually arrived at, but reports at the time suggested that the only thing the eminent authors could agree on that defined being British was that one lived in this country. This was clearly not exactly the epitome of citizen's pride. You can't imagine the USA, for example, having a similar problem with such a handbook. Having said that though, finally we do now have a handbook on being British which aspiring citizens have to study for their naturalisation process. However, more recent thinking from the present Conservative government has been that it should educate potential citizens in our British history rather than concentrate so much on the new rights and the welfare benefits which are now available to these new citizens, one of the main emphases of the first booklet. But what a strange state of affairs for a guide to citizenship to be so difficult to devise for so long, with seemingly no way of stating what becoming a citizen of Britain might entail?

For some years I directed a charity in the UK and my wife ran the trading arm of the charity, which offered an events venue service that would then donate all its profits to the charity, a favoured way of funding for UK charities. In our organisation we endeavoured to foster deeper human values and we placed great store on good human relationships with our staff and clients. And it made a tangible difference; people remarked on the friendly and uplifting atmosphere at our premises, and the good service, which clients often positively remarked on and were surprised by. My wife had established a good relationship with a local college who would send their 17-year-olds for work experience at our business. The principal of the college wanted to help raise the expectations of these kids, who often came from very difficult backgrounds, and deliberately sent them to our charity because of the values we upheld, and so that they could experience a workplace where people were actually happy working. A full time job became available at our premises and we let the college know that their students would have preference. One of the lecturers was visiting our place shortly afterwards and he related a conversation he had had with a 17-year-old student who was looking for work. The lecturer told the young man, who had previously spent a day of work experience at our business, about the job opportunity. 'So are you going to go for an interview, since they are likely to give you a job?' said the lecturer. 'No,' said the young guy, 'I don't want to work there. People are too happy.' The lecturer was shocked and dismayed as he cared deeply about advancing his students, and it was sad to hear him relate this tale. This story really made me think: how is it that a 17-year-old in London, with all their life ahead of them, doesn't even want to be happy? Just one story, but it made me ponder more on what this said about our country.

When I read articles in British magazines and weekend supplements about some new self-improvement regime or course—and it could be the latest yoga routine or a new diet or exercise programme—I've often been struck by the reporter's attitude. The reporter may well find the particular health course helpful and positive, but towards the end of the article, if not before, the reporter will invariably have to declare that he or she is a lethargic couch potato who will continue to overeat and to drink in excess. I realised that in order to be considered rational and objective, they have to display a 'healthy' or 'balanced' pessimistic world-weariness. Perhaps, without this, in our present British cultural milieu, you might not get published and could appear easily impressionable and perhaps even dangerously starry-eyed.

I'm stating the obvious when I say that the British media has quite a strong leaning towards the negative, towards dwelling predominantly on what is wrong, pulling down and deconstructing whoever or whatever seems to stand out positively. Foreigners I know are often shocked by the sheer nastiness of our tabloids, though the 'quality' papers do the same more subtly. The Levenson inquiry aired much of the darker side of our media in public. It piqued my interest to read that we even have an export market in gutter press. It seems that bottom of the barrel publications in the States, such as *The National Enquirer* and similar titles, have apparently been powered by the recruitment of expatriate Brits, who have a reputation for their proficiency in muckraking and aggressive gathering of news stories.

I noticed several years ago that I was unconsciously gravitating towards reading the obituaries pages in newspapers, and I did wonder if I was being morbid or wistfully looking back in time. Then I realised that obituaries are just about the only occasion when it is socially acceptable in Britain today for journalists' writing not to be imbued with, what is to my mind, a somewhat negative slant. This stance is far too often confused with being objective and healthily sceptical. On the occasion of death, it's acceptable to write about the positive achievements and qualities of a person, without one's balanced 'realistic' critical faculties being called into question. I would often feel inspired by reading in obituaries of the struggles and uphill battles that eminent people had had in their lives and how they had coped with them or prevailed. What a strange state of affairs, though, that these are the sole allowable occasions for writing in this vein?

Then for a touch of the ridiculous, I can't help but mention the upliftingly titled book, *Is It Just Me or Is Everything Shit?* It may be superfluous to state, but this is, of course, a British book. And in case you thought it was just a novelty title, the popularity of this edifying treatise has ensured a sequel, *Is It Just Me or Is Everything Shit, Volume 2*, with the helpful subtitle, *Because If Anything, It All Just Keeps Getting Worse*. And now we have *The Best of Is It Just Me or Is Everything Shit Volumes 1 and 2*. On top of this, I noticed in my local bookstore, the latest addition to this distinctively British self-help series, *Is It Just Me or Has the Shit Hit the Fan?* which has the helpful explanatory subtitle, *Your Hilarious Guide to Unremitting Global Misery*. I was amused, and it gave me more than a little pleasure, to see that there now is a riposte to the question posed by this series, in the book, *It Is Just You, Everything's Not Shit: A Guide to All Things Nice*.

Please excuse this litany of petty ills, but as I said, I think a few examples are necessary in order to make a serious point, and there is a pattern to these little stories. Hopefully, you'll bear with me through the process. There is also, of course, our famed poor service in shops, restaurants, well, just about anywhere really. When I lived in the States, on the East Coast and also West Coast, in California, I couldn't help but be struck by how the attitude towards service is hugely different. At first I dismissed the waiter's incredible interest in how I was enjoying the meal as obviously insincere and further proof of American superficiality. But then I realised, at first amazingly, that generally, American waiters really did mean what they were saying. It was just me as a jaded Brit, who took exuberant positivity as being clearly inauthentic. Returning to Britain, I was struck by how often people serving really don't seem to want to be doing it. It's as if they feel, 'Why are you bothering me? What a drag that you want to buy something!' Perhaps partly some remnant of our class system of not wanting to be in a servile position, but I think other reasons are more responsible for this attitude.

There are occasions when the sales assistant doesn't say a

single word and I am left wondering why I am emptily saying 'Thank you!' as an outdated habit when there has been no verbal exchange at all. Or sometimes I'm not afforded the courtesy of knowing that I have been recognised as even existing, because I can't bring about any mutual eye contact, let alone verbal exchange. The sales assistant is talking on the mobile phone or to another bored sales assistant during the whole 'exchange' and I have to virtually beg them to acknowledge me and be so kind as to accept my money. Of course, I also have stunningly different and very positive chance encounters with shop assistants or strangers that really do make my day, but I'm talking about a general national characteristic. And this is often highlighted even more by the very marked contrast of the enthusiastic service given by young Eastern and Southern Europeans who fill many of our shop assistants' roles these days.

Sceptical or Cynical?

We British seem, at this point in time, fairly slanted towards a certain pessimism and cynicism as a national characteristic. I know it's a common feature of all sophisticated, post-traditional cultures to be ironic and cynical, but our English version has a particular edge; we do, I feel, bring something extra to it. I've lived and worked in Holland and Germany and the States, and while cynicism is a definite feature in these places too, it's striking how we in Britain are just more vehement and down putting in our expression of it. Many of us will say that we are not cynical; we are sceptical, is the reply. And isn't questioning what is true a good thing rather than naively and lazily taking opinions, knowledge or facts for granted and accepting the given? Of course, scepticism is a valuable and important attitude, yet what has come to be thought of as scepticism in our present culture is often, I would suggest, actually cynicism. True scepticism is a questioning attitude towards knowledge, facts, or opinions stated as facts, or doubt regarding claims that are

33

generally taken for granted. The open-minded questioning of the genuine sceptic can only be helpful. What is often left out of the picture is that our questioning is heavily influenced by our underlying motivation. If one's motive is more to prove what's not possible, to ridicule and to pull apart, then the questioning is not scepticism, it's cynicism or what biologist Rupert Sheldrake has termed dogmatic scepticism, which is much the same thing.

I was on a panel in a public debate in London on the provocative subject of *Cynicism: The British Disease?* several years ago. I was interested to discover that fellow panel member Richard Wilson, author of a book on scepticism, *Don't Get Fooled Again* and also part of the 'Sceptics In The Pub' organisation, was not at all a cynic. He was very clear about the difference and I found that the two of us had much shared ground. The word cynicism in its original meaning referred to a school of Greek philosophers beginning in the fourth century BC, known as the Cynics. Funnily enough, their doctrine was not what we would recognize as being cynical. They held that the purpose of life was to live a life of virtue in accord with Nature, a simple life free from all possessions. Virtue to them meant self-control and the goal of life was happiness, which was to be found by living in agreement with Nature. Diogenes was the most famous of the Cynics, remembered for his asceticism (sleeping in a tub) and for his ethical seriousness. Nowadays the dictionary definition of cynicism, which is much more familiar to us, is: *an attitude of scornful or jaded negativity, especially a general distrust of the integrity or professed motives of others.*

One simple way, which I find helpful, of thinking about what the attitude of cynicism actually expresses is, 'It's not possible'. It doesn't much matter what the 'it' is; there's a prior embedded attitude that whatever new idea, project, scheme, solution is being suggested, it's not possible because it won't work. And it's always far easier to knock things down than to find constructive, new ways forward. Commentators and pundits in Britain are adept at pouring scorn and ridicule on new proposals and ide.. often brilliantly articulating their arguments with sarcastic wit. One of our most highly developed and subtle qualities in this country, our humour, is often used to devastating effect by our intelligentsia. It almost seems like some commentators don't actually want anything new to succeed, and seem to delight in pulling down and pointing out, with such sarcastic wit, what's wrong with just about everything. But why? Why do we generally tend towards a negative slant and take seemingly perverse pleasure in pulling things down?

When the gargantuan new Terminal 5 opened at Heathrow airport, it was objectively a well-planned project which came in on time and below budget. Yet there were teething troubles with the baggage delivery system, which apparently is normal in any new airport terminal around the world. Yet the British media pounced on this fault and that is all most of us would ever hear or remember about T5; certainly not the fact that it all works very well these days. Similarly with the Millennium Dome in London's Docklands, pilloried as the worst white elephant in history, for which no future use could ever be found. Funnily enough, rebranded as the O2 arena, it is now the most iconic, popular and profitable concert arena in Europe, with huge numbers of visitors, yet this is not worthy of a news story in Britain. Of course I am well aware that 'news' is, to a great extent, bad news, all over the world, yet we British seem to do this with a particular vengeance. Why do we tend towards this attitude? Where does it come from?

This dogmatic scepticism surfaces on the religious front too, or rather on the vehemently *not*-religious front. I'm referring to the atheism of a peculiarly militant brand that is not content to leave others to their faith, absence of faith, or agnosticism. The term Neo-Atheist is commonly used for this rather evangelical movement led by the likes of Richard Dawkins, the famous evolutionary biologist and author of *The God Delusion*. Where

tain would you have had the 'Atheist Bus
h saw our iconic red buses with huge adverts on
pfully informing the populace that, 'There's
od. Now Stop Worrying and Enjoy your Life'? Just
con... that statement for a minute is revealing. In those
few words it's actually saying quite a bit and pretty fervidly and
dogmatically. It's basically implying that the only thing keeping
you from a happy life free of worry, is giving up this pernicious
and superstitious idea of God. But why such a dismissive tone?

To move on to a different subject, I go to the gym regularly
and in different gyms I've been to in this country, I have often
pondered on the semi-permanent signs which get affixed to gym
equipment to inform patrons that a particular exercise machine is
not working. I wonder why the gym wouldn't just have it fixed
instead. Appealing to staff usually has no effect, as if there is an
underlying sense that this is just the way things are, it's not their
responsibility. Also a look of blank incomprehension is a common
response, as if they wonder, why would I expect things to work?
I must also mention a rather silly example, but a revealing one
nevertheless. I've always been struck when returning to Britain
and using the washroom facilities in Arrivals at Heathrow and
Gatwick airports, by the signs commonly fixed above the wash
basins, which in some cases have been there for many years.
These permanent signs bolted on the wall say: 'Warning:
Extremely Hot Water, Be Careful.' I always wonder why they
couldn't just adjust the thermostat setting to make the hot less
scaldingly hot, as they would in other countries? And these
airports are not alone, as I keep finding similar signs in many
public washrooms all over the country. I'm of course aware of the
irony in relating these examples that a common characteristic of
British culture is to complain while having no intention of doing
anything about it.

You may wonder why I haven't mentioned the binge drinking
culture of Britain as another example. Well, our drinking has a

longer pedigree and is more complex in my opinion. Interestingly we were apparently already binge drinking when the Normans conquered England nearly a thousand years ago. The Norman noblemen and knights certainly drank alcohol but they liked to keep their wits about them. They were amazed and horrified by their English Saxon peers who would just drink and drink and drink for a couple of days until they passed out.

While on the subject of history, another general and pervading characteristic I began to notice in Britain is that most people don't seem to know much at all about our history except for a few disembodied bytes of information of the Henry VIII or Hitler type. There seems to be a disconnect from any story of our history with no real sense of who we are and where we have come from; no narrative, just disconnected little packets of information about sundry kings and battles in our national past. Ofsted has produced a critical report on history teaching in secondary schools in England, concluding that 'students' chronological understanding was not sufficiently well developed: they had ... 'a poor sense of the historical narrative.' Historian Simon Schama is very concerned with this state of affairs and laments the loss of what he terms the 'long arc of time.' England is the only country in Europe where history is not compulsory for students past the age of 14, and many schools don't teach much history at all these days. The living thread of our national story appears to be in danger of being lost, leaving us floating in an unmoored present, awash with information, but lacking any thread of a narrative. As Schama says,

> Whatever else gets cut in this time of nicks and scrapes, incisions and mutilations, the cord of our national memory had better not be among the casualties. For even during the toughest trials it's our history that binds us together as a distinctive community in an otherwise generically globalised culture.

What's Below the Waterline?

It dawned on me that our disconnection from a living story is much more significant than being a small gap in our education: it is intimately connected with our sense of declinism and pessimism, in ways that will become clear as we proceed. Just because we are not in touch with any national story, does not mean that we are not profoundly affected by the past. Why do we muddle through in Britain? It is a tired stereotype about Britain, but there is truth to it, nevertheless. Why do so many things not work well or are shoddy in this sophisticated and advanced nation, in a way that would never be tolerated in many other Western countries? Why do many people not care or can't be bothered? Why are so many of our opinion forming intelligentsia, columnists and famous authors so cynical, wittily expounding on every failing in our society and seemingly finding little of merit in the country? Of course, at the same time there are very many individuals and businesses in Britain with a quite different attitude who positively embrace customer care and being responsive and efficient, yet these examples are always pleasantly surprising to us, precisely because they stand out from the norm.

A myriad of such peculiarly British examples have made me contemplate, and especially when I realised that, in spite of sometimes having a different view from my time living abroad, that culture is not just something 'out there', it's very much me too. I've come to appreciate how we are shaped and conditioned by our national cultural heritage to a degree which most of us might find surprising. I remember a particular incident which opened my eyes to my own cynicism. I was in a discussion about culture with an American colleague when, in the course of the conversation, she spoke about the Declaration of Independence in the United States, a living document for Americans which very much still inspires and informs them right up to the present. I found myself saying, 'Yes, it certainly was a momentous event when the USA crafted the Declaration of Independence, but mind you, there wasn't much to celebrate for slaves or Native Americans. I don't recall them getting a mention in the document.' I pondered afterwards as to why I said this? It may well be true, yet why do I tend to have to add a put down, and in that indefatigable British way, a witty one, at that? I didn't get this attitude from my parents, who were from an older cultural generation and never expressed a trace of cynicism. I trust I have given sufficient enough everyday examples to illustrate my point in this chapter without labouring the point. I have spent considerable time pondering and contemplating this rather pervasive seam of pessimism which seems to have endless expressions in contemporary British culture and which I certainly also express.

While of course all nationalities have their peculiar quirks, I have come to appreciate that this pessimistic and declinist tendency so alive in us today, has strong roots in our recent national history. It has found fertile soil for growth in the broader Western European cultural heritage, of which Britain is a part of, and which itself has been much affected by the traumatic experience of the world wars of the twentieth century. This will become clearer in the next chapter. In order to be in a position where we are able to take an individual and national step beyond this mindset, we need to understand its roots. I feel that facing and then hopefully integrating shadow sides of our national self-sense can work in a similar way to the integration needed with regard to shadow issues in one's personal psyche. Clearly, from what I said earlier, it's no wonder that our current amnesia about our national historical thread is intimately connected with all this. And this lack of a living story removes us from a healthy sense of rootedness and belonging. A developmental view illuminating how our sense of ourselves, our worldviews and culture has changed and evolved through the decades and centuries can be helpful in bringing clarity as to why we are as we are today. This is where I would like to turn our attention in the next chapters.

Chapter 3

Back in the Day

History is the version of past events that people have decided to agree upon.
Napoleon Bonaparte

In order to gain a fresh perspective on what it means to be British at this point in time, I feel we need to step back and understand some of the forces and patterns at play which have shaped us and are forming and influencing us now. These are by definition doubly hard to see in ourselves, firstly because we haven't consciously and knowingly chosen them, and secondly because they are shared by everyone around us in our culture. How do we start to see the lens we are already looking through and which inevitably colours and helps form many of our views and conclusions? To do this, I feel that it is helpful to look through a developmental lens at how we have become who we are in order to understand the eyes we are looking through now as a Briton, or of any other nationality for that matter. We obviously haven't just spontaneously arisen as sophisticated post-traditional metro people; there's a long thread of continuity and development through centuries up to this point.

Have People in the Past really been essentially the Same?

To start with, how do we see our own worldview? Borrowed from the German *Weltanschauung*, it refers to the framework of beliefs and ideas through which any individual, group or culture interprets and interacts with the world. How do we see the particular system of values which define our view? It's not an optional fancy philosophical add-on. It's important to say that

41

everyone has a worldview, and it is usually not consciously chosen, but absorbed unwittingly in our formative years so that we then express some individualised version of the prevalent worldview of our nation or culture. We may react against or reject our upbringing or culture or nation, yet in that we are still adopting a worldview. Even those who may feel they have in some way reasoned themselves out of a particular worldview and feel they are seeing the 'bare facts', such as materialists, are nevertheless espousing a worldview. Materialism is actually a metaphysical position in regard to the nature of reality; it's every bit another belief system and outlook on life in itself.

Many of us unwittingly subscribe to some degree to what has been humorously called the Flintstone Fallacy by Dutch metaphysician Jan Sleutels, though he is actually making a very serious point. He's referring to the Hanna-Barbera TV show that I certainly grew up on, where the Stone Age cartoon characters shared much the same worldview as us in the modern West. Actually to be more precise their Stone Age culture mirrored almost exactly, American culture in the mid-1960s, without the technology of today; and purely coincidentally of course, this just happened to be the time and culture in which the series was created. Fred Flintstone and Barney Rubble were just two middle American working class guys (blue collar in American parlance) apart from their stone tools and animal hide outfits; and their stone age wives Wilma and Betty, were stereotypical American housewives, replete with animal skin mini skirts.

Understandably, probably most of us have never really thought about this question and yet it is actually quite important. We tend to take for granted that we are all human beings and that there isn't really any significant difference between a Paleolithic man or woman and ourselves. We assume that our consciousness would be more or less the same; the only difference being that our Paleolithic cousins didn't have ipods or Facebook, and did their hunter gathering out on the steppes tracking mammoths instead of tracking the bargains with a trolley in Tescos. Watch a popular British TV fantasy drama show like *Merlin* set in the Dark Ages of King Arthur's time, and the characters are portrayed just like us today: the young women and men at court slouch around with a sassy attitude similar to someone you might meet in Starbucks. I half expect one of them to utter a common postmodern catch phrase like 'Whatever', or 'Cool' at any moment. We generally don't ascribe much, or any value to the way human culture and consciousness has tended to change and develop over time. And perhaps such contemplation also can seem unappealing to us, since it can easily suggest a certain attitude of superiority on our part. Part of why the TV series *Madmen* was so captivating is because unusually it portrays the world of early 1960s America and later periods much more truly to how it actually was; in other words it recognises the huge difference in culture and worldview back only 50 years ago; right down to the details of the ever present fug of cigarette smoke which has now all but disappeared from our screens and from our everyday life. Of course BBC Victorian costume dramas do go some way towards attempting to evoke the Victorian values of the nineteenth century, especially when they are based on novels written in that period. Yet generally we inadvertently superimpose our contemporary values and mindset upon whatever historical period is the subject of the film or series. Watch any version you like of Robin Hood, set supposedly in medieval England, and my case rests. And these differences are far from being just of fashion and technology.

A little journey into several points in our historical past will serve to illustrate my point. I find it fascinating to read accounts of what life was actually like for our forebears and to understand what they enjoyed, what concerned them, and to try to get some sense of how they saw themselves and the world. Written history doesn't go back very far in terms of our human ancestry and yet the subjective and cultural experience which our ancestors recorded in the last several thousand years since its advent is vastly different from our own. It makes me realise just how much we have generally changed and developed as a society and as individuals over the centuries. People glibly state that human beings have always been the same, but examine closely and it becomes clear how much we have changed and continue to change and develop. And again I don't mean merely the more peripheral expressions of culture such as fashion, customs or technology, even though these artifacts themselves stem from very different senses of ourselves as human beings. It's very hard to see through the eyes of people from previous generations, and the further back we journey, the more difficult it becomes. We unwittingly and inevitably project and impose our own values on their world.

Discovering Nature

Let me give a couple of examples to illustrate what I am saying a bit more vividly. And you don't have to go far back in time at all, to be in a radically different cultural world. It may surprise you to hear that it was only in the late eighteenth century that we discovered nature. I know that sounds ridiculous since humankind have obviously been in an intimate struggle for survival with nature for all of our history, and for all our prehistory, for that matter. Gradually we have learned to work with and to attempt to harness the powers of nature. This has been a key part of the story of civilisation. So what on earth do I mean by saying we discovered nature? I'm talking about the romantic poets such as Wordsworth and Coleridge who were among the first to 'discover' nature. When Wordsworth would be out rambling in the countryside and just standing staring at wildflowers—perhaps his beloved Lesser Celandine of poetic fame—local farmers would think that this character must have a screw loose and be more than a little nutty. People didn't gaze *at* wildflowers or *at* 'the natural world' or care for 'the environment' back then. They were *in* nature, toiling in the fields, digging the earth, in order to have enough to eat, to survive. The plants and animals were there to be used for human needs; you didn't have nature lovers then. The romantics were the first nature lovers, and they came into being well after the Western Enlightenment, and as a sensitive reaction to the one sidedness of that new worldview, which elevated reason and objectivity to being the only permitted reality and mode of perception. I see it as a development in culture and also of consciousness, for people to have become individuated enough and sufficiently differentiated from nature in order for them to see themselves as separate from nature and to objectify it. And in the case of the romantics, to then go a step further and to re-appreciate nature. Of course this separation and objectivity came to prominence with the Western Enlightenment, and as well as all the great gifts of that age, one consequence was also an unprecedented distancing from nature and an industrial exploitation of natural 'resources', rather than an appreciation of nature.

For the educated gentleman of those enlightened times, 'nature' was a rather ugly forlorn place and they would even pull down the blinds in their horse drawn carriages when travelling through wild country; not out of fear of attack, but because untamed mountains, forests, marshes, were rather unsightly and unattractive. Samuel Johnson, on his famous trip to Scotland only slightly earlier in 1773, found the nature he encountered tedious and called Scotland rather tactfully, 'A very vile country'. In his own words, speaking with characteristic disdain to a Scot, 'Your country consists of two things, stone and water. There is, indeed, a little earth above the stone in some places, but a very little; and the stone is always appearing. It is like a man in rags; the naked skin is still peeping out.'

As I write this, I am listening to Ewan Macgregor wax lyrical in a BBC TV narration over stunning helicopter footage of those same rugged and wild Hebridean islands. The abundance of stone, greenery and water all merged together is part of the magical beauty to my eyes and it's hard to tell if its lakes within islands or islands dotted within the sea. Nowadays most of us greatly value and seek to preserve what we can of the natural world, and we appreciate the intrinsic value of fauna and flora, and feel concern for the environment. We seek out such natural scenic areas for our holidays. Yet until the Romantic Movement started developing at the end of the 18th century, there was no such consciousness in people, at least in the West, about such matters. To be able to appreciate the beauty and intrinsic worth of nature is an important point in the development of worldview and values. The romantic consciousness was an expansion of imagination and the advent of a richer interior world. This equates, I would say, to an actual development of consciousness, indicated by the increase in capacity to be able to hold this greater complexity and to encompass more perspectives; to be individuated enough to be distinct from being embedded in nature while re-embracing it with greater appreciation.

Wordsworth and Coleridge remain two of our most popular poets today, because their sensibilities, so radical and startling when they unleashed *Lyrical Ballads* on the world in 1798, are now part of our own consciousness. The two poets warn the reader at the beginning of their revolutionary slim volume,

The majority of the following poems are to be considered as experiments....Readers..if they persist in reading this book to its conclusion, will perhaps have to struggle with feelings of strangeness and awkwardness: they will look around for poetry, and will be induced to enquire by what species of courtesy these attempts can be permitted to assume that title.

Of course the worldview of these early romantics was way way ahead of the mass of the populace and it would not be until a century or two later that their views would become commonplace in Britain.

A Brief History of Violence

Let me jump to a totally different example of a radical change in our cultural world from not so long ago either. I stumbled on a fascinating history of capital punishment in the world which included considerable data about Britain. It sounds rather morbid, I know, but bear with me. A whole swathe of offences, some 220 of them, were punishable by death up until 1815 in Britain. They were collectively known as the 'Bloody Code', though that name was not used at the time, as the courts, I imagine, would have thought this only fair punishment and probably not particularly bloody. Offences warranting the death penalty included such heinous crimes as 'being in the company of Gypsies for one month', 'strong evidence of malice in a child aged 7–14 years of age' and 'blacking the face or using a disguise whilst committing a crime'.

Up until the middle of the 19th century in London, which was in those times one of the most advanced and relatively 'enlightened' cities on earth, public hangings were a regular feature of life. And these were popular occasions, especially when a number of prisoners were to be hanged on one day. From accounts in the mid eighteenth century, crowds would line the streets to pelt the condemned with all kinds of objects as they were marched through the streets from Newgate prison to the site of the gallows at Tyburn, about two miles away. It was no coincidence that the day of the execution was named Tyburn *Fair*, for a good time was had by all—that is, apart from the condemned. If these seem like far off places, it's worth remembering that this regular procession, lined by gawpers and revellers, wound its way along High Holborn and then along the full length of today's premier London shopping destination, Oxford Street, ending at Marble Arch, which was known then as Tyburn. Crowds. Tens of thousands would gather at Tyburn to watch the executions. Think of that next time you go shopping in Selfridges on Oxford Street. It was only a very few generations ago.

In the early nineteenth century, executions were moved to take place right outside Newgate prison, yet the spectacle was still there for the crowds. A seat at one of the windows overlooking the gallows could cost punters up to 10 pounds for the best view, a very considerable sum of money at that time. A cry for 'Hats off!' went up before the execution, yet not, in case you are thinking, out of respect for the condemned, but so as not to block the view of those in the rows behind. In short this was a very enjoyable day out with the family. Family entertainment, and not even PG rating. School teachers would bring their whole class to watch the show and I read of a case of a teacher who took his class for a picnic instead of to view the hangings, and who ended up in trouble for this clearly anti-social behaviour. Even up until the 1850s, accounts tell of executions at Lancaster castle attended by thousands including organised school parties.

The point is that killings and violence were seen as good entertainment in mainstream culture less than two hundred years ago in this country, and Britain had more protection for the individual than the majority of other countries at that time. Up until about 1790, the punishment for treason in Britain was to be hung, drawn and quartered in public and this obviously was a particularly barbaric form of punishment. I will spare you the details but the initial hanging didn't kill the offender; that was just the milder part of the whole experience. You were very lucky if you died only from the hanging. The commonest type of treason was for passing forged coins, and not for dramatic plots such as trying to blow up the Houses of Parliament like Guy Fawkes. This punishment was only meted out to men; it was considered indecent to have women pulled apart in this way. But in case you are thinking that at least there was some embryonic stirrings of sensitivity for the female gender back then, the punishment for forgery for women was being burnt alive at the stake.

Go a bit further back in history and it gets considerably more brutal and violent still. When we imagine, say five hundred or a thousand years ago, it seems such a long time ago. But it isn't really. I was recently standing in an ancient church on the Suffolk coast looking up at a list of all the previous vicars carved on the wall. I was amazed at how far back in time the list stretched for nearly a millennium with Norman names appearing as the list went back further. But what amazed me much more than this, was how relatively *short* the list was. There's not that many generations and you are back in early medieval times. The murder rate per head of population in England (and across the world) was far far higher then, since generally it seems that people back then had far less self control or ability to self reflect on their feelings and emotions. From accounts of the times, it appears that people could very easily change in mood from merriment to murderous rage and kill others over almost nothing. Harvard psychologist Steven Pinker, in his monumental opus *The Better Angels of our Nature*, marshals overwhelming evidence to support his thesis that violence has declined throughout history. I've waded through the seven hundred pages of this tome and it really is quite convincing, once you get over the understandable objection that the world still isn't exactly a very peaceful place, and to many people looks more violent than ever. Nowadays, constantly bombarded by media images and reports of violence around the world, in a way which no previous generation ever could be, we understandably end up with a jaded and distorted view of how things actually are.

So Pinker looks at a very relevant statistic for the individual: what is *your* personal likelihood of being murdered at different times through history? Interestingly, much of his supporting data comes from Britain, perhaps because there are records available dating back hundreds of years and also probably because it's in English. Pinker conducted an internet question-naire about perceptions of violence in Britain: one of the questions asked being: which was more violent, fourteenth century Britain or twentieth century Britain? People surveyed guessed that fourteenth century England was about 14 per cent more violent than twentieth century England. In fact the murder rate in various parts of England plummeted by a factor of ten, fifty and in some cases a hundredfold between the fourteenth and the twentieth century. Our rural past in Merry England was not idyllic at all, and certainly was no Golden Age.

Pinker also drew my attention to the relatively unknown Norbert Elias, a Jewish refugee from Nazi Germany who taught at the University of Leicester for the latter part of his life. Elias wrote *The Civilising Process*, putting forward the theory that humanity is becoming more civilised gradually through history. Since conventional data from medieval times was hard to find, Elias studied all available texts to glean a sense of everyday life back then. It was especially the pictorial illustrations of daily life from these times which revealed to him a landscape which is quite startling, more so because it is not attempting to be sensa-tional, but merely portraits of everyday life. When I studied examples of these illustrations closely, the level of barbarity is unbelievable. The everyday picture of life which is depicted looks literally like scenes out of Hieronymus Bosch paintings, with its wanton and casual violence and cruelty in the foreground and background of these tableaux. Elias includes an interesting history of table manners through the centuries which explains how part of the rules and etiquette to be observed at mealtimes have arisen in order to better control people's impulses and to help prevent murderous arguments. So it came to be codified that table knives were only to be used for cutting meat and *never* to be pointed towards other diners. If you had to pass a knife, you only did it with the handle towards the person you were passing it to. After all, folk having a nice dinner together wanted some assurance that they weren't going to be viciously stabbed during the main course. These rules about knives were passed down to us today, where we all recognise that it is still bad manners to raise the table knife to one's mouth with food, yet we have no idea where it originated.

One popular entertainment prior to the 1800s was to suspend a cat over an open fire and watch it be burnt alive in the flames, or to tie two cats tails together and watch the poor creatures tear each other to pieces. Now I know cynics reading this will say, 'Well, what's changed? Plenty of people today would still like this kind of barbarity if we let them'. And yes, there are people today in Britain who are viciously cruel and violent, yet the overwhelming majority of us view such people as being sick and needing treatment, and in need of restraining and perhaps temporarily removing from regular society for their own and others' good. The vast majority of us don't have to restrain ourselves at all from such cruelty and brutal violence. I'm not saying we don't all sometimes have extremely violent thoughts, yet we don't tend to act on them and we have a very considerable capacity for self-reflection on our feelings and emotions. In addition, we just don't derive pleasure from suffering and cruelty. In fact the reverse is true in our society today; we increasingly have a natural sensitivity towards others and towards animals too. To put it bluntly, my point is that I don't have to resist a recurrent urge to grab my neighbour's ginger tom cat and roast him over the gas cooker in my apartment for the sheer fun of it. I prefer to give him a stroke.

We all have simply developed in sensitivity and compassion and empathy to such a considerable degree that we intuitively feel the fact that other people and animals also suffer, and empathise with them and want to alleviate it. This doesn't take away from what the Dalai Lama often preaches as he tours the world, in that we could all do to become more compassionate, and yet we generally do have a fair degree of compassion today;

much more than we give ourselves credit for. Compassion and empathy are justifiably much valued in our culture today and are, I am saying, an expression of a more inclusive, greater level of development of values and consciousness. It is being able to hold more perspectives; to empathise with how other people feel and increasingly, how animals might feel too. If you are born in today's Britain, you will grow up having a sensitivity towards other people, animals, the environment, which was in the past, only the attainment of a very few rare individuals, way ahead of their times, like a William Blake. And someone like Blake who, in his sensitivity towards suffering, whether human or animal, railed in his poem, 'A Robin Redbreast in a Cage, Puts all Heaven in a Rage,' was not appreciated or understood; he remained completely unknown in his lifetime; a weirdo.

In this way general cultural values and structures are absorbed as if osmotically by any child growing up in their environment, and it seems that culture and consciousness are in reality interwoven inextricably. Countless other such examples could be given to illustrate how radically different were the worldviews of our forebears. This can help to loosen up our modern assumption that people and society and culture have always been much the same apart from advances in technology and medicine. This presumed staticness is often unquestioned, and a further reason is that many of us also don't like the very notion of development, since it can easily seem to smack of superiority on our part. Yet actually, development honours the fact that we are shaped by the past and by our ancestors; we are the benefactors of their advances, and gratefulness might be more appropriate on our part.

No More Big Ideas, Please

Turning our attention to more modern times, the changes in our culture and worldview have similarly continued to be huge. As I have been remarking previously, it's gradually dawned on me over years, how the effect of our cultural background and national inheritance on how we think and feel is often greatly underestimated. To understand where we are now, and how we might develop, it's a simple truism, though very important nonetheless, that we need to see where we have come from. I think it will be instructive to first look at Britain as a Western European country and look at the legacy that lives on in us as our collective cultural history and inheritance.

If we think about the twentieth century, we can't avoid thinking of two cataclysmic World Wars leveraged by the power of unprecedented military technology, leaving untold millions dead and a ravaged continent in its wake. And there was the Holocaust, a genocide of a new order, a diabolical new precedent, characterised by a modern scientifically advanced nation attempting to cold-bloodedly and efficiently exterminate an entire race. No wonder Theodor Adorno famously said in 1951, 'There can be no poetry after Auschwitz.'

Many of the disasters of the twentieth century were either caused by or associated with the major -*isms* of those times: National Socialism, fascism, communism, Stalinism, and imperialism. It makes complete sense, therefore, that this would leave us modern Westerners today, and especially Western Europeans, with an inveterate mistrust of all -*isms*. And I'm including Britain in this sense as a European country since—well, just look at a map. The country is ever so slightly offshore, which led to Paul Johnson calling his polemical history of England, *The Offshore Islanders*, an appellation which I've always liked. Is it so surprising that for us living in an era which gratefully saw the end of the hegemony of some of the -*isms* responsible for visiting the worst excesses in history on humankind, we would have developed an extreme dislike of anything which smacked of imposition and mass movements and uniformity? Many of these fell more or less by the wayside. Plenty of other –*isms*, such as nationalism, patriotism, or capitalism, also of course, have a dubious historical record. One effect of this has been to justifiably create among sensitive people throughout Western Europe, including Britain, a wariness and aversion to such Big Ideas or utopian schemes, having had more than their fill of fascism, Stalinism, or any other brand of utopian project which wants to enlist masses of the populace in its service to the suppression of their individuality.

George Orwell was one of the first prescient enough to see and then chronicle the rising dangers from both the extreme Right and Left, first from his personal experience in fighting against Franco's Spanish flavour of fascism, but then also soon seeing parallel mechanisms at work in Soviet Russia. Orwell's *Animal Farm* and his *1984* illuminated these disturbing trends for a whole generation to see, and these two books together are still one of the biggest sellers, the two titles together having sold more books than those of any other author of the twentieth century. His terms like 'Big Brother', and 'Orwellian' itself among others, now have come to occupy a permanent place in our language and culture.

This is a good example of how a certain cultural attitude and sense of values—in this case encompassing a number of countries—has become part of our contemporary Western European outlook which most educated people absorb almost osmotically, merely by virtue of growing up today in Europe (and again, I'm including Britain in Europe here). This is part of why the British today tend toward a national mood of pessimism as well-being due to the declinism mentioned previously. Of course this pessimism is shared in many Western European countries as well as Britain. Yet to fully understand our strong and particular tendency towards a sense of decline and cynicism which surfaced from the iceberg below, in all those little vignettes in the previous chapter, we need to look into Britain's history of Empire; and this will be explored in a subsequent chapter.

An analogy made by a Canadian speaker at a philosophical conference I attended several years ago struck me as both amusing and really quite perceptive. Dr Greg Barker was comparing the cultural difference between Americans and British. To make his point he pointed out the difference between Star Trek and Doctor Who, both hugely successful sci-fi TV programmes; the former, of course, being very much a US product, the latter quintessentially British. The future as portrayed in Gene Roddenberry's Star Trek is an optimistic one of order and higher values where humanity has reached a more evolved and positive condition. There are, of course, major threats and problems to deal with, but all of this takes place within a context in which an essentially good cosmic social order will prevail. By contrast, the world and the future according to Doctor Who is a completely different matter. The good doctor battles diabolical enemies, muddling through an endless succession of evil alien forces intent on destroying the earth. The overall impression is of a cosmos teetering between imminently potential catastrophes whereby the forces of good, that is, our intrepid Doctor, are hanging on by the merest thread.

Personally, I found it quite revealing to think of the difference between the two programmes as representative of significant cultural trends within the two countries. The USA did, of course, emerge from World War II as, in an important sense, the sole victor. Not only was her homeland, save for Pearl Harbour, untouched by the ravages of war, but she emerged not only as a winner but into an era of unparalleled economic prosperity. By contrast, as described in the first chapter, the picture in Britain (and other Western European countries of course) was considerably less rosy during the post-war years. War had devastated many of the cities and also the economy, and it was the second of two world wars of the century. As also referred to, Britain showed an impressive capacity to reinvent herself. Nevertheless there was a prevailing sense of uncertainty and, to a large extent, crisis of identity, which made confidence and clarity of purpose considerably more remote than that enjoyed by the USA.

To my mind, the contrast drawn between the underlying premise of Star Trek and Dr. Who says a lot about how, moving into the second half of the twentieth century, the two nations viewed themselves and the values of the two countries at that point in history. The dislike and wariness towards Big Ideas, idealism and *-isms* is more pronounced as a European phenomenon than a US one, partly because these *-isms* were fought out on European soil with such disastrous effect in the twentieth century. To be clear, I am not saying that this is in any way right or wrong, just that our outlook, our views, and our psyches are much more a product of the culture we live in and its history, than we would imagine. And it can only be beneficial to have more awareness of cultural factors which may sometimes unconsciously motivate our actions.

The European (and British) cultural view is now so very far removed from the idealism and triumphalism of the Victorian era and of the period up until the First World War, with its unprecedented total industrial warfare. Up until then, the future beckoned and people were so confident of their purpose and of the great virtue of progress itself. To give a taste, here is John Ruskin in a speech in 1870 at his inaugural lecture at Oxford University, speaking in a way that is so foreign to us today that it sounds absurd, embarrassing or downright offensive:

There is indeed a course of beneficent glory open to us, such as never was yet offered before to any poor group of mortal souls. But it is with us now, "Reign or Die". And this is what England must do, or perish: she must found colonies as fast and as far as she is able, formed of her most energetic and worthiest men.

And in case you are wondering, this was for Ruskin's appointment as Slade Professor of Art that he gave his famous 'imperial duty' speech. It does make you wonder about the curriculum of the Art department under his leadership.

Nowadays many people, especially intellectuals in Britain and the rest of Europe, are very doubtful that 'progress' is even a good thing at all. John Gray, political philosopher and author of *Heresies: Against Progress and Other Illusions*, goes as far as to argue that the very belief in progress itself is the cause of many of the ills in our society, and for the disasters of history. And he is certainly far from alone in his view, for this view of progress as the problem itself, strikes a chord in many sensitive people, concerned over how we seem to be destroying our delicate earth. I made the point in the Star Trek story of how American attitudes are significantly different from Western European and British ones. This is in part also because the USA, being a newer country, retains (for good and for ill) some of its original pioneer spirit, and still has greater confidence in the future than Europeans now have. However American attitudes are also moving more towards European ones in this regard, as they see their global hegemony start to wane; this shift is much more pronounced on the more liberal East and West coasts.

To get a sense of our current Western cultural zeitgeist, just look at the preponderance of dystopian movies in our times: no more idealism, but instead dark futures. The typical scenario is a post-apocalyptic wasteland after humanity has all but destroyed itself and the few survivors eke out a precarious existence while avoiding murderous bands of zombies or cannibals. From *Mad Max* to *The Road*, from *Twenty Eight Days Later* to *Robocop*, from *The Walking Dead* to *Waterworld*, the dystopian future is all but ubiquitous these days. If I think about it, an idealistic positive future would seem ridiculously naïve to many of us, unless it's a Disney animation meant exclusively for children.

During the periods of time I spent living in the USA, Australia, Holland and Germany, I observed many similarities with Britain of course, and yet also many differences. I would be struck, perplexed, dismayed, as well as sometimes very heartened too, every time I returned to Britain, by our particular cultural character. The downside of Britain with its declinism, pessimism, lack of connection with our history or sense of shared story, prompted me into an ongoing contemplation as to its origins; since apart from all the pan-Western and European factors that are partly explanatory, I was convinced there were other significant factors at play as well. I became fascinated by the subject and I read many of the current books on Britain, England and Britishness, which were all interesting yet I felt that generally there was a missing element: there wasn't a living story linking past to present, nor was there generally any sense of what I have referred to already as a developmental view. I'll illustrate and explain what I mean in the following pages, rather than try to define it right here, since it is a different way of looking which has many nuances.

Chapter 4

Shining a Light on Cultural Evolution

What we mean by maturity in people's thinking is not a matter of how smart they are, but it is a matter of the order of consciousness in which they exercise their smartness or their lack of it.
Robert Kegan

The life of man is a self-evolving circle, which, from a ring imperceptibly small, rushes on all sides outwards to new and larger circles, and that without end. The extent to which this generation of circles, wheel without wheel, will go, depends on the force or truth of the individual soul.
Ralph Waldo Emerson

Distinct Patterns of Development

In order to have a sense of where we are as a nation and how on earth we got here, I want to shine a developmental light on some broad contours of our British story and the times that we are living in now. Let me start with a story which first opened my eyes to this different way of seeing: A number of years ago I met an unusual man called Don Beck. He's the main proponent of one particularly clear approach to human development called *Spiral Dynamics*. A genial Texan psychologist and consultant with the drawl and dry humour of the Lone Star State, he has a great sensitivity to people and their life conditions, and tirelessly traverses the globe, speaking to whoever is interested in his work.

I attended a conference led by Don Beck in London a few years back, intriguingly entitled, *From Rule Britannia to Cool Britannia to Integral Britannia - Summit on the Future of Great Britain*. Being archetypically Texan, Beck could at that time inadvertently act as a magnet for the mass, or more accurately, morass of bad feelings harboured by Europeans for his Texan compatriot, a certain George Bush Jr. And Don Beck can be mischievously enigmatic as to his own political persuasions, sometimes incensing liberals by dropping a choice non-PC comment. I've heard him playfully float the notion to an audience as to whether they would like global governance with one person, one vote? When liberals nod affirmatively, Don will reply, 'So do you like Chinese food?' Yet I've come to know him as a person who has a deep care for humanity and one who is dedicated to resolving conflict - not by simply striving to impose peace, but more significantly by working towards development between conflicting parties, which can potentially and ideally lead to a more lasting resolution.

True to form, Beck, partly mischievously I think, played the London conference audience a music video by Norman Lear entitled, *Born Again American*. I found it actually quite a moving video portraying a range of ordinary Americans expressing what they sincerely felt was best about their country; simple heartfelt expressions of people's love for their country, the US of A. Don Beck asked us to reflect on this American video and to contemplate what our homegrown British equivalent of this might be, as a way for us to connect with what is most deeply positive about our own culture. Yet the initial effect of playing the video was to release a veritable flood of reaction and indignation at this seeming American cultural imperialism, and its (to our British sensibilities) crass patriotism. But I think Beck deliberately wanted us to be confronted with our own annoyance and disdain, to provoke and reveal our own contemporary British values. It was clear to me that such a simple and straightforward expression of love by ordinary Americans for what they felt is best about their country was very distant from us British today, especially this sophisticated audience. But Beck's gambit got us all engaged and helped stimulate a productive conference.

In recent decades an impressive cross cultural body of evidence has emerged from developmental psychology and other social sciences, which very much points to the conclusion that the minds and worldviews of human beings, and by extension, our societies, do develop through certain recognisable broad patterns or stages. I'm talking about the complex sets of values and structures which define our deeper sense of ourselves. These are far from rigid and linear categories, but flowing and living with many variations in details, and yet it really seems that recognisable patterns do keep being corroborated by research, which despite local flavours, clearly transcend whether people are from a particular country or culture. So the pattern really does appear to be cross cultural and applies to the development of human culture and consciousness. For the purposes of this book on Britain, I am focussing exclusively on the Western world, acknowledging that for example there may well be deep and significant differences, in for example, Eastern mindsets and worldviews. The Western researchers include well-known names in psychology such as Maslow, Kohlberg, Loevinger, Gilligan, Graves and Kegan. While they differ in exact quantification, they do very much point to a certain stage-wise development of value systems in individuals and in cultures. Though varying considerably in expression according to the particular society, these value systems can be generally recognised both now and historically as well.

Spiral Dynamics is one of these approaches and was originally created by Don Beck's colleague and mentor, psychologist Clare Graves. Graves' research demonstrated how each stage of human development is formed and influenced by its relationship to the preceding stages. Each stage of development arises in response to the needs and problems of its particular times and life conditions. It's important to say again that this is not an attempt to categorise people in types or put them in pigeon holes; it is a way of describing the whole value systems which people hold. As

Don Beck himself says, 'The focus is not on types of people, but types in people.' And to underscore this, I've always loved founder Clare W. Graves' statement: 'Damn it all, a person has the right to be who he is.'

And this is not just theoretical. Don Beck has had decades of experience applying this knowledge in real life situations such as his work in South Africa during the transition from the Apartheid system in the 1980s, when he made literally dozens of trips there to help the enormous cultural transition necessary on all sides and to try to help prevent more bloodshed with apparently quite some success behind the scenes. He worked to shift the dialogue from the polarisation of black versus white, to one about understanding the very different values held by people, which are not racial at all.

My role was to shift the categories people were using to describe the South African groupings from 'race,' 'ethnicity,' 'gender,' and 'class' into the natural value-system patterns and the dynamics of change. Many were able to connect across these great divides to find the basis for a sense of being 'South African'.

What *Spiral Dynamics* elucidates is how the development of consciousness and culture proceeds through certain specific main stages which stand out clearly throughout history and can also be seen in the present time. These stages develop in a particular order and direction, though these are broad trends and there is of course much individual variation and anomalies. Beck's *Spiral Dynamics* is just one approach to development and there are various others, yet there is clearly quite a broad congruence in these models, which tends very much to substantiate their overall reality. Beck again:

Each level of existence, or meme,* (*Beck's vMemes or value memes, as distinct from Dawkins original usage of the word) is more like an emerging wave, a fluid living system, than a rigid hierarchical step. Once a new level appears in a culture, all of the previously acquired developmental stages remain in the composite value system. In (Integral philosopher) Ken Wilber's language, each new social stage "transcends and includes" all of those that have come before. For this reason, the more complex thinking systems have greater degrees of freedom.

It was Jean Piaget who famously demonstrated stages of cognitive development in children. While this now sounds entirely reasonable, even perhaps obvious to us today, it was hugely significant at the time. Other researchers extended this developmental approach to adults. And many researchers realised that there is a definite parallel between individual stages of development and the development of cultural and historical worldviews, though they can't be exactly equated. Renowned social philosopher Jurgen Habermas, for one, has very much endorsed the similarities between psychological and historical development. This is a whole subject in itself and beyond the scope of this book, yet for our purposes, it's helpful to see the parallels. I'm suggesting to hold this perspective lightly for now as a potentially useful lens, while being aware that there is always more complexity to the picture.

Just to be clear about what I don't mean: this can superficially look like some odious way of categorising people or cultures; of ranking them, some superior, some inferior. Looking at people and societies in that crude evolutionary manner brings to mind the social Darwinism of the late nineteenth and early twentieth centuries which used the biological concepts of Darwinism, of the struggle for existence and survival of the fittest, to justify all manner of harsh social policies which made no distinction between those able to support themselves and those unable to support themselves. This ideology has also been used as justification for ideas of eugenics, of manipulating the genetics of populations, though it thankfully fell into complete disrepute through its enthusiastic adoption by the Nazis.

These are broad patterns, and people and cultures can't just be plonked in some neat category. Human beings are much more complicated, extraordinary, variable, perverse and amazing than anyone can predict. Reality is much more complex and nuanced than that, and people are a complex mesh incorporating various shades of value systems in the same psyche. Also, of course, there is more to human development than just the growth of our values: emotional and cognitive developments can be, to a fair degree, independent of a person's worldview and values. And then there are the towering rare figures through history who buck categorisation and sometimes seem to be many centuries ahead of the general curve: the greats, like Plato, Gautama Buddha, Lao Tzu, Gandhi, etc. Development seems to be much more meandering and fitful than it is linear.

Yet I am convinced that a broad pattern of development can be discerned through the centuries, though I have to admit that when I first heard about these various systems of categorising human development I thought they sounded ridiculously simplistic. I thought that though maybe possessing a grain of truth, they probably had more to do with the originators' desire to neatly categorise, than with actuality on the ground. Yet as I learned more, I came to see how they did answer a lot of questions I had had about Britain and the world in general, and that these models were really tracking actual human development. And also that these models, properly understood, were the antithesis of any kind of crude ranking or labelling of races, nations or any ethnic group.

Through the Centuries & Now

I hope that as I proceed, the relevance of this way of looking as a means for shedding fresh light on our present day situation in Britain will become apparent. So to continue this short introduction to a developmental view, I want to outline the main stages. To keep it simple, I will use commonly accepted generic terms for these main stages rather than the particular and more technical terms used by *Spiral Dynamics* or other systems; each system has its own terms, yet, as I said earlier, there is a broad similarity between them.

The main stages proceed from what can be broadly termed *pre-traditional* to *traditional*, to *modernist*, and then through to *postmodern* consciousness and whatever may be beyond. And it is not that we each occupy only one of these stages; usually several exert their influence and yet we tend to have a centre of gravity around one or two particular levels. It's important to hold these distinctions lightly when we speak of a stage of consciousness or level of development. We're speaking of patterns of values, which are not fixed or isolatable; they are living currents inter-acting with life conditions in real people, and yet these generali-sations are pointing to something which has validity and is real and which has different expressions in different countries. Also, a later or more complex higher level shouldn't be thought of as necessarily 'better' or more intelligent. What's *'best'* is the level of consciousness, value system and worldview which is *best* adapted to the particular life conditions a person is in the midst of. And yet because, as Beck says, each new stage transcends and includes those which came before, there are potentially greater degrees of freedom available for people with these later emerging and more complex value systems.

In Britain and the West, the most relevant stages of devel-opment to what I am discussing, are the traditional, modernist and postmodern waves, yet a little discussion of the other stages will, I feel, be helpful.

Pre-traditional & Traditional

Briefly, the earliest arising pre-traditional wave of development that we still see in the world today is what could be tribal consciousness. Clans and tribes have been a universal mode of organisation between human beings for untold thousands of years, and this still continues today in places like the rainforests of the Amazon or Papua New Guinea. This kind of society, which can be hunter gatherer communities, should not be thought of as primitive or as lacking intelligence, since the people are extraordinarily adapted to their life conditions. They have various senses developed which have become absent or vestigial in us moderns; for example, their attunement with each other, 'feeling' in ways that can seem like ESP to us, living in tune with nature and perhaps in touch with subtle realms through their shamanistic practices. There's a sense of enchantment to their world, and their world really is a magical one. This worldview is so far removed from ours today that we can only feel a faint resonance deep in ourselves, and our attempts to enter this world tend to be strongly retro-romantic, and wishful thinking. Such indigenous groups of people are perfectly adapted to their life conditions as long as they are left undisturbed, which looks increasingly unlikely today, with the pressures for logging and rain forest clearance for farming ever encroaching on their world, and with the relentless juggernaut of modernity sweeping everything in its path.

Today in Britain, tribal consciousness still has some resonance yet our life conditions have changed so enormously that different values systems now predominate. While foraging in Asda between the aisles with the shopping list demands certain skills, it is a long way from the enchanted spirit world of foraging and hunting in the rain forest. Yet a sense of belonging and kinship with family and community and connection to the land is for us moderns a healthy sense of tribal consciousness as part of our nested system of values. And football matches with our fervent tribal allegiance to our home team can be a fantastic release for tribal energy. However, today in Britain, we have increasingly lost touch with one valuable element of tribal consciousness: a shared sense of continuity; a sense of a story which gives us meaning and rootedness.

It can sound fanciful to speak of the evolution of consciousness, since being by its nature immaterial, there is obviously no direct material evidence of consciousness existing now, let alone as different stages in the past. To put it bluntly, there is of course no fossil record of consciousness where we might observe any possible development over time; no fragments of ancient minds; no museum displays in glass cases to ponder upon. And yet we can trace the effects of minds or consciousness by the artifacts produced by people from the past: by the stone axes, the statues, the paintings on cave walls, and gradually with the advent of the written word, by their stories and records. Gary Lachman speaks of what he calls the 'the imprint of human imagination' in his intriguing *Secret History of Consciousness.* 'It is the mind pressing itself on the material world. And it is through these "mindprints", that we can trace the further evolution of consciousness.'

Princeton psychologist Julian Jaynes came up with the most startling theory of all about the historical origins of consciousness as we conceive it, in his *The Origin of Consciousness in the Breakdown of the Bicameral Mind.* According to Jaynes, ancient peoples did not have an interior world; they didn't think, 'Hmm, I wonder what I want to do today? Should I go for a spot of mammoth hunting today or shall I just stay in the cave and sharpen my stone axe instead?' or anything remotely of that sort. From his study of *The Iliad,* the characters in this earliest of Greek books, dating from around 1250 BC, listened to 'voices' which they heard in their heads. And they took these voices to be the voices of the Gods. The characters in *The Iliad* are passive and mentally inert with no sign of a private mental space and no self-reflection. There was no sense of, or word for will or volition, nor introspection. The 'bicameral' in the title of his book, meaning two-chambered, refers to the right and left hemispheres of the brain, which until around 1250 BC, according to Jaynes, were functioning completely independently. The 'voices of the Gods' emanated from one side of the brain, telling people what to do. A controversial theory from a controversial man who had little time for his own field of psychology, which he described as not much more than bad poetry disguised as science. Yet it does make us stop and question our assumptions and projections upon past peoples and how they perceived themselves and the world.

To return to our narrative, the next emerging pre-traditional value system is that which has been called 'warrior' consciousness. Each stage starts to emerge partly as a reaction to the limitations of the preceding stage. Warrior consciousness is the breaking away from the conformity and perceived stasis of tribal culture with a new bold self-assertiveness, and the beginning of an independent self. Yes, it's an aggressive raw egocentric self, violent and ruthless, and has led to the warrior cultures of warlords like Attila the Hun and Genghis Khan, and in Britain we remember Celtic warriors such as Boudicca, Queen of the Iceni. But it was also a violent creative breakthrough of the human spirit. At its best it expresses the noble qualities of heroism and adventure, breaking into the new, and has led to warlords and the early empires of our world. This kind of warrior consciousness is still very alive and active in places like Somalia, Iraq and Afghanistan, where it best matches the prevailing life conditions.

While this pre-traditional worldview is not a large part of the Britain of today, we can still find elements of warrior culture in street gangs; where what is most important is 'respect'. Any perceived disrespect merits punishment and often leads to revenge and ongoing skirmishes with rival gangs over honour and respect. Other citizens can live in an urban neighbourhood which, unbeknownst to them, is strictly divided by postcode or streets into rival gang territories; the gang members see the rival gang members trespassing on their turf while we see nothing of this subculture most of the time, unless we inadvertently become a victim of it. In some significant ways we really don't all live in the same world. Also we find elements of this value system in rock stars, with uninhibited rebellion and self-expressiveness. This warrior element is still very much part of all of us and can be reactivated in the right conditions, such as the heroism of a firefighter or the fighting spirit of an athlete. We are each a composite of different shades and degrees of all these values living in us. It's important to note that each stage of culture has a healthy aspect and a pathological aspect and each provides an intrinsic and enduring value to the whole developing process; what Don Beck calls the spiral of development that both individuals and cultures go through as they develop.

Traditional consciousness came into being, as have all these value systems, as a response to life conditions, and in particular as a reaction to the chaos and brutality of the previously predominant pre-traditional warrior culture. The traditional system brought order and the valuing of the importance of community and higher purpose; now the common aspiration became to sacrifice one's self for the greater good of the community or society. Historically this marked the birth of the great religions of the world with their mythic order and significantly, with their written texts which concretised this new higher order. Traditional consciousness values higher truth, often religious in God's name, but also in secular societies as well. This was a more complex emergence which provided a civilising foundation with its upholding of law and order which crucially allowed all kinds of social, political, and cultural structures to flourish in a way that was not possible in the time of the warlords. Right and wrong and black and white are clear here, and must be obeyed.

This level was the prevalent structure in Britain along with warrior consciousness, until the stirrings of modernism in the Renaissance and then more dramatically with the advent of the Western Enlightenment in the seventeenth and eighteenth centuries. Yet don't think of traditional consciousness as standing still during these many centuries. It has changed a great deal through that time. This was medieval Britain and it was also Protestant Britain in later stages; and even today, the traditional worldview, though greatly updated, is still a key component of a considerable number of Britons. It's 'traditional' in the sense of that structure which upholds a higher order and sacrifice of self for the greater good, and not in terms of any particular content or appearance, which may shift dramatically over the centuries. A contemporary Briton may have a traditional centre of gravity for his values and at the same time work as a software developer.

Robert Bartlett, a leading authority on the medieval mind, manages to convey what a vastly different worldview was the norm in Britain in the period between the ninth and the fifteenth centuries. It was a traditional world of mythic order where the King's right to rule was divinely ordained by God; there was order and stability providing one abided by the rules, and a freedom from the previous chaos of warrior culture. Medieval life centred on the great power of the church which mediated for the people between God and the forces of the devil. Yet it was religious in a way that I think we are unable to truly comprehend today; life was inseparable from the religious view. You couldn't not be religious then; you just couldn't conceive of 'religion' as an optional category. The real world for the medieval person was not *this* one, but the *next* one where you went to after a very short span in this world. And where you went: heaven, hell, or purgatory, was of course, all important. The supernatural was ever present and there was no clear boundary between the living and the dead, who were always present. Your local church was a fortress to help protect your soul on the perilous journey from life to death and beyond; the devil was a constant menace and could appear to tempt you at any moment perhaps as a crow or a dog. Angels and demons battled for your soul and this was everyday reality, and miraculous tales were faithfully recorded and repeated to all as gospel truth. For us today, this is a bridge too far and it's impossible for us to enter into this medieval worldview; we can appreciate their beliefs but we can't enter into them nor see through their eyes. When you next look out on the rolling hills of the British countryside and see the familiar church towers of perhaps half a dozen or more old churches dotted across the landscape, poking through the tree tops, imagine these as the veritable citadels and bastions which they were, in the battle against evil.

In contrast, a revolutionary act took place in the medieval world in 1336 which may surprise you. The Italian poet Petrarch climbed a mountain, Mount Ventoux in France. What's revolutionary in that, you may ask? Clearly people had climbed mountains before, but these climbs were always for utilitarian reasons like for grazing sheep or to cross a pass, or in the case of Moses ascending Mount Sinai in order to receive the stone tablets from God. What was radical was Petrarch's motive for climbing a mountain. In his own words in a letter to his former confessor, 'My only motive was the wish to see what so great an elevation had to offer.' This was unheard of. You just didn't do such a thing. The medieval world was a full and complete one as described above and yet it was in effect, a hermetically sealed one. Such enjoyment of nature, and enjoying the view, was not part of that world, as we have touched on earlier with even the much later eminent Dr. Johnson. Petrarch, in his climbing a mountain for the thrill of it, was stepping out of the medieval worldview, and revelling in space and perspective. Gary Lachman goes as far as to call this act 'the true beginning of the "space age",' rather than being inaugurated by the Russian satellite Sputnik in 1957.

Generally in England, up until at least the seventeenth or eighteenth century, not to believe in God just wasn't a choice, and the mythic order was enforced. In fact with the Puritans, a more extreme protestant reform movement, (they preferred to call themselves 'the godly') for a brief period after the English

Revolution in the mid sixteen hundreds, we had crackdowns by Cromwell on entertainment and festivals, partly supposedly for national security but also in an attempt to reform the morals of the nation. Definite shades of the Taliban here, and it's interesting to see how similar and recognisable stages and worldviews emerge cross culturally yet with their own distinct characters. Such 'talibanisation' didn't go down well in England and this attempt at enforcement soon had to be given up. Puritans had to give up their idea of England as a theocracy, though that was what the even more radical New England Puritans attempted for their communities. Interesting that we managed to export most of our religious extremists to the American colonies.

Modernity

Following this emerged the next stage: modernist consciousness, with the trumping of mythic order by the liberating power of reason, rationality and individual achievement and effort. The Western Enlightenment in the seventeenth and eighteenth centuries was the flowering of reason and rationality, breaking away from the conformism and superstition of the 'mythic order' of traditional society which had dominated for centuries in a feudal society supported by the power of the Church. It was the birth of the modern world, of realism, of the rights of man (and to some degree, women), of freedom of speech, of democracy, of achievement and progress. Science was released to provide us with a more objective truth, and technology developed rapidly in the Industrial Revolution. Many advances and freedoms for the individual came from modernism and for many, our lives were greatly enriched and extended. All this of course is very recognisable in British history; this country being the cradle of the Industrial Revolution, and Britain more than any other single country, probably did the most to help form the modern world as we know it. Modernism gained ascendancy and flowered in full force in Britain with the Industrial Revolution, and to this day it is still the greatest influence on a large proportion of the British population.

What on Earth is 'Postmodern'?

The postmodern system of values is the most recent emergence, and again, it, like previous systems, arose in response to the increasing pathologies and inadequacies of the preceding stage; in this case, modernism. Already even at the end of the eighteenth century, a few leading edge individuals, starting with the Romantics such as William Blake, Wordsworth and Coleridge, began to become disenchanted with the downside of modernism with its inherent limitations in asserting objective material reality as the only valid way to see the world. At first these were lone dissenters, yet as time went on and especially in the second half of the twentieth century, the devastation caused by the results of modernism in wars, the destruction of the environment by rampant industrialisation, in the way the West was running roughshod over all other cultures on the planet, led many to doubt whether this was really any 'progress' at all. Also Britain and other Western nations had been able to use their superior technology and weaponry and organisation to conquer and colonise a large part of the world. Because of these ever more self-evident pathologies of modernism, leading thinkers began to fundamentally question the whole Western Enlightenment project. This emerging sensitive and compassionate consciousness really came into its own as a mass movement in the 1960s and for the purposes of this discussion I am calling this movement, postmodernism.

A little digression and explanation is needed right now. *Postmodernism* is a slippery and elusive term because there isn't really any clear consensus about what is meant by it. We can of course say that it's whatever has come after modernism, but that doesn't help that much, and also various academics don't even feel that there is any such thing as postmodernism and that it is merely an extension of modernism. And it is true that some achievements often associated with postmodernity such as human rights were already the gifts of modernism. The term postmodernism is often used as a wide ranging and general label for certain movements in art, architecture, literature, literary criticism, or for certain trends in contemporary philosophy. I am not a philosopher, and expert philosophical distinctions are not within the scope of this book, yet it is important to have a sense of the way I am using the term 'postmodern' for the purposes of this discussion. I am using it in a broader sense as a new worldview, an organizing principle in thought, action, and reflection, linked to many changing factors in modern society, similarly to how I have described the previous worldviews. It's also more difficult to perceive or talk with clarity about this worldview today because we are so much *in* it as I have mentioned previously, and we don't have the advantage of hindsight.

Postmodernism has been and still is to some degree, a reaction to the assumed certainty of scientific and objective efforts to explain reality. It sees reality as being constructed and inter-preted by each of us rather than our even being able to know if there is anything objective or 'out there'. We each interpret the world in our own relative way and so postmodernism is very sceptical of overarching explanations which claim to be true for everyone everywhere. I find it interesting that postmodern philosophy has been a particular emergence in France with famous names such as Foucault, Lyotard, Baudrillard and of course Derrida. In France, postmodernism has been influential at the high end of culture yet not at a popular level, with the country remaining a largely modernist society. Conversely in Britain, postmodernity has been far more influential at the pop end of the cultural spectrum, starting with the explosion of the 1960s and all the mass ramifications in popular culture. The emerging pluralistic postmodern consciousness and worldview in Britain from the 1960s onwards, addressed the excesses of modernism with its inclusiveness, its concern for the environment, and by emphasising the fact that every culture is worthy of respect and has its own inherently valid point of view. The 1960s popularised the need to take into account everyone's point of view, and gave birth to multiculturalism, environmentalism, women's rights, animal rights, gay rights, and curbing the harm done by industrialisation. The emphasis was on the individual and it was the coming of age of the Baby Boomers.

Sometimes only the excesses and the over emphasis of the so called 'Me' generation are remembered when we look back at the 1960s, but as outlined above, many great advances for Western culture and globally too, were a direct result of this new worldview and consciousness. Here we need to distinguish between some of the beginning emergence of postmodernism which can be strongly anti-modernist, and a more mature healthy postmodernism, which is constructive and has the wonderful capacity to hold and accommodate many different and even conflicting views in a way which no previous stage was able to do.

In a way we are all like Russian dolls; a nested hierarchy of systems of values and worldviews; they are all within us. We all have these sets of values in our make up and we're talking of people's centre of gravity value-wise, which determines which stage or stages of consciousness we tend to act and live from. Also any of these levels can be reactivated if conditions evoke them. For example in a major disaster, we may easily revert to earlier stages as the dystopian movies love to point out. It's not a simplistic linear historical story, nor some ladder; we are talking of trends and directions, and evolution seems to be a messy and meandering business. The past is not gone at all, but lives within us far more than our modern minds tend to realise.

In fact, cultural philosopher Jean Gebser, who independently came up with broadly similar categories to those discussed above, which he saw as changes in the structure of consciousness, cautioned against using such words as development and evolution, or direction and progress. This was because he felt that such terms were inapplicable as a way to describe what he saw as an unfolding of consciousness. He preferred to call these historical changes in the structure of consciousness, 'mutations.' Gebser noted that concepts of linear time and progression are ones which only emerge with what we are calling here the consciousness of modernism, and were not previously any part of the worldview of people, back say, in medieval times. Since today we are all so heavily conditioned by this modern mental-rational structure, we find it hard to think of time as other than purely linear like a straight line. Gebser provided much evidence of how he saw signs of this fixed sense of 'straight line' time now starting to break down, as a new structure of consciousness, which he called 'integral', emerging in many fields such as literature, visual arts, philosophy and science. A different time sense, was for Gebser, one of the clearest characteristic signs of the new consciousness which he was identifying. Gebser's view can help loosen our thinking to appreciate that although the categorisation I've been making is a very useful tool, at a deeper level, time still remains much more mysterious, as does the whole subject of the past.

Over the years, I've come to appreciate how these forces and patterns of development have been playing out in my life and in the culture around me, growing up in Britain, and then through adulthood. I realise how much these currents and dynamics are a formative stream in all our lives; how the past lives and expresses itself now, as us. This evolutionary lens has afforded me a fresh angle on understanding the British; it sheds light on an important strand regarding where we have come from and where we may possibly be heading and on why we may feel and react and respond as we do. Not only that, it helps us reconnect with and appreciate how we are the beneficiaries of our forebears and their cultures. We can begin to separate out the healthy aspects of previous stages from the prejudices and horrors of those stages, instead of rejecting much of it, and thus leaving us feeling disconnected from our rich history. For example, we can value and appreciate such positive qualities of the traditional worldview as personal responsibility, honesty, fairness and the value of sometimes deferring personal gratification. This can now be separated from the pathologies of that worldview such as fundamentalism, dogmatism, racism and sexism. And while not condoning such prejudices today, it can give us a better and more sympathetic understanding of why we and others may still feel and express those same tendencies. This will be explored in the subsequent chapter. We can grow into a fuller affinity with different layers of our British culture and be more accepting of our own deeper psychological layers as well, neither avoiding and rejecting our national past nor hankering after it nostalgically. This would help us to both reclaim and better integrate our national history as part of ourselves.

Chapter 5

A New Story

A people are as healthy and confident as the stories they tell themselves. Sick storytellers can make nations sick. Without stories we would go mad. Life would lose its moorings or orientation....Stories can conquer fear, you know. They can make the heart larger.

Ben Okri

Following the preceding short overview on development, I'd like to put a little flesh on those theoretical bones to show what it can look like in practice in Britain: to help understand what it means to be British today, with the various and sometimes competing forces and currents pulling on and motivating us. To do so, I'll take several modern British figures as examples of how this all plays out in actual human beings. As I've repeatedly said, it's not neat and demarcated, but more a swirl of competing energies, which nevertheless do show recognisable patterns within all the other dynamics at play in any person's life. And where better to start than with my own case.

How Development Plays out in Actual British People

My own traditional and modernist upbringing was solidly middle-class and aspirational. I was gently expected to do well and achieve at school, and religion was absent and not talked about at home; we lived in a new build house in a freshly created cul de sac in the suburbs, and the sense was of optimistic progress providing you work for it. Mild shades of pre-tradi-tional warrior consciousness would surface now and then in my love for groups like The Who, a band the rebellious side of myself identified with in my adolescence. I remember going to a show of theirs in a North London ballroom in the 60s and being awed by their legendary finale where they smashed up all their equipment. I have strong memories of defiantly trespassing in the grounds of the local suburban golf course belting out aloud the defiant words of the Who song, 'Anyway, Anyhow, Anywhere', as I stomped along in the woods.

I had a phase where I became a weekend wannabe mod complete with de rigueur ex-army parka and chrome accessories on my Vespa SS180 scooter and joined a group of friends—'gang' would be too strong a word. My thrill riding wasn't helped by my shortsightedness and I felt it would be way too uncool to wear glasses. A crash after a dare attempting to take off from riding fast over a humpbacked bridge, did bring me down to earth in more ways than one. These were mild shades of warrior, yet I knew the intoxicating wild surge of energy and power which that consciousness evokes.

Studying zoology at university opened my eyes to the extremely reductionistic bias of science, especially in the way it was taught at that time. I studied zoology for my degree because of my lifelong love for nature and here I was dissecting dead creatures all the time while almost being asphyxiated by the stench of formaldehyde. Rejecting these modernistic values, I felt drawn by the 'come together' spirit of the times (almost the byword of egalitarian postmodernism) and helped found an idealistic community more in touch with spirit and nature in my twenties. Communal values, consensus in decision making; care for the world and making a smaller environmental footprint all inspired me in my new postmodern values.

I'm firmly postmodern, and yet when the triggering moment comes, I can be traditional in an instant. My eyes get moist and pride and a sense of gratitude swells up within, when I hear a replay of Churchill talking of his 'broad sunlit uplands' in his *Finest Hour* speech at the darkest point in WWII; similarly if I watch a History Channel programme about *'the few'* in the Battle of Britain. These kind of emotional responses to WWII used to confuse me as a young adult in my days of anti-war pacifism. Although I detailed the traditional stage as being the norm in Britain for a long long time before modernism, there are still many many people in this country who are strongly grounded and expressive of that traditional value set.

Now to move on to the first of my modern historical examples to illustrate what I mean. A renowned figure who to a significant degree embodied the above systems of values in Britain was of course, Winston Churchill himself. He was a prime example of traditional consciousness. With his unwavering conviction in the high moral purpose of Britain's fight against the evil empire of the Nazis to literally save Western civilization from barbarism, he was the perfect war leader to unite the country. Loving his country and wedded to the great traditions of Britain and Empire, he had the iron will and strength to inspire and rally the country through the darkest days of the great struggle in WWII. He stood unambiguously for what's right and Good, for God, for Britain, for The Empire and for Christian civilisation. Offering at first only blood, sweat and toil, he inspired people to give themselves for a greater good. And it worked; he was *the* man for the dire living conditions in 1940. Thank goodness we had him. Imagine having a postmodern Ed Miliband or a Nick Clegg in 1940; they'd probably want to do some focus group studies first; perhaps a cultural exchange programme with the Nazis?

Come the end of war at last in 1945, it may seem ungrateful of the British electorate that they dropped Churchill in an instant for a socialist welfare government, and Churchill himself was stunned and dismayed. Yet Churchill was a wartime leader, not a peacetime leader, and people intuitively knew it. They wanted jobs and houses now, and Churchill was not the man who best met those life conditions.

The downside of traditional consciousness can be seen in Churchill in his unchanging intolerance, dogmatism and prejudice. His traditional outlook led him to hold onto The Empire doggedly and irrationally. He certainly didn't regard Indians as equals and was rudely dismissive of Gandhi, and in the next chapter we will see how this prejudice had still greater effects. Churchill loved his wife 'Clemmie' with a depth and consistency that is moving, writing to her whenever he was away from her, and at the same time, in his earlier Edwardian political days, hear his very conservative views on women generally. 'The women's suffrage movement is only the small edge of the wedge, if we allow women to vote it will mean the loss of social structure and the rise of every liberal cause under the sun. Women are well represented by their fathers, brothers, and husbands.'

Richard Dawkins, the well-known evolutionary biologist, is an interesting and classic present day example of a modernist, both very positively and also I feel somewhat negatively as well. A great scientist, who embodies the scientific and Enlightenment ideals of reason dispelling superstition and advancing objective knowledge. A believer in progress by extending the good effects of science and technology, he tirelessly promotes this view. He wrote the renowned *The Selfish Gene* as well as various other books on biology and popular science. He's a brilliant populariser of science and the scientific worldview, and a strong proponent of the view that only that which can be materially proved and measured by science, is real. Though he's a modernist through and through, I've seen him on film at Charles Darwin's original home in Kent, reverently holding an original notebook of the great naturalist, and the passion and yes—dare I say it, devotion—in Dawkins towards his hero was striking. The devotion even looked religious to me. So even Richard Dawkins can be traditional at times too.

Yet these days he is even better known for his outspoken writings on atheism such as *The God Delusion*. While many scientists may be atheists, agnostics or believers, Dawkins has taken his own atheism much further and seems to be almost on a crusade against religion. One way in which modernism can have a pathological aspect is in taking the materialist scientific view too far and saying that only this mode of perceiving and interpreting the world has any validity. This leads to scientism rather than open minded scientific inquiry. Dawkins seems to feel it his duty to expose and debunk the supposed dangerous ignorance of believers everywhere and to sweep away the tide of superstitious mud of their irrational belief in higher powers. This mission to eradicate superstition is curiously reminiscent of the late nineteenth century when the belief in science and progress was at its zenith. Take this classic Dawkins statement: 'It's the genes that, for their own good, are manipulating the bodies they ride about in. The individual organism is a survival machine for its genes.' He makes it clear what in his view, life is actually all about; a view which though incisive and fascinating, to my mind leaves a tremendous amount about life out of the picture. Dawkins is a modernist who takes this worldview to the more extreme end of that spectrum.

When we come to postmodern consciousness, one classic icon has to be John Lennon who was one of the key figures in the first widespread emergence of postmodern values in the 1960s. First obviously with the Beatles who helped define the character of that time and with their interest in Eastern spirituality and the power of love to bring people together; this is a very different and more inclusive worldview than modernism with its focus on reason and progress. *All You Need is Love* comes from a very different worldview than any Elvis or Chuck Berry song. Also in Lennon's post-Beatles years, think of his *Imagine*, and then *Give Peace a Chance* which became the new peace anthem for anti-war movements, especially the Vietnam war. Supporting all manner of groups of disadvantaged people, and celebrating the feminine, Lennon exemplified the inclusivity and egalitarianism of this new value system. Retiring from music in 1975 to become a househusband and spending all his time for the next five years with his newborn son was almost unknown in those times. John Lennon was a great believer in the postmodern view of truth, which simply put is, 'whatever is true for you'. As Lennon said it himself,

> When I was 5 years old, my mother always told me that happiness was the key to life. When I went to school, they asked me what I wanted to be when I grew up. I wrote down happy. They told me I didn't understand the assignment, and I told them they didn't understand life.

The Genuine Gifts of Postmodernity

Of course, this initial phase of postmodernity has much developed and matured since Lennon's time to become far less naive and stereotyped and more integrated in British life. I don't want to give the impression that postmodernism today looks anything remotely like late 1960s counterculture anymore. The point is that the values of this system have infused the mainstream in Britain to affect us all greatly. This isn't fringe or alternative any more. The alternative has become the mainstream, has become the status quo. You can't turn on the news today without hearing reports and discussions about how might we better care for this or that group of disadvantaged people, or a report exposing some area of inequality or discrimination still existing. Sensitivity and compassion are now an intrinsic and much valued part of our society, and failures are rightly decried. Care now extends beyond our borders and we recognise the intrinsic rights of different cultures around the globe. Issues of care for the environment, equality of opportunity for women, finding consensus whenever possible, preventing discrimination, are all mainstream now. Gay rights, women's rights, sustainability, holistic approaches to health, better treatment of animals, multiculturalism, diversity, health and safety issues, are all part of the great gifts of postmodernity. This is all only in the last fifty years.

Yet one aspect which we usually don't give ourselves credit for, is the sheer capacity that ordinary people like us now have to be able to hold multiple and often contradicting perspectives; to be able to accommodate so many differing views and to recognise that each person or group has a right to their own view, and to be able to see each as having intrinsic validity. This is an emergence of a very sophisticated and complex consciousness which is now commonplace. We don't automatically back our own ethnic group or our own locality or our government or our nation against another nation. We can hold and weigh up many factors increasingly as a world citizen with what can be called a world-centric stage of consciousness. I think this is extraordinary and remarkable compared to any previous generation in history. This more sensitive segment of the population has been identified by sociologist Paul Ray as 'cultural creatives' in the book of the same name he co-authored. This study describes the roughly one quarter of the population in the States, (though they estimated a similar proportion in Western Europe) as having developed beyond the standard paradigm of modernists. Also the World Values Survey from the University of Michigan, following trends for the last three decades, shows Britain along with many other countries in the West moving towards ever greater degrees of self-expression progressively through the years, and away from survival values, in a Maslowian values sense.

Clashing Value Systems in Britain Today

This doesn't at all mean that most people in Britain are motivated by postmodern values—because most certainly aren't—but it does mean that pluralistic postmodern values are starting to gain ascendancy in the public cultural sphere. Everyone has to go along with these values to quite a degree, at least publicly, even though of course a great many people, including many of our politicians or business leaders, have modernist or more traditional values. To these people, this all seems like loony liberal PC nonsense or insanity. Modernists feel that bleeding heart liberals are always making special cases for everyone and awarding them the special and coveted status of victims who have been wronged by some lack of equality and need help and compensation. Even when some new road or housing development is planned, a green group will invariably discover a rare invertebrate or lichen on the site which needs protecting, perceived from the modernist point of view as seemingly only a pretext to stop progress. While those with postmodern sensibilities feel the drive for progress and expansionism of modernists as being heartless and uncaring of people or Mother Earth.

My first encounter with some of the downside of the early and anti-modernist strain of postmodernity came in the back to nature/spiritual community I experimented with in my twenties in a rural part of Kent. It was when in our weekly community meeting of the twenty or so adults living there, I found that a small toddler could stop the whole meeting. If this small beautiful being happened to feel like wandering into the open space of our adult circle, he or she could sabotage any discussion and command attention while none of us adults felt we wanted to, or could in any way stifle or repress that fresh young being's natural expression. The strong resolve not to repeat some of our own past upbringings where children were to be seen and not heard, haunted some of us, no doubt. So the meetings could sometimes be hijacked at will by a toddler. At the time, this troubled me, but in my egalitarian naive postmodern idealism, I couldn't figure out exactly why. Or rather I actually could figure it out, but I shied away from the authoritarian and oppressive sounding direction that my thinking was pointing; that is, just deal with the toddler. The dislike of hierarchies and their oppressive nature and the extreme value relativism which can be a pathology of postmodernity, meant that I was in a philosophical pickle trying to navigate this one.

Each stage arises in response to and partly in reaction to the stage before it, and starts in a few pioneering individuals and then spreads if the emerging worldview better matches the life conditions. Like all value systems, there is a healthy and a pathological side of each; a dignity and a disaster to each. So our British and European outlook, at least among sections of the population and especially among a very influential intelligentsia and opinion shapers, is postmodern pluralism, and it's a necessary and important corrective to the excesses of the steamroller of modernism and its unrestrained 'progress' and industrialisation. And those of us who are born in these times are the beneficiaries of this hard won evolution. The dignity is in its sensitivity and compassion and desire to re-include all those who had previously been marginalised. It hates the racist and sexist exploitation of modernism, and values pluralism and multiculturalism. Consensus, working together and inclusiveness are its hallmarks, and non-violence its means.

Yet postmodernism often doesn't see the benefits of traditional and modernist levels and wants to pull down their hard won and time honoured order and structure as being inherently oppressive; which is harmful to people at those levels and akin to kicking away the ladder which enabled you to get to your vantage point, and which would not be there for others. In its urge to dismantle all hierarchy, which is seen as inherently oppressive, postmodernism has had an adverse effect on the healthy side of traditional British order and structure and discipline. Take the lack of discipline in schools and in general in Britain exemplified by the all too common drunken weekend rowdiness in town and city centres. Granted, I speak as one who rebelled against the almost military discipline and general whackings for minor infractions in my own secondary school days, but it has to be said that the conditions in my day hadn't changed much from scenes straight out of *Tom Brown's Schooldays*. Okay, that was oppressively traditional, and well gone, thank goodness. Yet now, the licence to do what one wants whenever one feels like it, the emphasis on rights rather than responsibility, has also had an undermining effect on the development of traditional values, which incidentally are still as essential as ever in childhood as a foundation for growth. Parental authority has declined to a great deal. Kids need boundaries to develop, and this depends first and foremost on parents. Extreme value relativism, which is one of the downsides of postmodernity, leads to an inability to distinguish between the value of what went before, from the unhealthy part to be left behind. It wasn't all bad in the past and we throw out the healthy developmental aspects at our peril. Psychologist Dr Aric Sigman claimed that a generation of young people is growing up with a sense of entitlement because adult authority has been eroded. He cited 'apologetic messaging' and gave the almost incredibly hard to believe example of a Court Service leaflet which stated: 'We would be grateful if you would not bring your knife into court'.

Another aspect of this postmodern downside is in its inability or unwillingness to make value distinctions at all. This can lead to absurd results. Granted, every person is worthy of respect and each person has a view which has inherent validity, yet in order to function and discern and make wise decisions, we obviously all need to make choices; which means valuing one thing or view more than another. And some views are definitely better or wiser than other views, dare I say it. Cultural critic Terry Eagleton can be relied upon to be humorously incisive.

> The liberal state has no view on whether witchcraft is more valuable than all-in wrestling. Like a tactful publican, it has as few opinions as possible. Many liberals suspect passionate convictions are latently authoritarian. But liberalism should surely be a passionate conviction. Liberals are not necessarily lukewarm. Only the more macho leftist suspects that they have no balls.

Eagleton touches on another important point: passion and conviction needn't equate with authoritarianism or a more fundamentalist attitude. The understandable wariness many in Britain feel today about passion or conviction is unfortunate for it tends to dampen and stymie our creative spirit. We need renewed passion and conviction if we as individuals and as a nation are going to rise to the challenges we face today. In Britain today, passion and conviction can so often put people off for another reason as well. So reflexly do we tend toward pessimism, that as many life-hardened folk will sagely inform us, if you don't expect anything, then you won't be disappointed when it doesn't come to pass. This passes for profound wisdom in some circles.

Being cognisant of developmental stages can help us navigate more skillfully through the complex changes and upheavals in our rapidly changing country and world as we inexorably globalise and people are thrown together like never before. I remember having my eyes opened in a conversation with a friend of mine who was at that time the Ambassador to a West African country and a specialist in overseeing aid to African countries. We were talking about Western aid to developing nations and I brought up the issue of corruption and how I understood that aid doesn't always reach those most in need. My friend acknowledged this, yet told me how an important African official might have an extended family or clan who are dependent on him, who look to him for help and support. If he doesn't distribute part of the Western aid to his perhaps 200 extended family members, then that would be seen as immoral and violating his and their own indigenous and tribal code of ethics. This made me stop and think. It could be easy just to write such people off as corrupt, yet in doing so we are imposing our particular Western values and not understanding a legitimate moral code which is very relevant to their life conditions.

The West insists on installing a version of our own democracies (our particular cherished values) on far flung countries, be it Iraq, Libya or Afghanistan. Yet the authentic structures in Afghanistan are much more tribal and clan loyalties with their own complex customs and values, rather than an abstract imposed Western notion of government run from far off and almost foreign Kabul. Democracy in the way we seek to impose it, has little meaning to many people there. When I used to watch reports from the British army in Afghanistan on the TV news, I often wished that there could have been more understanding and sensitivity to these issues. Amazingly, we apparently had no experts from Britain on the ground who could speak Pashtu or Dari, the languages spoken in Helmand province, or who had any understanding of their venerable culture. TV images from that period would initially show, for example, British soldiers searching women's quarters in some village in Helmand for possible Taliban insurgents, with seemingly no understanding of the offence and disrespect it creates in a warrior and tribal culture. Fighting back and seeking revenge is an honourable response from the men in that value system. Westerners can easily be perceived by traditional believers as dangerous atheists; dangerous because they have no fear of God and hence are perceived to be unconstrained by any morality and are surely therefore capable of heinous crimes.

The United Kingdom was formed by the Act of Union in 1707, incorporating Scotland into the union. In 2014 we had the referendum for independence in Scotland, which was defeated, yet not by a huge margin, and so Scotland remains in the Union at least for the foreseeable future. At the time I thought about what would happen if Scotland did become independent, or rather I thought about what *wouldn't* happen; because much has thankfully changed and developed in the intervening three centuries, and the issue doesn't stir up so much passion for many of us, except for campaigning members of the Scottish National Party. And note that it's 'national' not 'nationalist' for the SNP. If independence had occurred, there would have been a big party in Scotland and then life would have continued much the same on both sides of the border, with everyone accepting the result, just as the SNP did following the 'no' vote. Certainly there wouldn't have been anything resembling the ethnic horrors unleashed after the breakup of the former Yugoslavia. The most discord would have been over the currency and how to divide up the offshore gas revenue from the now Scottish North Sea, and how much national debt the Scots had to shoulder as their fair share.

Yet why wouldn't there have been violent ethnic conflict yet alone ethnic cleansing erupting, with Hadrian's Wall having to be rebuilt and fortified? For the simple reason that we have collectively developed. Thankfully we have come a long way since the days of King Edward I's battles with Scottish independence leader William Wallace in the late fourteenth century, popularised by Mel Gibson in *Braveheart*. Mirroring similar English cruelties, it was said that our real life *Braveheart* hero had a sword belt made for him out of the flayed skin of a vanquished English adversary, the unfortunate Hugh de Cressingham, Treasurer of the English administration in Scotland at that time. Taxmen have never been popular and apparently the English didn't like poor de Cressingham either. People in the UK don't now define themselves primarily by their national or ethnic identities. It's part of our identity, yes, a significant part, but only a part. More important is that we are all first and foremost human beings and individuals worthy of respect.

Earlier, we examined our now instinctive wariness towards - *isms* in Britain and Western Europe in general. Just to return once more to this subject, this was to lead French philosopher Jean-François Lyotard to famously declare in 1979, 'Simplifying to the extreme, I define postmodern as incredulity towards metanarratives.' In other words the very essence of postmodernism in his opinion, is a mistrust of great overarching stories or universal claims of any kind. Understandable certainly, from our recent history, as I said earlier. Eagleton again from *The Meaning of Life*:

> In the pragmatist, streetwise climate of advanced postmodern capitalism, with its scepticism of big pictures and grand narratives, its hard-nosed disenchantment with the metaphysical, "life" is one among a whole series of discredited totalities. We are invited to think small rather than big.

Skeptical of notions of progress, of seeing any linear narratives anywhere—and the big one is in history—the liberal postmodern view has inadvertently become the view of many of us in Britain. And as I keep repeating, we have benefitted enormously from this emergence. Many more of us than ever before in the past have the luxury and leisure to contemplate and criticise modernity precisely because of the freedom and standard of living modernity has enabled for us.

The Value of an Evolutionary Perspective

This has been a brief sweep through part of the vast field of development furnished with a few examples, and is only meant as an orienting guide; there are many views and much is disputed and I can't in any way do the subject justice in this short space. Yet sometimes, keeping it more simple is helpful in order to see the forest, as it were. It helps to know where we've come from and what is driving us, and if development is real, then obviously it doesn't stop with our view now at this particular snapshot in time. And we are in need of a more encompassing view at this point: towards a view which honours and includes all the advances bequeathed to us from our history and culture, and yet which is not backward looking; instead embracing more complexity to meet our exponentially changing and complexifying life conditions. An evolutionary worldview such as I have been suggesting in this chapter can go a long way towards recontextualising our past and present, providing greater depth and breadth to make wiser and more considered choices as we meet the moment. It then becomes possible to include both the directionalism of modernity and the pluralism of postmodernity into a more integral view which transcends both while honouring the contributions of each. Variously termed a developmental or integral evolutionary worldview, or a process perspective, this is certainly a kind of metanarrative, yet it's hard to have serious objections to at least the simple fact that we are part of a vast deep time process. This is also now scientific orthodoxy with our current knowledge of cosmological development of the universe and of life, and yet the implications haven't even begun to seep into our personal psychological relationship with the world.

One particular underpinning for this view has come from process philosophy and it has been influential in a quiet way. It is a respected if not so well-known academic field which owes a lot to the one person with which the discipline is most associated with: Alfred North Whitehead. He's a candidate for one of the most important people you may never have heard of, yet I believe Whitehead's ideas will be found to be increasingly more relevant in this century as the years pass. So a brief digression about Whitehead's work can be very pertinent as a backdrop for understanding our changing culture in Britain. Whitehead was an English mathematician who co-authored with Bertrand Russell, *Principia Mathematica*, one of the most important twentieth century works on mathematics, a landmark three volume colossus (1910–13). Whitehead's interests were, like his friend Russell's, much wider than mathematics, and leaving Cambridge he moved to London University where he engaged in work on the philosophy of science. He was later in life invited to Harvard to teach philosophy, a completely new discipline for him, and it was then that he fully developed his comprehensive system of philosophy which has come to be known as process philosophy. I was amused and somewhat amazed to read that apparently the first lecture course on philosophy that he ever attended was the one he himself gave at Harvard. His most famous work is *Process and Reality*, which was taken from the lectures he had given for the Gifford series in Edinburgh in 1927.

Whitehead sought to unify science and religion and formed a radical philosophy based on process. He saw reality as a process and he questioned the illusion of solidity whereby we assume the foundation of the universe is matter. He turned conventional conceptions upside down by saying that the universe was not made up of material objects, but of events, and he was thus perhaps the first philosopher to recognise the radical implications of quantum physics. He spoke of the 'fallacy of misplaced concreteness' that we unwittingly attribute to everything. It is hard with our rational minds to conceive such a different way of perceiving whereby what is most real is the fact that the universe and every *thing* in it is actually more truly an interdependent developing process than being made up of discrete separate 'things', and of course, that includes us, too. Integral evolutionary writer Carter Phipps identifies our unconscious habit of attributing concreteness and fixedness to reality as one of being under 'the spell of solidity' which needs to be broken to see clearly. And if you think about it, it is more like a spell since it doesn't correspond to what we now know about the nature of things from quantum physics and cosmology.

Process thought sees reality as being made up of experiential events rather than enduring inert matter or entities. Since we are also completely part of this process, what is at core most real, are relational encounters and events. We are a developing story. Distrusting of big ideas, yet yearning for meaning since human beings are meaning-making creatures, you can easily see how this could form the basis for a new creation story or origin myth for our time. It has been called by various people, the 'Universe story', and it's a story which is thoroughly undogmatic since it is very wide open and constantly open for revision. Whether or not the Big Bang continues to be the most accepted theory as to the origin of the universe, we are still a process. As process aficionados would say, 'It's process all the way up and all the way down,' and so everything is up for questioning and modification as to how exactly it all happens.

Darwinian evolution precipitated momentous change in the nineteenth century, but the change potentially resulting from the adoption of an evolutionary outlook in the much broader sense I am suggesting, could be larger still. I mean evolution in the sense which transcends biology, being a wide set of principles generating change, development and novelty. There is an ever growing spectrum of people of widely varying backgrounds and fields who broadly share a developmental vision and this loose body includes sociologists, psychologists, futurists, politicians, theologians, scientists and entrepreneurs. There are as many interpretations as there are advocates, which is only natural in such a broad emergence.

Process philosophy is just one strand among many in this new worldview, as are the various developmental theorists and researchers I mentioned earlier. Paleontologist and priest Teilhard de Chardin, one pioneer of a comprehensive evolutionary way of thinking, asked, 'Is evolution a theory, a system, or a hypothesis?' He answered himself by saying that evolution is much more than this: 'Evolution is a line which illuminates all facts, a curve that all lines must follow.' Julian Huxley, the famous evolutionary biologist and first director of UNESCO, early on saw the extraordinary implications of evolution way beyond his own field of biology. He pithily summed up our human situation in an elegant and profound way: 'We are nothing else than evolution become conscious of itself.'

This sentiment has always stuck in my mind for it embodies the startling realisation that you could say that we are in essence, development and evolution itself. Yet there is an added and crucial twist: we are becoming conscious and self-aware of being part of a process. It is this understanding that can help us in finding our place again in the world, in our country, in our community and in our own bodies. For thoughtful people today in Britain and elsewhere can't help but feel at least to some degree partly alienated. We just don't belong like we used to in the distant past when the village was our life and community and the stars and planets were like the enveloping and comforting raiments of our hermetically sealed world. We now know too much. We became estranged following the advent of the superstition-crushing rationalism of the Age of Reason; some of us then romantically attempted to re-embrace nature and a sense of belonging, yet we are still troubled by our relentless doubting minds with our embedded Cartesian split. With a process perspective, there is no split between ourselves and the world; no mind/matter division; no alienation. Our bodies are fully part of the world; we are in the world completely.

Becoming both more Traditional and less Traditional at once

English philosopher Owen Barfield made the distinction between what he called the lost 'original participation' we once had in earlier times, and our now needing to come to a new 'final participation' (not that anything can be called final when evolution is the context) where we have a much more complex and self-reflective understanding yet see ourselves as intrinsically and inseparably part of our world. Of course it is one thing to have a cognitive and theoretical understanding, and quite another for this to become a person's living emotional outlook. It's very early days for an evolutionary worldview, yet this is how any new emergence begins and starts to spread: if it works; that is, if it better matches the living conditions of the times than the prevailing worldview.

One of Integral philosopher and developmental theorist Ken Wilber's most memorable and helpful contributions to the subject is his recognition that each new emergence and stage 'transcends and includes' what has come before. So we are not in any way separate nor superior to all the struggles and developments in humanity which have come before. We embody them, learn from them, increase our capacities as a result, and can be grateful for them. The more we are conscious of what is forming us, the various stages and sets of values buried deep in our cultural and collective consciousness, and yet still living within us and influencing us—or being able to be reactivated at any moment—the better integrated we can be to have a healthier outlook to meet the challenges of the next moment. So that we don't just react to the past, which is such a common feature of a less self-aware development. Now we can value the great emergences of the past without looking back at them in any way nostalgically. We can see the value of such past qualities now in contemporary society, upgraded and relevant to our situation; not reaction and rejection, but rather transcend and include, and integration. We can recognise again the importance of qualities such as heroism, forcefulness, order, self-sacrifice for a greater cause, conviction, passion, achievement, progress; and also of the qualities of kinship, belonging and a certain re-enchantment of life—not in the way they originally emerged but in a re-contextualised manner for our own life conditions. All these qualities restored healthily in our emotional palette would be invaluable for the Britain of today.

In an interesting way, this points to us becoming both less traditional and more traditional together. This conscious embrace widens and deepens our psychological and ethical capacities and palette. This is an expanded sense of our own development which is not linear, but expands out more like a sphere with greater breadth and inclusion and which stretches back through time all at once. This is an important way I feel in which we can expand our capacities for understanding, for complexity, for empathy, compassion, and for insightful decision making. As

Emerson said in his famous essay, *Circles*, 'Our life is an appren-
ticeship to the truth, that around every circle another can be
drawn; that there is no end in nature, but every end is a
beginning; that there is always another dawn risen on mid-noon,
and under every deep a lower deep opens.'

What is Our Story?

Weren't you moved by those human footprints recently
discovered on the Happisburgh beach in Norfolk? It is the oldest
record of humans outside of Africa anywhere in the world,
nearly one million years ago. The first Brits? Perhaps hard to
label them as Britons, since Britain was still part of the continental landmass back then, this apparent family group would
have shared the estuary of a river thought to be that of the
Thames earlier course with the megafauna of the time:
mammoths, hippos and rhinos. The footprints, men's UK size
eight, and smaller ones of children, were soon washed away by
the tide, but they gave us a tantalising glimpse into our far
distant past.

We carry and embody the achievements of those generations
who came before: the hard won learnings of millennia of living
and surviving on these northern islands; the desires, fears,
dreams and imagination of earlier ancestors; the advances in
culture and consciousness; the great strides in perspective and
understanding. We're part ape, part prehistoric hominid, with
even earlier reptilian contributions. We are the whole spectrum
of individual and collective consciousness, such as it has
developed so far. And the urge of life is ever to become more. It's
a complex mesh of strands of development and yet in various
very real ways, we don't all live in the same time or even in the
same world. History lives in us and we live in history. All periods
of history still coexist and are being enacted today in various
parts of the world. For traditional consciousness, the truth is in
the Bible or the Koran and other sacred books, and secular

communist manifestos as well; for modernists, the truth is in scientific fact; and for postmoderns, the truth—well, it all depends on the context, doesn't it?—and the truth is always subjective.

This too is a partial understanding, and great advance no doubt that it is, it also needs to be transcended and included within a worldview which includes our valuable new sensitivity and individuation and yet which rehabilitates a healthy form of progress; since development seems to be part of the very grain of life and of the cosmos itself. It wasn't just a cultural fad of modernist white men. Many thousands of years of human culture and development are alive in us throughout the world. And what does that mean for us now entering into a more developmental consciousness, those who are starting to see that we are the process of life itself? This is our story; a big story, a new story, which is gaining ground and one which doesn't run contrary to reason. And human beings have always told stories, perhaps unconsciously and intuitively because our existence actually is a story. As eco-theologian Thomas Berry said, 'It's all a question of story. We are in trouble just now because we do not have a good story. We are in between stories. The old story, the account of how we fit into it, is no longer effective. Yet we have not learned the new story.'

There's also the uncomfortable insecurity that there is no guarantee at all that our future in Britain or the rest of the world for that matter, is going to turn out well. These dynamics of development can fluctuate wildly in the short term. Some processes can turn out to be destructive, and decay and degeneration are also a part of nature. Evolution in all its dimensions seems to be a messy, meandering, erratic and open ended business. There is no inevitability to the process, no Hegelian absolute certainties. It's up to us to do whatever we can to shape that story; our story.

Having said all this, you may be wondering about the

relevance of this somewhat more philosophical outlook and what it actually means in relation to being British at this point in time. Well, plenty, as I hope to convey in the coming chapters, which are informed by this view. Having a deeper time understanding can only be helpful in order for us to make wiser choices. I don't want to reduce what I am trying to convey to fit some simplistic developmental grid of categorising our lives. It's one important and overlooked element among others which I will go into later. And an evolutionary view is certainly congruent with adopting a needed new story which is more in tune with our times.

A bigger view on our history and our development in Britain is in my opinion invaluable in helping us negotiate our challenging and often polarised times; for a post-colonial Britain where we are unsure of who we are and still coming to terms with our loss of premier status in the world; a Britain disconnected from the thread of its long history, where the teaching of history in schools has become ever more reduced and relegated to isolated factoid bundles about the Henrys or Hitler; a Britain which currently has lost its faith in our political elite and the two party system; a country now finding itself adrift with an unbalanced and overly negative view of itself.

Chapter 6

The Setting Sun

Our ignorance of history causes us to slander our own times
Gustave Flaubert

The discussion of development brings us to the practical question of how might a sensitive Briton today come to terms with the long and chequered history of this nation we have inherited? I hope to show how related this might be to the current less than optimistic outlook which was highlighted in Chapter 2 about the downside of British culture and why we tend towards seeing the glass as always half empty. A new understanding beyond modernity and pluralistic postmodernity is called for in order to meet our current challenges and opportunities. This is where a developmental lens can help us to better understand and integrate our British national past: for example, our vast colonisation around the world—The Empire. Is The Empire anything to do with us, or with you or me today? Does it remain undigested and unassimilated in our collective psyche, affecting us now? Let me start with a personal story.

The Flag Test

A visible shock and look of almost horror rippled through the faces staring at me when I unveiled 'it' during my lecture. It was when I pulled out the transgressive object from where it had been hidden behind the lectern where I was standing and held it up to the audience. It was as if I had suddenly displayed some hard core porn image. What was this offensive object which could surprise and shock such an urbane and broad minded gathering? I had held up the national flag of Great Britain, the Union Jack. I reassured the audience that no, I was not a recent convert to the

BNP, or even UKIP, and I certainly was far from having any far right leanings at all, my general political persuasion being towards the left. I have done this experiment several times during talks I have given about Britain and our values, and it always gets a similar response. I named it half jokingly, 'The Flag Test'. When people would dismiss out of hand my notions that there might be something unresolved with our sense of national identity, I would bring out this dreaded symbol, which was often sufficient in its visual simplicity to evoke a non-intellectual visceral response. Case would rest.

Now it has to be said that I haven't repeated this experiment since the London Olympics in the summer of 2012 when there was for once a super abundance of Union Jacks being joyfully waved at the athletes. Of course the Olympics is a sporting occasion where flag waving is a part of all national cultures and it was a very special event; the last Olympics in the UK being in 1948. So I might not get that same shocked response in quite that way now, as we have become recently more habituated to its presence, but I am bringing this flag issue up to make a point. It is, in fact, simply a common or garden flag, just a symbol. Every country has one. The kind of thing Americans typically display with obvious pride on flagpoles on the front lawns of their houses, and virtually everywhere else too, come to think of it. The kind of thing that some of the most post-traditional countries such as Denmark, Holland and Norway love to exhibit on their national days, and also display more generally as well. Whenever I would go to Copenhagen to lecture, which was for a certain period fairly regularly, I always used to notice the Danish kids as I came out of arrivals at the airport, waiting to welcome back friends or relatives from abroad. They were invariably each waving a little Danish flag. Go to Holland around their famous Queen's Day (King's Day now) and see the entire country painted Orange in honour of their national holiday.

Why is it for us British that our flag has become the property of right wing political extremists, or a tourist souvenir, or at best, an acceptable way to express support only when it comes to sporting events? Why are we so uncomfortable with it? Funnily enough, even when I was at the London Olympics, I happened to be sitting at an open air table eating lunch and right opposite me were two English academics. I couldn't help but overhear them chatting about their teaching work at university and also I pricked up my ears when they started talking about the flag. There was an area at the Olympic park sponsored by British Airways, and BA staff gave out these usefully waterproof plastic mats for sitting down on the damp grass. And they were emblazoned with the Union Jack. I was amused to overhear one of the academics say that he had one of these mats in his bag which he was keeping because it was helpful for sitting on the damp grass, but he was embarrassed about being seen with it. He opened a corner of his bag to reveal the edge of this shameful object to his commiserating colleague.

The Undigested Empire

A developmental perspective can, I feel, go a long way towards both making sense of such phenomena and more importantly, in indicating how we may come to a more integrated and healthier relationship with our country and its history. A few years ago, I had been racking my brains for a while about why do we British tend to have this pessimistic glass-half-empty attitude to our country and to life? I had a Eureka moment sitting in the sauna of my local gym after a workout when it occurred to me that a key part of the problem was 'THE EMPIRE.' We haven't gotten over the Empire. Of course, this idea had occurred to me before since it is hardly original and I had previously dismissed it as a ho-hum truism. But this time the insight landed deeper and I realised there really is considerable truth to this point. I blurted this out without thinking to a bulky Caribbean background bodybuilder who also happened to be in the sauna, and he replied in a very matter of fact way, 'Oh yeah, of course the British haven't got over the Empire.' I then started to look into our British relationship with the Empire and found it quite revealing, in more ways than I had imagined.

British psychologist Nick Beecroft has made the state of our collective national psychology a particular interest of his, which he has chronicled amongst other issues on his website and series of books, *The Future of Western Civilisation*. In connection with this, he went to the Cenotaph and conducted on-the-spot video interviews with people attending the Remembrance Day commemoration. Simply asking them, in their participation in the ceremony, what they were proud of or why, he was met with bafflement. Again and again people involved in commemorating the self sacrifice of the British war dead struggled to articulate any response to these two simple questions. And this is among the self-selected group of people who actually turned out for this remembrance occasion. It is hard to imagine an American equivalent, in a country where the founding fathers are revered as if the War of Independence ended only yesterday, being so lost for words.

In this period of my Empire research I took part in an interesting experiment. It was suggested by a friend of mine, Richard Olivier, whose company Olivier Mythodrama teaches leadership skills to executives using drama and especially the works of Shakespeare. I was telling Richard about my interest in the subject of being British and the ambiguity that surrounds our national self-identity and the relationship to the Empire. He put forward the idea of running a Constellations-type workshop where the theme would be exactly this. Deriving most particularly from Bert Hellinger, the Systemic Constellation process is a method gaining acceptance in family therapy. It can help resolve deep issues which may span generations of family history, with destructive patterns often being rooted beyond the individual. I was at first somewhat incredulous at the notion that one could take a topic like a confusing aspect of being British, as the subject for any kind of therapeutic workshop, yet he assured me that it was perfectly valid. I hadn't at that point realised that the Constellation process is not just applicable to family dynamics but also for family, organizational, community, and social systems.

So still only half believing in the idea, I invited a group of friends and associates along one evening for this experimental Constellation process. I was to be the client or seeker and the invitees were to either act as what they call 'representatives' or they would actively contribute by observing with full attention, while Richard Olivier was the facilitator. It began by me being asked to state my issue and confusion regarding Britishness to the group, which I did. Then Richard invited me to select group members to represent symbolic elements of the issue of Britain and the Empire itself. I had to position each representative in the Constellation space in the large room where the session took place. There was someone to represent current British culture; one person to represent the effects of the Empire; another to represent Empire from the British point of view; and one for the Empire from the colonised subjects' point of view, etc.

If you're not familiar with this process, it's interesting to note that the representatives were not role playing or acting but using their bodies and intuition to perceive the element they were representing. I was literally amazed by the strength of emotions that emerged between the participants and which was unquestionably genuine. It seemed as if people were channelling deep currents of unconscious unresolved elements in the national psyche. Also what was striking was how intractable the issue seemed to be with no point of contact, let alone any reconciliation, with the elements being completely opposed to each other (the representatives physically had come to symbolically stand with their backs to each other). Richard questioned whether we wanted to stop after an hour or two yet everyone wanted to carry on. Eventually a representative for the thread of communication emerged to attempt to bridge the seeming chasm between the opposing elements, and a certain degree of resolution was reached. Everyone was stunned by the undeniable power of the forces between us which had erupted and been worked with, seemingly out of the blue. It showed all of us who participated just how much of this recent and hugely influential phase of British history has simply been swept under the carpet.

Following examples like this, and various others, I've realised that the Empire and its loss affects us British quite profoundly, and that the most important reason isn't even the most obvious one. The most important reason in my opinion is in the *perception* of decline among British of all ages, and its association, either consciously or more often unconsciously with loss of the Empire. And perception of decline is not the same as actual decline, as I will explain. I realised that the national tendency toward pessimism and cynicism which I've elaborated on, is closely bound up with our perception of decline.

Phases of the British Empire

But first of all, we need to look at how we arrived here; a little history and a developmental lens is useful. Let's look back to the demise of the Empire. Coming out of the devastating Second World War in 1945, the immediate concern in Britain was reconstructing the country, and then soon after, this hitherto great nation was suddenly facing into a void. The void was the loss of Empire. This country, which, only a short time previously, had seen itself as the Master of the World. The most powerful country on earth whose navy ruled all the oceans of the planet for more than two and a half centuries, whose dominion extended over sixty countries enveloping the globe. This had been the nation whose restless and eager commitment to trade had created a new world order, had birthed the capitalist economic model, laying the foundations for a global economy as the preeminent paradigm it has remained until this day.

Even those of us born in the post-1945 era can quite likely recall the map of the world on the classroom wall at school in the fifties and even into the sixties with all its pink swathing which signified the extent of British rule. It was somehow reassuring to see all that pink and to feel the unstated pride which went along with it, which was quietly confirmed by my teachers. I remember the many hours as a child when I would pore through the different volumes of the illustrated *Children's Encyclopedia* by Arthur Mee, an ardent Empire supporter, though of course I didn't know his political slant as a child back then. This was *the* children's reference book at that time. During a meeting I had with Rowan Williams, ex-Archbishop of Canterbury, during research for this book, he related a similar formative experience as a child with Arthur Mee's ten volumes. Sitting cozily by the fire on the floor, holding one of the heavy ornate volumes which I would take out from the wooden cabinet in the living room, I would read of the marvels of the world and of the benevolence and advances which the British Empire had brought to the world. The tone throughout was pride in Britain and of the Empire, and like a patient mother, Britain would lead all those unfortunate peoples who through no fault of their own, hadn't had the good fortune to have been born in Britain, to a golden future. The pink seemed to straddle and embrace the whole world. An Empire so vast that the sun could never set on it, as the phrase says. Until the 1940s that is...

Seemingly overnight, after the Second World War, all this was gone. And what took its place? A sense of guilt, avoidance, pessimism? Our new-found liberal sensibilities understandably tended to view the fact of Empire, with all its transgressions and illiberal connotations, as a matter of embarrassment and shame. And since it was embarrassing, it was all too easy to sweep the whole thing under the carpet and, well, vaguely acknowledge that it was an unconscionable episode in our history and quickly move on. Liberals were pink, but pink with embarrassment and shame. After all, in our now global village with pluralist sensibilities, how can you feel good or comfortable about your own country in the not so distant past having taken over, often by brute force, and ruling and exploiting sixty countries around the world?

This way of dealing or rather not dealing with the enormous legacy of our past with all its ambiguities became, I would suggest, a powerful influence on our national psyche. We'd reached the zenith of power, wealth and influence and now it was all downhill, either crashing down the slope as we went to the dogs or entered a lingering yet inexorable decline. Where else could we go now, but downhill? So why should we bother now? Why should we really bother too much about anything now? What's the point? Now we had no overarching aim, no purpose, no metanarrative. We could still make witty pessimistic jokes as we slid into decay. You can still have sarcastic fun on the way down; a kind of groovy decay. The optimism and idealism of previous times seemed like a sick joke now as our small rainy group of islands with the now embarrassingly grandiose name, 'GREAT' Britain, faded into obscurity.

I cannot remotely do justice to the complexities and huge scale of the British Empire and its history and demise in this short book, and don't intend to try. This isn't a history book, it's more concerned with our relationship to the past and those influences on us today, which is often quite different to what the facts might be. I want to bring out a few salient points with which to help understand our uncomfortable and confused relationship to the Empire and especially its psychological legacy on our national psyche. To do so, a little background on the long human history of empires will put the Empire into context. And a few examples will hopefully help illuminate some of the worst of the Empire and also, in addition, what may even have been beneficial about the Empire. In order to come to a healthy relationship with our national psyche, we need to face the whole thing, but in context, not in isolation nor solely with retrospective postmodern sensibilities. We British currently need such exercises in connecting us with our own history. After all, it's a truism that oppressed peoples make every effort to remember and proudly keep alive every scrap of their history and culture; while countries which have been oppressors often tend to have an amnesia about much of their own history. Even though there is of course the parallel truism that the victors are the ones who write the history, this tends to be more focussed on glorious victories in battle than in preserving their culture. And it certainly avoids entirely the iniquities of their oppression.

The British Empire was not a monolithic unchanging beast. It had different phases and aims, and like everything else including even empires, it developed over time. In a simplified nutshell, the Empire had its inception at the end of the sixteenth century with the British beginning as pirates robbing the Spanish and others of their own plundered gold on the high seas. We were laggards in the European empire building game, and had to catch up with the Portuguese, the Spanish, and the Dutch. Then the Empire grew into primarily a trading enterprise in the eighteenth century, which at best was amoral, and of course was often infinitely worse with our slave trading. And then in the Victorian age, empire came to acquire a moral purpose with an explicit mission to bring civilization—of an enforced and paternalistic British kind naturally—to benighted peoples in all the colonies. In this latter phase of Empire, the Victorians brought a moral mission with their perceived destiny to do nothing less than to redeem the world. As Macleod Wylie, said in his *Bengal as a Field of Missions* in 1854, in the height of this latter phase of triumphal empire building, quoted by Niall Ferguson.

When the contrast between the influence of a Christian and a Heathen government is considered; when the knowledge of the wretchedness of the people forces us to reflect on the unspeakable blessings to millions that would follow the extension of British rule, it is not ambition but benevolence that dictates the desire for the whole country. Where the providence of God will lead, one state after another will be delivered into his stewardship.

Moving into the twentieth century, the by then global British Empire was profoundly impacted by the upheavals of the unprecedented global wars of those times. Entering into this decline and dissolution phase of the British Empire, though managing to survive WWI, the Empire was dealt a mortal blow in WWII, during the conflagration between what were essentially, other rival empires. Emerging from WWII as a bankrupt victor, Indian independence now loomed large for the Empire, occurring soon afterwards in 1947. Then on to the fifties and early sixties when we divested ourselves of the vast majority of the colonies in a very short time and with remarkably little discussion. It was never a General Election issue and decisions were made by ministers, governors or military men with virtually no pressure from public interest one way or the other. The British public by now weren't interested and didn't want to know, and they weren't consulted. As Paul Johnson said, 'The way in which the English disposed of their Empire was almost as confused and unsystematic as the way in which they had acquired it.'

The greatest empire there had ever been in human history, just disappeared, without fanfare and for the most part without much bloodshed. It just happened and all I personally remember growing up in that time, was repeated official flag lowering and raising ceremonies briefly reported on the evening TV news, as yet another country gained their independence. Prime Minister Harold Macmillan's famous speech delivered in Cape Town in 1960 unforgettably marks this shift in attitude in Britain. Known forever afterwards as his 'wind of change' speech, Macmillan said that there was an awakening national consciousness sweeping through Africa and he shocked his audience by stating as fact that 'the wind of change is blowing through this continent.' He spoke of the right of black majority populations to rule themselves and he directly criticised the apartheid system. The audience was shocked because he was speaking to the white supremacist South African parliament, the very architects of apartheid. The writing was on the wall and the British had now given up on Empire, and wanted out of it as quickly as possible.

How do we sum up the British Empire? How do we assess this momentous period of British history, and because of its effects, world history? Of course from our postmodern pluralistic worldview nowadays, there can be no justification whatsoever for building an empire. Trading and then invading and forcing peoples against their will to be subjects of the British Empire or of any other empire, obviously cannot be condoned in any shape or form. Even way back in the 1770s, Edward Gibbon had written, 'A more unjust and absurd constitution cannot be devised than that which condemns the natives of a country to perpetual servitude, under the arbitrary dominion of strangers'.

Yet the almost universal belief in the superiority of white Europeans at that time sanctioned tremendous cruelty and injustice to be inflicted on peoples, races, countries, around the world, and the effects reverberate to this day. From Macleod Wylie's 'manifest destiny' view of Empire quoted above, fast forward what seems like a million light years, but in reality is only 150 years, to now. Writing in The Guardian in 2003, renowned British Rastafarian poet Benjamin Zephaniah had this to say about Empire after being offered an OBE (Order of the British Empire - surely the title could do with a little update?) in the Queen's New Year's honours list.

Me? I thought, OBE me? Up yours, I thought. I get angry when

I hear that word "empire"; it reminds me of slavery, it reminds of thousands of years of brutality, it reminds me of how my foremothers were raped and my forefathers brutalised....OBE—no way Mr Blair, no way Mrs Queen. I am profoundly anti-empire.

How to make sense of all this and everything in between? We need a slight digression at this point into the history of empire building. Again it helps to bring a developmental lens to bear on this whole European colonial period of the last several centuries and its place in history. The European and British colonial period need to be seen as part of humanity's developmental continuum, rather than in isolation as some uniquely shameful aberration of history. Otherwise empire inevitably appears as a weird and terrible freak of human greed, cruelty and racism, unleashed by those now thankfully DWM (dead white men).

The Long History of Empires

Empire building has a very long history and has been part of the organic way human society has come to develop greater organisation and complexity over many many centuries. The white Europeans were not the first empire builders, conquerors, exploiters, nor were they the first slave traders. They were part of a long development. All of which is no condonement; it is though, true. The word 'empire' comes from the Latin *imperium*, meaning power or authority. An empire by definition is an extensive group of states or countries ruled over by a single monarch, an oligarchy, or a sovereign state, and this has been for thousands of years, part of the trajectory of human development. Human society has inexorably become ever more organised and sophisticated in the last few thousand years and empire building is inextricably bound up with that process.

'We Didn't Start the Fire' sang Billy Joel in his hit song of the same name. Indeed so. The song lists rapid fire references to the headline events around the world in each of the years since Billy Joel was born in 1949, while in this story of empire we are talking about a much longer time span, covering millennia. Humanity's increasing organisation into what might be termed empires goes back several thousand years at least, and was increasingly enabled by advances in technology. The Bronze Age, dating from about 3000 BC, so called because of the discovery of the hard metal alloy which could be forged from copper and tin, made it possible for tools and weapons to become more sophisticated, and for power to be projected. In more fertile areas of the world, populations grew and towns with marketplaces became cities governed by royal families with courts and then armies to protect their territory. Kingdoms arose and trading between them became the norm since different empires had different resources, whether in agriculture, mining or forestry. Desire for resources often led to one kingdom conquering another with great wars being fought by expanding empires wanting to increase their wealth and power. And I don't think I need to detail the horrors of what we know about the violence, subjugation, suffering and cruelty which took place under these various ancient empires.

In case you may be tempted to feel that power-hungry rulers and empires are the root cause of violent conflict, it seems pretty well established that groups of human beings have always fought. Steven Pinker's study of the history of violence mentioned earlier makes it clear that even the seemingly most peaceful hunter gatherer tribes, past and present, have feuds and have a homicide rate considerably greater than that in any modern nation state. Although nation states and empires have resulted in the violent deaths of millions over millennia, the advent of nation states has also resulted in lowering the homicide *rate* impressively below the homicide rate in tribes and clans. This comes as a shock to many of us today who tend to romanticise indigenous peoples who live much more in accord with nature as being only peaceful. I was reminded of how contentious even saying this kind of thing is, when I recently went to hear Jared Diamond, the famous geographer and author speak at the Royal Society of Arts about his book, *The World Until Yesterday - What Can We Learn From Traditional Societies?* In spite of the main thrust of his book being about what we can learn from traditional societies, especially the wide range of societies he has studied in New Guinea over decades of close involvement, he was picketed at the RSA by Survival International. They took issue with him for stating in his book that on average traditional societies are more violent than modern nation states, and they clearly felt (erroneously in my opinion) that by doing so, he was denigrating these people, and should be stopped in some way.

Just to give a few examples of historical empires: already from about 2000 BC there was the Assyrian Empire, one of the first large empires comparable in organisation to the Roman Empire. From all accounts the Assyrian rulers seemed to have positively revelled in violence, torture and massacres. In India the Maurya Empire dating from around 300 BC was a very powerful empire which it has been estimated, controlled about a third of the then world's population; according to the Greek explorer Megasthenes, who travelled to India, its empire had a staggeringly vast army of 600,000 infantry, 30,000 cavalry, and 9,000 war elephants. In the West, the Roman Empire was one of the largest empires up until modern times, controlling vast swathes of Europe, the Middle East, North Africa, incidentally with a single currency which was legal tender throughout a larger area than that covered by today's common currency of the EU. Then in the seventh century the Islamic or Arab Empire grew and conquered across North Africa, the Middle East and part of Iberia. This empire, whose different successions are often known as the Caliphate, and which continued on as the Ottoman Empire until the twentieth century, was the largest ever empire until surpassed by the Mongol empire in the thirteenth century. In

Africa there was the powerful Ashanti Empire of West Africa in the eighteenth and nineteenth centuries with great military power helped by early adoption of European firearms. Empire has been a universal human phenomenon.

Genghis Khan (his name literally means universal ruler) is popularly known today in Britain as a joke byword for ruthlessness and brutality; and certainly he was incredibly violent. He gave opponents a choice: either a city would surrender to his forces and submit to his complete domination and rule, or if they elected to fight, then the consequence would be that every last person would be butchered when Genghis Khan won (which unfortunately for those who elected to fight, he invariably did). Afterwards, severed heads of the vanquished were stacked in huge pyramids. Yet Genghis Khan with his warrior culture, brought a kind of rough and brutal order to the Mongols, where before his rule, there had always been low level anarchy and the mayhem of tribal feuding, raiding, stealing and killing. His empire was governed by the legal code which he developed, containing laws that prohibited blood feuds, adultery, theft, and bearing false witness. He encouraged religious tolerance and instituted a degree of meritocracy in his army and government rather than the usual blood ties. So to dismiss him as a byword for savagery would be a very partial judgement when one sees the important stabilising order and dare I say it, civilising influence he achieved, which in that warrior world at that time could only come by brutal enforcement. Nothing else would have worked.

Following this quick breeze through empire history, this brings us to the European colonial period initiated by Portugal, Spain, and then the Dutch. All of them were, like the subsequent British Empire, maritime empires with the initial impulse of trade and then subsequently leading to conquest. Portugal and Spain initiated this first phase of European empire, with the impetus to explore, powered by the new ideas and capitalism emerging from the Renaissance at the end of the fifteenth century. With superior firepower and innovative technology, nothing could stop the European powers in their ambitions, and they were joined by the other powers of Britain, France, Germany, Belgium, Italy, Russia and then Japan too; all looking for trade, riches, glory and territory.

Slavery & Abolition - Two Sides

One of the very worst and most infamous aspects of this European colonial period was the slave trade and Britain became a leading transporter of slaves to the Americas and the Caribbean. I want to go into this in more detail since slavery has understandably left one of the biggest shadows and is inextricably bound up with our feelings towards the Empire. The slave trade made some British very rich (the slave traders, plantation owners and the ports of Liverpool and Bristol particularly). It has been estimated that perhaps up to 12 million African slaves were transported all told by European traders; only Portugal transported a greater number of slaves across the Atlantic than Britain. It has to be seen though that slavery has had a very—and I mean very—long history indeed. Our rightful repugnance towards slavery today and our inability to comprehend why on earth people would have allowed it to exist, is actually a sign of how much we have developed over the recent centuries. We simply find it impossible to enter into the mindset and worldview of those in the past for whom slavery was just a fact and normal part of existence.

Take for example, Christopher Columbus' epic 'discovery' of the Americas (from a European point of view of course. The indigenous folk, I'm sure didn't previously feel undiscovered). Howard Zinn in his wonderful alternative history, *A People's History of the United States* opens his book in early October 1492, naturally enough, with Columbus' first landing on the islands of the Bahamas after crossing the Atlantic from the Canary Islands.

Columbus encountered the very hospitable Arawak natives who came down the beach to greet the great explorer and his sailors, bearing food, water and gifts. Columbus wrote in his log, 'They have no iron. Their spears are made of cane.... They would make fine servants.....With fifty men we could subjugate them all and make them do whatever we want.' He proceeded to take some of them captive to guide him to where he was convinced lay treasure troves of gold and it's certainly a far less romantic view of the 'discovery' of the New World. His interest was in gold and slaves.

Slavery did not make sense in original hunter gatherer communities, so we don't see slavery in those types of tribes. Yet in the oldest records that we have, slavery is already mentioned as being an established institution in the majority of ancient civilizations throughout the world. The classic and much admired Greek civilization with its free thinking philosophers and experiments in democracy, depended on a huge number of slaves, as did the Roman period. It's been estimated that two to four fifths of the Athenian population were slaves and that perhaps 100 million people were slaves throughout the Roman era. Letting in this fact gives a different gloss to fabled Greek democracy.

And slavery was also a very established part of African and Arab societies for a similarly long time as well. The British and other Europeans bought their slaves from African slave traders, who sold their fellow Africans. One academic study estimates that 90 per cent of slaves shipped across the Atlantic were enslaved by Africans and then sold to European traders. Varying yet substantial proportions of many African kingdoms were slaves before the Europeans arrived. And even after slavery was abolished by the Western powers, it persisted in the Middle East and Africa, notably in East Africa, and Zanzibar where apparently 90 per cent of the population were slaves. In fact one estimate puts the largest slave population remaining in the world in the 1890s to be that of the Sokoto Caliphate in northern Nigeria. Two million people as slaves is the estimate. The Arab slave trade was vast and long lasting. I found it shocking to learn that even as recently as the beginning of the 1960s, Saudi Arabia's slave population was estimated at 300,000, slavery only being abolished in 1962. Mauritania had the unenviable distinction of being the last country to officially criminalise slavery in 2007, though the practice still continues today unofficially in Niger and Sudan. Terrible as this whole global human story is, which has been perpetuated by all countries, it also has to be said that never had so many slaves been forcibly transported to another continent as by the Atlantic slave trade.

Sugar was the biggest business of the eighteenth century British Empire. All because we had discovered a very sweet tooth and couldn't get enough of the addictive white stuff. The business depended on slaves transported to the Caribbean to work on the sugar plantations in what were horrendous conditions. It was an immensely profitable business which made fortunes for plantation owners and many many others connected with the trade in Britain. Yet the other side of this particular story is that Britain went from being one of the leading slave trading nations to becoming the leading abolitionists in a few decades. It doesn't in any way wipe away the former inhumanity but it does give a more nuanced, and I feel accurate view, of an evolving empire and a people who were evolving in their values. As Niall Ferguson says in his *Empire*, 'It's not easy to explain so profound a change in the ethics of a people. It used to be argued that slavery was abolished simply because it had ceased to be profitable, but all the evidence points the other way: in fact, it was abolished despite the fact that it was profitable.'

The anti-slavery movement in Britain was one of the very first mass public mobilisation campaigns. Although Quakers had spoken against slavery for a long time previously, it was the Society for the Abolition of the Slave Trade formed in 1787, led by figures like Thomas Clarkson and Granville Sharp, which got the movement rolling. The rise of Enlightenment ideas turned some against slavery, and the rise of Methodism in the mid eighteenth century brought evangelicals and non-conformists to the cause. And the presence of freed slaves in Britain, many of whom had fought for Britain in the War of Independence with America, helped bring the cause home to the British. William Wilberforce was their voice in Parliament and part of an influential network of high minded Christian abolitionists.

Mass petitions were organised and by 1792, an amazing 519 petitions had been presented to Parliament with over 390,000 signatures. Pottery magnet Josiah Wedgwood had ceramic anti-slavery badges produced with a Black man in chains pictured saying, 'Am I not a man and a brother?' And these became widespread emblems of protest. Ordinary people who were apparently all avid consumers of sugar—after all, that's why the sugar and slave trade was so lucrative—boycotted sugar or only bought sugar guaranteed to have been produced from 'non slave labour' such as from the East Indies; this was perhaps the earliest forerunner of today's ethical Fair Trade campaign and of the phenomenon of the consumer boycott. The *Abolition Project* relates an example where an ordinary person, James Wright, a Quaker and merchant of Haverhill, Suffolk, took out an advertisement in the local General Evening Post on March 6th, 1792, telling his customers that he would no longer be selling sugar. Here's an extract of what he said,

.....Being Impressed with a sense of the unparalleled suffering of our fellow creatures, the African slaves in the West India Islands.....with an apprehension, that while I am a dealer in that article, which appears to be principal support of the slave trade, I am encouraging slavery, I take this method of informing my customers that I mean to discontinue selling the article of sugar when I have disposed of the stock I have on hand, till I can procure it through channels less contaminated, more unconnected with slavery, less polluted with human blood.....

Many people supported the campaign against their own self-interest. In Manchester, for example, a substantial percentage of the city's population signed petitions in support of abolition of slavery in spite of the fact that the city was profiting greatly by the slave trade. Eventually the government had to take notice of the turning tide of public opinion and the rise of a powerful ethical pressure group. A bill was passed in 1807 (The Slave Trade Act) making it illegal for British ships to carry enslaved peoples between Africa, the West Indies and America. And this bill was passed in the face of determined opposition from powerful vested interests.

Slavery itself was finally abolished in British territories in 1833. In a strange twist, now Britain had become a major force for abolition, Royal Navy ships were tasked with policing the oceans on a moral mission to intercept and stop ships carrying slaves, since slavery was still continued by other countries, most notably Brazil and the USA. There was a British West Africa Squadron which patrolled the African coast and naval officers received a bounty for each slave intercepted and liberated. I think it is hugely significant for our human species that this movement was the first to attempt to abolish an entrenched custom which had hitherto been part of the fabric of societies throughout the world for all recorded history. And it succeeded to an extraordinary degree despite what still persists as modern slavery.

Shadows and Shame

As I said before, it's impossible to summarise so vast a subject as the British Empire during its three centuries of existence around the world. With the colonial powers dividing up territory between them, particularly in the 'scramble for Africa', they took no account of the inhabitants and their different kingdoms, tribes and ethnicities as they carved out colonies. The result has been that the post-independence countries have been left to deal with the very difficult legacy of ethnic groups and tribes lumped together or separated by the vagaries of colonial map makers and the arbitrary boundaries which they drew.

In addition to the slave trade, there were a number of other awful and regrettable courses of action that were taken by the British Empire at various times. And there are some just as important policies of inaction by the British Empire which also had devastating consequences for colonised populations. These are not generally part of our received knowledge of the Empire; they didn't figure at all in my educational history at school. For example, the disastrous Irish potato famine in the late 1840s was a real famine and wasn't created by the British. Yet the British government's relative inaction in the face of a natural catastrophe led to a vast death toll in Ireland, inexcusable from such a rich country towards its close neighbour. The inaction seems to have stemmed from a combination of laissez-faire economic doctrines, a Protestant belief in divine providence and a deep set ethnic prejudice towards the Catholic Irish.

The killing of Aboriginal people in Australia by British colonists was ongoing in the nineteenth century with one of the worst episodes being the wiping out of the majority of the Aboriginal people of Tasmania in the so called *Black War* by British colonists and the survivors' relocation; certainly a very shameful aspect of our history. While in China we also could make no claim to hold the moral high ground in Britain's foisting highly addictive opium on the Chinese market in order to pay for Chinese tea to service our thirst for the drink. *The Opium Wars*, starting in 1840, where British warships forced the Chinese to concede to Britain's trade terms, have been long forgotten in the UK. But not so in China where these events are still a key part of educating children as to what the imperialists did to them. The

Opium Wars mark the start of what the Chinese refer to as the 'century of humiliation.' The Chinese national psyche still carries this sense of humiliation from those days and it affects their attitude today as a major world power.

The Mau Mau 'rebellion' in colonial Kenya in the 1950s was one of the most bitter and vicious fights waged by the British colonial powers in their counter insurgency campaign against a rebellious section of the Kikuyu population of Kenya. It was vicious on both sides. The colonial powers created internment camps with widespread mistreatment and torture in an unconscionable way, all the more so given the fact that this was the middle of the twentieth century. It was only in 2013 that the British government officially recognised the abuse and torture of Kenyans by the colonial administration of the time, and agreed to pay compensation to the victims. India, being already a relatively wealthy and far more venerable civilisation than that of Britain, was particularly exploited. Historian Piers Brendon in his article, *A Moral Audit of the British Empire*, says

> From the time that Britain had begun to transform its commercial dominance into political ascendancy, India was bled white. During the 1760s Bengal was so squeezed that the province, which the Mughals had called "the paradise of earth", became an abyss of torment. It was ravaged by war, pestilence and famine. A third of the population died of hunger, some driven to cannibalism. Although relief efforts were made, British "bullies, cheats and swindlers" continued to prey on the carcass of Bengal and some profiteered in hoarded grain.

Churchill's apparent role in leading to a vast number of people being left to die of starvation in the Indian famine of 1943, has only more recently come to light. Perhaps one to three million perished during its course in Bengal. Journalist Madhusree

Mukerjee's well researched book, *Churchill's Secret War*, has unearthed documents proving that Churchill repeatedly refused to have food aid sent to relieve the famine in spite of the many pleas from those around him. Citing his not wanting to divert precious food from the war effort elsewhere, he thwarted every attempt to aid the starving Bengalis and seems to have been driven by racial hatred according to Mukerjee. Churchill famously disliked Gandhi, convinced that he was just a cunning lawyer dressed in a loin cloth for effect. 'It is alarming and nauseating to see Mr. Gandhi, a seditious Middle Temple lawyer, now posing as a fakir of a type well-known in the East.'

The Empire in Context

Now to look at the other side of the balance sheet of Empire, in order to come to a fuller and more nuanced picture. The British Empire was a 'liberal' empire founded on principles which were held, at least theoretically, to lead to subject peoples being given their right to self-rule. As an example of these Enlightenment values to which the Empire at least purported to pledge allegiance, let's revisit the story with Mahatma Gandhi. Adolf Hitler admired the British Empire before WWII and was wont to give his helpful advice as to how the British could deal with the rising independence movement led by Gandhi. 'Shoot Gandhi' was the Fuhrer's eminently practical advice to British Foreign Secretary Lord Halifax, in 1938, about how to rule India. 'And if that does not suffice to reduce them to submission, shoot a dozen leading members of Congress; and if that does not suffice, shoot two hundred, and so on until order is established.' Sound advice from the Fuhrer's perspective. In most empires of the past, that was simply what would have happened. Gandhi's inspired adoption of non-violence was a potent moral force for change, yet it could only be effective if his opponents were in some, even slight way amenable to it; that is, if it is sufficiently close enough to their own values for some degree of resonance and empathy.

Clearly using non-violence against the Nazis would have just made it that much easier for them to roll their Panzers right over people. Hitler even said, 'If we took India, the Indians would certainly not be enthusiastic and they'd not be slow to regret the good old days of English rule.'

Integral philosopher Ken Wilber has suggested that there have only been a couple of instances in the entirety of recorded history where non-violence has been effective as a policy or tactic: namely, in the cases of Gandhi and of Martin Luther King in the Civil Rights struggle. And they only worked because they were up against opponent countries which held Enlightenment values which recognised the sanctity of the individual and human rights and due process under the law. At least that was the theory and yet clearly, to some degree, those countries actually strived however imperfectly, to embody those values. Genghis Khan would not have been impressed by Gandhi and neither would the Britain in say, the time of King Edward I. This 'great and terrible king' (the title of a biography of this brilliant and ruthless warrior) would not even have been able to comprehend such a bizarre notion as pacifism.

It is precisely because peoples and countries can and sometimes have developed to have a higher centre of gravity in their values, that Gandhi's more evolved method of struggle could be so effective against the might of the British Empire. For despite its many flaws, there was in the later periods of Empire, a spreading in the colonies of the features of British society at home. It was of course all very paternalistic, with the idea of educating the poor benighted people, giving them institutions just like in Britain to eventually make them, well... British; that is, civilised and self-sufficient. The most significant of these features was the idea of liberty. Although that sounds rather ridiculous, if not downright offensive at first sight for a conquering nation and empire to talk about 'the idea of liberty,' bear with me. Niall Ferguson says,

What is very striking about the history of the Empire is that whenever the British were behaving despotically, there was almost always a liberal critique of that behaviour from within British society. Indeed, so powerful and consistent was this tendency to judge Britain's imperial conduct by the yardstick of liberty that it gave the British Empire something of a self-liquidating character. Once a colonized society had sufficiently adopted the other institutions the British brought with them, it became very hard for the British to prohibit that political liberty to which they attached so much significance for themselves.

It's helpful in understanding this 'liberal critique from within British society' mentioned by Ferguson, to look at the long term British political landscape. For centuries, and ever since the Glorious Revolution of 1688, the political scene in England was not based upon a single religious culture as in many European countries such as Italy or France where one religious tradition was dominant. Nor was it divided between a religious right wing party and a more secular left wing party as was also common in various European countries. Since the late seventeenth century, the political landscape in Britain has been divided between the two cultures of Anglicans and Nonconformists, both of which were religious. On the Nonconformist side, the Whigs (who later of course, became known as Liberals) had sympathies with and supported the Dissenting tradition with its criticism of the State and its desire to place all people on a more equal footing. Consequently British politics, especially from the left, has had a strong religious flavour and moral fervour to its campaigns for change. Richard Tombs makes this point strongly in his *The English and their History.*

This religious fervour provided an inexhaustible dynamism in campaigning for virtue, for rights, for justice, for equality, for self-improvement; and it certainly prevented English political life from descending into a complacent torpor. Tireless campaigns for religious equality, for the abolition of slavery, against alcohol and prostitution, for the rights of women, for human rights abroad and in the empire would have been unimaginable without this relentless and demanding conscience.

And this wasn't necessarily the case at all with other European empires. Even George Orwell, who bitterly hated The Empire from his own experience in 1920s colonial Burma, acknowledged it as much better than any other empire. Piers Brendon, quoted earlier, writes, 'It was vastly superior, in moral terms, to the French, German, Portuguese and Dutch empires.'

Think of the Congo, a country run personally as a serf fiefdom by King Leopold of Belgium, who bled it dry and decimated the population, literally halving it, leading to this appalling adventure being commonly cited as genocide. Even this atrocity was completely eclipsed in sheer horror by the Japanese Empire's actions in the 'Rape of Nanking' during its imperial expansion in 1937 into China and then through South East Asia. The extreme wanton savagery of the Japanese imperialism in Nanking is too horrendous to describe—I've read accounts of it—and perhaps would have made even the Nazi SS blanche. And this episode of Japanese history has not to this day begun to be admitted or dealt with in any significant way by the Japanese, which cannot but affect them adversely and especially the Chinese, who bitterly resent the lack of any acknowledgement.

Of course less bad doesn't equate to good or justifiable when it comes to empires or anything else. As I've said previously, we are hopefully evolving beyond the age of Empire at this point, though many people have made convincing cases that there is in effect an American Empire which has replaced the British one.

The American style of empire, because of its history of having fought successfully for independence and to free itself from being a colony, is of a kind where empire must never cross a line by permanently occupying another country. The American way and rule of empire is to invade and then withdraw, and if necessary, go in again (and maybe again too). The colonisation, in other words, mustn't be permanently physical; it's remotely exerted by trade and financial and cultural influence. This 'soft' form of colonisation can also have very pernicious effects on the inhabitants of other countries.

The British Empire in its later incarnation enabled free labour movement (after slavery was abolished), pioneered free trade, free movement of capital and introduced British institutions such as law and governance. There is evidence that former British colonies were more likely to have transitioned to democracies after independence than countries which were formerly ruled by other colonial powers. Funnily enough, while speaking of different empires, what finally finished off the British Empire was not in the end, the budding independence movements of the colonies. It was instead the conflagration of WWII where empire was pitted against empire. The British Empire fought against the empires of Germany and Japan, resulting in what Ferguson aptly terms a Pyrrhic victory, which destroyed all of the empires. And ironically, without the Empire, and its large number of soldiers, most especially those from the Indian subcontinent, Britain would likely have lost.

Former colonies have had to deal with all the negative consequences of having been colonised, both practical and psychological. India in particular, was a great, advanced and wealthy culture when the British first set foot on the subcontinent in the sixteen hundreds; in fact one whose ancient culture far predated that of the British. Being the 'jewel in the crown' for the colonisers has meant great exploitation for that country and I am always struck from my visits to India over the years, how remarkably little resentment is generally felt by Indians towards their former colonisers. In fact the two nations seem to have quite an empathy, in spite of centuries of occupation and all the oppression which undoubtedly took place. Prime Minister Dr. Manmohan Singh gave an impressive speech at Oxford University in 2005 in which he expressed the self-confidence of India as an independent great nation which has transcended the history and harm of the Raj in his country,

> Today, with the balance and perspective offered by the passage of time and the benefit of hindsight, it is possible for an Indian Prime Minister to assert that India's experience with Britain had its beneficial consequences too. Our notions of the rule of law, of a Constitutional government, of a free press, of a professional civil service, of modern universities and research laboratories have all been fashioned in the crucible where an age old civilization met the dominant Empire of the day. These are all elements which we still value and cherish. Our judiciary, our legal system, our bureaucracy and our police are all great institutions, derived from British-Indian administration and they have served the country well. Of all the legacies of the Raj, none is more important than the English language and the modern school system. That is, if you leave out cricket!

Integrating Imperial History in our National Psyche

Empire is not in itself a particularly funny subject but somehow Monty Python managed to give us a new perspective on it. Their classic sketch, 'What have the Romans ever done for us?' imagines ancient Judean wannabe revolutionaries hearing a rallying call against the colonial power of Rome from their leader played by John Cleese. As they go on they are forced reluctantly to concede, blow by comic blow, that the Romans had, in fact, given them a lot: the Romans made roads and constructed aqueducts, they had brought sanitation, public baths, made the streets safe and brought order and so on and so on. Two thousand years later this is funny and we can see the advances which we derive from the Roman colonisation period. If there's a straight road in Britain, we can assume it's a Roman one. But if you were an ancient Briton experiencing these devilish foreigners with their superior technology and organisation taking over England, it would be a very different story. You naturally enough wouldn't appreciate any of these so called advances and would just want to fight back at these exploiting invaders with their fiendish and robotic military discipline. The point is, it's hard to assess the overall effect until a considerable time afterwards, as historians well know. We are too close to relatively recent events. Hence a deeper time developmental perspective is very illuminating.

Now that we've highlighted some of the complexities and paradoxes of our Imperial history, it's no wonder we British haven't digested and integrated this experience. There are still a fading few in Britain who glory in the Empire, yet for most of us that is a jingoistic and outdated position. Liberals are embarrassed or ashamed of our exceedingly un-PC past and avoid the whole subject of the Empire. Others don't consciously know much about it at all, and it just persists as a vague shadow.

I was listening to Melvyn Bragg on his insightful regular BBC 4 radio programme, *In Our Time*, on the subject of The British Empire. As always on this show, Bragg moderates and asks questions to a panel of eminent academics, all specialists on the particular subject of the week. I was struck by how the academics reacted when Bragg asked them about the dynamism of Empire and the innovation of the Industrial Revolution; to them this clearly smacked of racism and cultural superiority and they were at pains not to make any value judgement, at least none that could possibly be construed as being in any way favourable toward any aspect of Empire. Bragg said how it's hard in today's Britain to speak like he was doing, for fear of being seen as un-

PC. When he pressed them as whether they thought that anything good came out of Empire, the most the professors could venture was that there was a mixing of peoples and cultures and they could concede a certain positivity in that, though one was careful to say in the same breath that it was at heart all a relationship of power between coloniser and colonised.

Empire is clearly an as yet unintegrated shadow in our national psyche. I feel that a very good argument can be made for Britain to formally apologise for some of the worst aspects of colonialism. Governments in all countries are always leery about any such admissions, fearing they may lead to vast financial reparation claims from the countries involved; yet such apologies would help towards healing the trauma of the past. It would not only help atone for our nation's past wrongs, it would also be healing for our national British psyche. Dr Shashi Tharoor, an Indian MP, in his much viewed speech at the Oxford Union debate in 2015 about whether Britain owes reparations to her former colonies, while arguing that Britain does indeed have a debt to pay, concluded his case by saying,

> As far as I'm concerned, the ability to acknowledge a wrong that has been done, to simply say sorry, will go a far, far, far longer way than some percentage of GDP in the form of aid. What is required is accepting the principle that reparations are owed. Personally, I'd be quite happy if it was one pound a year for the next two hundred years, after the last two hundred years of Britain in India.

William Roger Louis, an American historian of the British Empire has called for the release of all the still confidential and secret files from the likes of the Colonial Office and the Foreign Office still held in the National Archives. This would help in bringing a full transparency to what actually happened in the British colonial period around the world. This is a moral obligation to our former colonies and would serve in acknowledging the darker side of Empire.

The legacy of the Empire is not at all distant or academic. I experience it every day in Britain. We all do. Sitting on the Tube in London I am endlessly fascinated by the sheer extraordinary diversity of people, nationalities and languages in every carriage. More in one single Tube carriage on the Victoria line than a great Victorian explorer of the past would be likely to meet in a lifetime of travel. Sixty countries worth of Empire plus another twenty-seven countries worth of the EU all mixing in London and all over the country today. This is one very real and tangible conse-quence of the Empire. Yes, there are very justifiable concerns about continued levels of immigration, yet the London, and I would say the Britain of today as well, is a far more vibrant, dynamic, and interesting place than the homogeneity of the staid country where I grew up in the 1950s. Of course there are problems with this extraordinary multicultural mix, yet somehow, it does work. This in itself is a promising sign as to what a post-colonial, post-traditional future could be like.

Chapter 7

The Myth of Decline

Civilizations die from suicide, not by murder
Arnold Joseph Toynbee

There are many, especially younger people, for whom all this Empire business may seem irrelevant and bygone history. After all, they weren't born then. Yet there is another shadow which has been cast which still affects us all, including young people too, in a more unconscious and pervasive manner than all which I have related so far. And this is our British perception that we as a nation are in decline across the board. This view insidiously affects our national self-esteem and I feel has a lot to do with our prevalent national mood of pessimism. The Empire story plays very heavily into this perception of decline, but it is more interesting than that.

What has informed my understanding significantly was when I came across George Bernstein's well documented and contrarian history of modern Britain, *The Myth of Decline: The Rise of Britain since 1945*. I mentioned this book briefly in the first chapter, and yes, that isn't an error, I did mean to write 'The *Myth* of Decline'. I'll explain. Bernstein is an eminent Professor of History specialising in British History at Tulane University in the States. I ended up having a long conversation with him, quizzing him on his research in this field and am very grateful for his invaluable help. One interesting fact is that he is American and not British, an advantage to being objective on this subject which is closer than close to us natives.

It's All Relative

I'm making the important distinction between *absolute* decline and *relative* decline.

Of course, there is relative decline in Britain *compared with* other countries in the second half of the twentieth century. Being the first industrialised country in the world gave Britain a unique preeminent position and it is only natural that other countries would catch up and also overtake Britain. After all, many countries are far larger and have much greater natural resources for growth. We could on the contrary take it as flattery that much of the modern world has taken our model and run with it. But inherent in our British *perception* of decline, though unarticulated, is that we are in some kind of terminal decline and are 'washed up' in some fundamental way as a nation, or 'going to the dogs'.

To give an example of this distinction, poverty used to be measured in an absolute sense, and there is no question that poverty declined dramatically after the advent of the welfare state post WWII to very low levels compared to *absolutely* any period at all before then in the whole history of this archipelago of islands. Yet when a relative standard to measure poverty was later adopted in the 1970s, measuring poverty by comparing people's household income relative to the national average, e.g. 50 per cent of the national average, the result is very different, and understandably shows a greater degree of poverty. It is closer towards a measure of inequality rather than a measure of absolute poverty. And this has validity as a measure, since gross inequality certainly ought to be reduced, yet it is tracking something different than the absolute level of poverty.

So I was curious as to how George Bernstein had come to his controversial view that Britain since WWII was actually not fundamentally in decline, when for everyone here, that is an unquestioned and often unconscious given. He told me that it started when he studied the figures and saw that the period from 1945-1973 was 'awesome' in terms of economic growth and progress in Britain and how poverty had declined, and yet no one was talking about it or acknowledging this fact. This led him to a wider re-evaluation of the accepted narrative, culminating in his book.

Firstly, to examine our perception of economic decline which has affected our national self-sense. Most Britons have a perception that we declined after WWII and slid into freefall in the 1970s, with the jury out on whether Margaret Thatcher saved us from certain ruin or compounded our predicament, while benefitting just a fortunate section of the population. Since then, it is assumed that we are still in a mess and vaguely continuing our inevitable slide downwards. The economic facts back up Bernstein's contrarian view. Britain's annual growth rate from 1951–73 was higher than in *all* previous time periods including the most powerful periods of empire, and this growth was really impressive, given the devastation of WWII. This goes dead against our perception of failure. Interestingly, industry was actually quite backward in the Industrial Revolution period in Britain because that revolution only occurred in a few key industries.

Our perception of failure in this period has much to do with the fact that the rest of the industrial nations were catching up with Britain and what really got under our collective skin was that France and Italy in particular, were doing better than us. We were shocked and engaged in much soul searching and introspection. Stepping back though, it was only natural that countries which had lagged behind Britain in the days of its global economic preeminence in the past, should catch up and perhaps overtake Britain. To put things in context, however, Britain's performance was comparable to the USA in this period. This rate of growth was not matched in later decades and this was the case for other countries as well, with the 1970s oil crisis for example, being one of the factors outside any country's control. Certainly the 1970s were a poor period for British productivity and manufacturing, and the UK's poor manufacturing competitiveness, poor industrial relations and poor management were real problems. The old industries which had been the powerhouse of the Industrial Revolution such as steel, textiles and shipbuilding were all in decline and the writing had been on the wall for a long time. These industries faced the greater competitiveness of emerging industrial countries with much lower costs. So I don't want to suggest there were no real problems with the nation; of course there really were and still are. We are still only newly emerged from the prolonged economic recession in Britain and in most other Western nations of the last few years.

Understandably there has been much thought given as to what went wrong and what is the matter with us? Our predilection to focus on what is wrong can often blind us to what is right. The inference is that there is something wrong with us a nation; that we are to blame for our predicament and that if only we had done things differently.... But maybe that's not true? Of course retrospective wisdom is a wonderful commodity and all kinds of mistakes and poor choices have inevitably been made by governments, both left and right. Yet British governments after WWII focussed on improving the social well-being of the populace and giving resources to that end and have been blamed for our economic decline ever since. Again I am reminded of Ken Loach's stirring documentary *The Spirit of 45*, highlighting how radical was the positive transformation of British society and well-being from the creation of the welfare state at a time when there seemed to be no resources to fund it, in the rubble of the aftermath of war. The vast changes for the better in British society and culture since WWII are to my mind genuinely revolutionary and mark a significant and permanent change, in spite of concerns about the NHS or the welfare state being dismantled, or of the recent severe global downturn.

Maybe the different British governments weren't all just one unmitigated cock up? Of course we could have been better served by our governments, but we need a measure of proportion.

Maybe it wasn't all a mess or a disaster and that the country has actually done pretty damn well, considering the enormous transition through world wars from Empire to welfare state? Granted there are always problems, sometimes big ones, but that's the nature of life, isn't it? What if no one is to blame for our awful predicament because we're fundamentally not in such an awful predicament? Such thoughts would have to positively impact our national self-image and self-esteem. Of course, one can counter with what about the very real current problems of sluggish productivity or intermittent economic growth, youth unemployment and personal and national levels of debt, etc, etc? And I don't want to minimise these and other crucial issues, yet I am deliberately taking a longer term view to point out what is not fed to us by the media, with its endless daily drip feed of woes.

The other major factor in our perception of decline is Britain's decline in power and status, and this is wrapped up with the Empire. I am indebted again to Bernstein for helping me question what actually was lost with the demise of The Empire. Strangely enough, Britain never had the global power we all assume that it did. Linda Colley in her *Captives: Britain, Empire and the World* shows how the seeming economic domination and military successes of the Victorian phase of the British Empire has prevented us from appreciating how relatively small and weak was Britain's actual state in the previous centuries of empire. In 1715, the British army was only comparable in size to the army in the service of the King of Sardinia. We can look at an old world map and see vast regions of pink seemingly signifying our global power, but Britain was never a 'superpower' in the sense that the USA became in the latter half of the twentieth century. We never had anything approaching that level of unilateral military power with world-annihilating banks of nuclear missiles or such overwhelming economic clout. Britain was a great power among a few other such great powers in the world. Britain never had the ability to project power in Europe, which is where it would have been most important. Britain had the largest navy in the world, but has never had much of a standing army. To deal with say France in the past, it has always had to rely on the assistance of other great powers. Two world wars showed also our reliance on the USA for its help for any war on the Continent.

Better off Without The Empire

We also particularly have an exaggerated notion of the power of the Victorian Empire. Pink patches on the map don't necessarily equate with increased power or wealth. That may well have been more true for the seventeenth and eighteenth century Empire but actually is not true for the later phases of Empire. In fact much research indicates that certainly from the mid nineteenth century onwards, the Empire had become a net liability for Britain. Yes, really. It's a no brainer to most of us that the Empire provided us with untold riches by our exploitation of the colonies, and now that that has all dried up, we are left impoverished. In Lance Davis and Robert Huttenback's, *Mammon and the Pursuit of Empire: The Economics of British Imperialism,* they analyse the costs and benefits of Empire, concentrating on a prime period of Empire, the five decades from 1865 up until the beginning of WWI. In this study they found no evidence of any continued exploitative profits during this period. In other words, the Empire wasn't a net source of wealth to the British economy by this time despite the fact that some British businessmen did make fortunes. This doesn't take away from the fact that in India, there was a systematic exploitation of resources and a great draining of wealth from that country by Britain throughout the whole colonial period.

Also returns from empire investment were not high in comparison to earnings in the domestic and foreign sectors of the economy, and what empire profits did exist, were earned at a substantial cost to the taxpayer. It was an expensive business funding a navy to protect the myriad far flung colonies around the world. Navies cost much more than armies because ships are so expensive. And it was impossible to defend such a far flung empire anyway. The idea of Britain patrolling the seven seas sounds glamorous and all powerful, yet it was more a public service enabling the development of free trade and globalisation without giving much return on investment. In the nineteenth century, the main benefit of still having the Empire was India's provision of troops for which Indian taxpayers had to foot the bill. Of course these troops were to defend the Empire, so it becomes a rather circular argument. And great numbers of Indians did serve in the British army and also many died in service of The Empire in various conflicts.

Britain was one of the 'Big Three' in WWII, and to me, those famous pictures of Roosevelt, Stalin and Churchill meeting together, immediately come to mind. I particularly think of that publicity photo of Yalta, in the Crimean winter in 1945, where the three leaders are sitting together in armchairs outdoors, wrapped in greatcoats after discussing and arguing over the future of the world. Britain attempted to keep a seat at the super-power table by spending vast amounts on her own independent nuclear deterrent to maintain our status, but it was impossible, since we had never been that powerful. Yet British leaders and many others believed that Britain's empire defined its power. The Empire actually became larger between 1880 and 1914, which meant more colonies for the navy to defend, which in turn meant more spending to keep the navy up to that expanded task. Bernstein says of this,

> Given this reality, the new colonies added after 1880 not only did not increase Britain's power, they may well have reduced it. They meant more territory to defend without furnishing many more resources for defending it. Thus by 1914, we are

faced with a paradox: Britain claimed some quarter of the world's population within its orbit, and it was all the weaker for it.

The British have absorbed a myth as self-evident truth: that the loss of empire in the post WWII period marked national decline, when in fact The Empire was impossible to defend, too costly to maintain, and irrelevant to Britain's actual power. The loss of the British Empire was much more a psychological symbol of decline in status and power than an actual decline. Yes, of course Britain has declined relative to huge emerging countries the size of continents such as China, Brazil and India. It's great news that more countries are developing. However, this sense of decline as a way of seeing ourselves is deeply rooted and it is widely believed by the rest of the world too. Admittedly with our recent global recession, some people in Britain are relatively poorer than they were at the start of the downturn in 2008, and this is a real issue. There is also evidence of inequality being on the increase, which is a real concern for fostering a healthy society. Yet this only makes it harder than ever for us to accept that the vast majority of people in Britain are far better off in every sense of the word than they ever were under the Empire.

When US Secretary of State Dean Acheson made his famous comment about Britain in 1962, 'Great Britain has lost an empire and has not yet found a role', it cut deeply to the bone with the British, provoking anger and humiliation, even though it's actually quite a helpful observation. Politicians, both Conservative and Labour have not helped the situation by finding it expedient to promote the narrative of decline of Britain as an easy way of attacking the other side. Prominent conservatives saw the 1960s as proof of our social and moral decline, and pointed to socialism as the deeper source of this malaise and decline. Think Mrs Thatcher and her strain of neoliberalism. You might think that Labour wouldn't embrace the narrative of decline, having themselves created the idealistic welfare state, but to be able to blame the other side for the worsening state of the nation was too great a temptation. Bad news just sticks better. The Conservatives had been in power from 1951 to 1964 and Prime Minister Harold Macmillan in 1957 had optimistically said in a speech that, 'most of our people have never had it so good.' It was actually true but mouthing such a statement in Britain was bound to backfire; as it did.

Labour couldn't resist taking up Britain's decline as a central issue to fight the 1964 election. Harold Wilson's phrase from that time, 'thirteen years of Tory misrule,' is indelibly imprinted in my mind, as if it were complete fact. And both left and right have continued this catchy narrative of decline ever since. Think of David Cameron's memorable phrase, 'Broken Britain'. This marketing message lodges in our subconscious and you don't remember the arguments for or against, but the phrase remains. *The Sun* ran frequent stories under the banner of 'Broken Britain' from 2007 until 2010, when the Conservatives came into power, and then the newspaper perhaps not so mysteriously dropped the slogan. So there has been a bias in favour of decline as a narrative in the political arena throughout the last few decades.

I'm reminded of the interesting survey and history of gloom and doom by Arthur Herman, *The Idea of Decline in Western History*. The 'idea of decline' appeals to many people, especially intellectuals, in a similar way that conspiracy theories are very attractive and almost addictive to a certain type of intelligent mind. In particular, Herman feels that too few intellectuals now support the Western Enlightenment liberal project, preferring narratives of pessimism and decline. Pessimism is popular, not only in Britain. In a way, this outlook is filling a vacuum in worldviews, and is a kind of worldview in itself. As French intellectual Pascal Bruckner says about modern Western Europeans in his fiery treatise, *The Tyranny of Guilt: An Essay on Western Masochism*,

Among Moderns there is a fascination with the theme of decline, a simple inversion of progress that attracts both experts and moralists....Anyone who cherishes the idea sees himself as a superior intelligence who has grasped the hidden process of history... For the country or the culture concerned, the news is not necessarily bad: falling is more noble than vegetating; it shows that one had risen very high.... There is a certain charm in decay, especially when the cataclysm is slow and mixes distinction with melancholy.

Interestingly, the French and the British find themselves in a similar position as having both been once proud Imperial powers, and have many similarities; which is probably why we profess not to get along with each other. In recent years, the famous French pride in their culture has given way to an orgy of introspection and self-denigration about what is the matter with their country because France can no longer see itself as number one. It's no longer the torch bearer for humanity nor the premier world language, their empire dismantled, and its much vaunted social system bankrupt. The French currently have their own flavour of cynicism. *The Independent*, reporting on President Hollande in March 2013:

> In a speech this week in Dijon, the French President rebuked his citizens for their pessimism, what he calls their torpeur. "A certain number of our citizens think that everything is too difficult, that France has no future," he said. This is a persistent characteristic. Opinion poll after opinion poll has measured it.

Recent French books such as *The French Suicide* and *Submission*, among others, continue the dominant theme of French pessimism about their national future.

Just as with Britain and France, all nations have their own gifts and also tend to have their own knots, traumas which have frozen the creative flow and still adversely affect the national character and expression in some way. In Turkey, for example, imprisonment can be the punishment for a Turk who dares to bring up the subject of the genocide of Armenians carried out by Turkey a century ago, such is the total and irrational official denial of this shameful aspect of their past. In fact, Germany is to be commended as being probably the first and only country ever to make a concerted and sustained effort to come to terms with its history—in Germany's case, the Nazi era. Austria, in contrast, has tried to present itself following WWII as a victim of Nazi aggression, in spite of the popular elation and strewing of flowers when German troops marched into Austria in 1938. Consequently, not much has collectively been faced there regarding their energetic involvement in Nazism, in comparison with Germany. However, even with Germany's commendable attempts to integrate their past and move on, the shadow of their Nazi past still hangs over the German spirit. Germany's great reluctance to lead in Europe despite being the greatest economic power in the EU, or to play a full military part in international peacekeeping and assisting with world problems, is testament to the enduring cultural shadow which is still cast. This stuff is real, and not just old stereotypes in the Xenophobe's joke book.

What also underlies much of what we are speaking about in this chapter is that we don't in Britain today (and in much of Western Europe either, for that matter), have a bigger story or myth which puts our lives, aspirations, our nation, and our world in perspective; no living story to give us greater meaning and purpose to existence. As discussed in the previous chapter, at this point in our development, for most of us, several centuries after the freedoms and advances gained by the Enlightenment, all that is no longer any source of inspiration or meaning. And particularly in Germany's case, the last thing they would want would be another grand 'utopian' project. For many of us, God, church, nation, obligation, direction, even notions of progress are fading or discarded, and no longer provide any overarching and meaning-making story. No manifest destiny for us; none of that God is an Englishman tosh any more for us. While naturally enough, we're still pursuing greater material advancement in Britain, we somehow sense that nirvana won't be found by eventually reaching universal social equality; the allure isn't as shiny as it used to be, and deeper down it doesn't give the same fulfillment. We can see that the Scandinavians are much closer to social equality than us and have almost achieved this socialist Holy Grail and yet they don't seem any more fulfilled or happy than us. Soon we'll all be kitted out homogeneously in our Ikea flats or houses; what then?

We can't be like the USA where the founding idea of the nation is still very much alive to many of their citizens. They have a living story for being American in a way which would seem absurd for us to adopt. 1776 can almost seem like yesterday to Americans, as if you might still meet a founding father or two if you popped into the right bar in old Beacon Hill in Boston. Yet there is also a downside to this living story. The frontiers of the Wild West back in the eighteenth century seem to remain real and alive for many Americans in the twenty-first century as if they were still those historical pioneers. It helps explain the otherwise unfathomable reaction of many Americans following every mass shooting, towards any attempt to modify their sacred right to bear arms (and even possess a small personal military arsenal) as enshrined in their Constitution. Each nation has to face and integrate its historical iniquities, and it can be easier for us to be objective about other countries. Speaking of the USA, perhaps even more important for that nation to come to terms with, is the long shadow of slavery. This 'original sin' of a trauma underlies so much of the deep racial tension in the States, in spite of it being such a multicultural nation made up of immigrants.

Towards a more Healthy National Psyche

Western Europeans including the British, broadly share a lack of national self-esteem in our attitude towards our past colonial exploitation and towards our crimes of the past. From Bruckner again,

> Let us recall this very simple fact: Europe has more or less vanquished its monsters, slavery has been abolished, colonialism has been abandoned, fascism defeated, communism brought to its knees. What continent can boast such a record of accomplishment? In the end, the preferable won out over the abominable. Europe is the Shoah plus the destruction of Nazism, it is the Gulag plus the fall of the Wall, the empire plus colonisation, slavery and its abolition - each time, a specific form of violence has not only been transcended but delegitimized. This is a double progress of civilisation and law. We are not talking here of falling into extreme nationalistic pride of the kind defended by the extreme Right which seeks.....to provide a glorifying vision of history ....but we have to be proud of ourselves *against* our crimes because we have recognised them and rejected them.

Can we allow ourselves a small moment of pride and achievement in this? Or do we feel instinctively to deny it and be cynical? A healthy national self-esteem is not an insular 'nationalism' with all its negative connotations setting 'us' against the 'other'. Pride can be positive, and is not necessarily separative nationalism. In fact, how open can we really be to others while we dislike ourselves? Just as in personal psychology, if there is not a basis of healthy self-love, it is not possible to love others. What message do we give our children and to recent immigrants if we ourselves lack national self-esteem? Such an attitude does not engender respect from others. Having said all this, I hope it is more clear why we have a national tendency at this point in time towards pessimism and a glass-half-empty approach to life.

The more we can start to make room in ourselves for the living story which is us, which is our national thread through the centuries, the more we can recontextualise our history; particularly the Empire phase which has been such a psychic block preventing our being able to appreciate our rich national history and development. We are estranged from our own story partly because of a postmodern bias against seeing any direction or meaning in history and more particularly because of our own shame and embarrassment about Empire. We are left with an amorphous and deadening feeling of decline which is taken to be somehow factual. We can begin to accommodate the whole spectrum of Empire which is currently undigested and unassimilated in our collective psyche: the indignities, the suffering and horrors inflicted in past centuries, the traumas caused as a direct and indirect result of Empire, the exploitation. It is the very willingness to face into our own historical iniquities which allows us to become more human, and without it, we remain, much as we may endeavour to be different, stuck in old grooves.

We can also in retrospect accommodate the positive legacy: the spreading of Enlightenment values, of human rights and the institutions and advances of modernity and democracy, of development itself. And an ironic benefit is how the development of an increasingly more benevolent Empire led to its only course being that of becoming self-liquidating, and hopefully heralding the end of the age of empires. With the dawning of a more inclusive developmental perspective, our national collective history could be better integrated into a more healthy national self-sense and perhaps also in helping to shape a new role for Britain in the world; forming a new living story for us where at present there is only a void. After all, the country which first brought about an earlier globalisation and mixed cultures on an unprecedented scale could have much to offer the world from our integrated experience. Having untangled the psychic knot of Empire and our felt sense of decline, we can look now at who we are as a nation and what does nationality even mean today.

Chapter 8

It's Your Country

And above all, it is your civilization, it is you. However much you hate it or laugh at it, you will never be happy away from it for any length of time... Good or evil, it is yours, you belong to it, and this side of the grave you will never get away from the marks that it has given you.

George Orwell

Fair Play

I still remember as a child, the shock when my ordered view of the world collapsed. Strangely, while I can't recall what was the trigger, it's etched into my psyche how my sense of certainty and goodness was shaken that fateful day. Like realising Father Christmas wasn't for real. It was when I woke up to the sickening realisation that *Life* wasn't fair. Up until then, it had never occurred to me to question the cast iron 'fact' that Britain was fair, the world was fair, Life was fair. And then my awful epiphany that fairness was not a universal quality. While similar rude awakenings no doubt happen to children all over the world, this one about fairness has a particularly British flavour. Fairness is a value we British hold most dearly. I was absolutely convinced that Life was fair; I mean, wouldn't there be a law against unfairness?

Trevor Phillips relates how when the Equality and Human Rights Commission, which he was head of, opened in 2007, they undertook a public attitude survey to find out what the public most wanted the Commission to promote and protect.

Fractionally behind a concern with being safe, the most important thing for people was fairness. Overwhelmingly respondents were more receptive to the idea of fair play than they were to the language of 'rights'. If you think that's uncontroversial, think for a minute how a French or American group might answer. Rights would be right up there, the rights secured by their revolutions and laid down in their constitutions. But we do things differently here. Fairness sums up our belief in cooperation for the common good. It is made possible by a robust rule of law and stable institutions.

Foreigners make fun of our almost religious ritual of queuing and we can be duped into feeling that we are being uptight, if not severely anal about this obsessive habit. Americans don't even have a proper word for the phenomenon apart from the rather inadequate 'stand in line'. I can't bear it if someone jumps the queue and doesn't wait their turn, and we seethe with anger at anyone who transgresses this unwritten law of Britishness. But it's not such a weird reaction of ours. It's because pushing ahead of others who have been waiting is not fair! And we think our society should be fair, or at least striving to be so. In a time when it often seems that we are devoid of any sense of what being British means or if we even think there is anything to feel British about, a value like fairness still resonates down the mists of time. Fair play is an article of faith across the political spectrum in Britain and we are outraged by injustice; Churchill and Orwell, opposites in many ways, both held it dearly. Fair play as a British value runs deep and has roots stretching way back into our historical development as a nation. It is part of who we are, and one facet of the elusive heart of Britishness.

Which National Identity?

So to start with, who are we as a nation, and which nation are we even talking about, given the range of views on Britishness and Englishness; and Scottishness, Welshness and Northern Irishness for that matter? Although as I said earlier, I don't intend to spend too much time attempting to delineate Britishness from Englishness, or from the other regional identities, we can't ignore the fact that the Act of Union in 1707 between England and Scotland created the new entity of 'Great Britain', a united kingdom (Wales was already part). Going back much further, you could argue that the ancient 'Britons', as they have been called, predated this more 'modern' Britain by a long margin. But I'm not concentrating on the distinction between British and English, nor on the other regional identities of Scottish, Welsh and Northern Irish, important though they clearly are.

Books about the English or the British tend to give lists of peculiar habits and characteristics of ours which are supposed to be definitive of our nationality, but inevitably they are superficial and also tend to be rather silly stereotypes: we are tea drinking, warm-beer swigging, cricket loving, Marmite scoffing, fish & chip enthusiasts; reserved folk who are very polite and at the same time repressed and feeling permanent embarrassment for the mere fact that we exist; saying sorry for having our own foot trodden on by someone else. We all immediately think of many British people we know and experience every day, who are not remotely like this stereotype. Even if we update the stereotypes, as some do, to include such things as the now favourite national dish of chicken tikka masala, it still isn't any more helpful. And with the extent of immigration in recent times, these stereotypes have even less value. In fact, these British peculiarities can begin to become a kind of in-joke which recent immigrants are on the outside of.

I mean what do Russell Brand, Annie Lennox, Diane Abbott, David Attenborough, Van Morrison, Mo Farah, Alex Ferguson and Stephen Fry remotely have in common? Apart from the fact that they are British, that is. And that is the interesting connection. For in spite of all I just said, I am convinced that there is a thread which runs through the people who are born here, and perhaps even more interestingly is absorbed and also runs through those many people who weren't born here yet have made Britain their permanent home. I will return to this point. Sometimes it's easier for us to be clearer about what we are not and what we are against, than being clear what we are and what we do stand for. Currently the prevailing mood seems to be that we are against the EU and Brussels and so we are not European. But who are we now? Books like Jeremy Paxman's, *The English*, while entertaining and full of amusing anecdotes, have curiously little to say about who we are now, and focus more on tales about old identities and outmoded national values.

I live in a bastion of Britishness, a borough where one of the highest proportions of all its residents identify with what they consider their country: Britain. I also very much consider myself British and am very happy to think of this as my primary national identity; so I guess I live in the right place. Where is this stronghold of Britishness in our Sceptred Isle? Well, what might come to mind could be somewhere like Tunbridge Wells or a small village in comfortable Hampshire or Dorset, or any location where the *Daily Mail* or *Express* dominates the dailies. But Royal Tunbridge Wells residents are far less than half as likely to identify themselves as British than in my home borough. It's the London East End borough of Tower Hamlets, which doesn't have a 'Royal' epithet either. Data from the 2011 census shows very clearly that all the boroughs in the country with the highest number of respondents picking British as their primary identity are London ones. And it pretty much correlates with the much greater ethnic diversity of these boroughs. It's repeated outside London too, where the 'most British' places are Slough, Leicester, Luton and Birmingham, all places with high levels of ethnic diversity. Elsewhere in England, much greater percentages of the population picked being English as their primary identity: in Tunbridge Wells, 63 per cent picked English in contrast to Tower Hamlets 25 per cent. When you think about it, it does make sense that areas with a high percentage of immigrants would be more likely to feel at home with being British rather than English; 'Black English' doesn't sound as appealing as 'Black British'.

I'm just making the point that who we are and who we think we are, is not a simple question to answer. Our sense of ourselves and our identity is not fixed and changes over the decades, yet alone centuries. Yet I feel that there are facets and qualities of our national identity, character or culture that are valuable to recognise, and qualities can submerge and become invisible only to reappear later in a new guise. These days, it can appear to many that we have no real national identity left, and the *Daily Mail* and its fellow travellers bemoan the disintegration of British character. In this view, the indomitable Dunkirk spirit has sunk beneath the weight of a growing population of welfare dependent wastrels who are work-shy and marinated in their feelings of entitlement without responsibility. On the liberal side we have the more individualistic view which at its most extreme end, says, 'I'm a human being, and I make my own choices. I create my own identity and I don't feel any particular allegiance to this pompous little island Queendom; this oppressively stitched together and patently "dis-united kingdom" whose main reality is faded memories of The Empire. Yes, everyone has to be born somewhere—on some patch of the planet—but big deal. So what? We should celebrate our human unity as one family. Hasn't all the patriotism about nation states whipped up by scheming politicians for their own devious ends been the cause of so much division and so many awful wars?' I don't hold with either of these extremes. We are not just 'nothing' and while I share the sentiment of being first and foremost, a member of the human race, we are not merely some kind of free floating global human beings. Yet neither can we hold onto outdated sentimental views of our past which don't exist any more.

We are our country. It's part of who we are, whether we like it or not, or whether it fits in with our political or intellectual persuasions or not. All the influences of the past carried forward through our culture, absorbed in our formative years and reinforced by the sheer immersive field of unspoken collective societal agreements, transmitted by example all around us; solidified and constantly reinforced in language and verbal cues; by our media, our parents, our education, our friends. We are shaped and formed by the past, by the struggles, failures, sorrows and achievements of those who have collectively made a shift in the glacial flow of shared human, and specifically in this case, British culture. You could write a similar narrative for any nation of course, but I'm focussing on the specific British one, because it's ME; it's YOU. It's US.

It's your civilisation, as Orwell said. You can deny it, avoid it, make fun of it, convince yourself with fine words that you are beyond it, but you will still be influenced by it. Reacting against it is still being under its influence. You can move to another country, be an expat for life, but you will never escape it; you will always be British whatever you do. You can no more remove yourself from your nationality than you can remove yourself from your physical body; you can attempt to be disembodied yet the flesh is still here as long as breath lasts. You can't not be your nationality; the sarcastic millennial hipster is as British to his fingertips as the more traditional British Legion member retiree in Bournemouth. We are our history, our country, our landscape. This living beast of Britishness is always changing, ebbing and flowing, erratically developing, complexifying; always changing, yet a thread remains and holds a collective identity. The collective baton is thrust upon us, and we don't have a choice about it as we lurch, stride, struggle, stumble or flow into the future.

History is not an arcane and irrelevant speciality. It's our story, the story of who we are and how we've come here. As radical jazz musician Sun Ra liked to point out, 'They say history repeats itself. That's his story. You haven't heard my story.' It wasn't history he was interested in, but his story—my story, our story. History is full of inconsistencies, failures, shameful episodes and horrors which seem to repeat themselves; the learning curve is often excruciatingly slow. There are no guarantees of course that the future will be any better, or that 'progress' is always a good thing, yet this is the adventure we have choicelessly embarked on as part of being alive. And also, and more significantly, it's the struggle of the creative impulse of human beings, the spirit of humanity in particular times and circumstances, to overcome obstacles, to explore; to more creatively and adequately respond to living conditions, leading often to advances across the board, technically, scientifically, culturally, ethically, artistically, spiritually, and humanly. And there are cul de sacs and mistakes and awful deviations too. Every culture has its own distinctive thread, greatly influenced by steps or advances made by neighbouring cultures.

It's erroneous for us to retrospectively judge the horrors perpetrated by our ancestors by the more 'enlightened' view of the present. It's not to deny the tremendous cruelty and oppression of times gone by, but it's also not to entirely dismiss our past. I'm talking about coming to a more holistic sense of ourselves, including in our self-sense, the deep roots of our historical and cultural legacy and the land and landscape which has shaped us. And the good news is it's not all shameful. There is a tremendous amount to be thankful and feel fortunate about what has been bequeathed to us by our forebears. Our liberal discomfort at the iniquities of Empire has caused us to significantly dissociate from our entire history as a nation. In this version of reality, The Empire was solely a 'most evil regrettable episode', and thus we have largely shoved this whole phase of several centuries out of conscious awareness, leaving just the clouds of an unexamined sense of collective guilt and shame. I mean, conquering somewhere in the region of 60 countries by force doesn't sound a particularly nice thing to do, does it? Nice people just don't invade other countries, plant a flag, claim ownership, and then oppress and exploit the poor indigenous inhabitants, and bleed them dry. So because of this, we have tended to cut ourselves off psychically from history, cut off from our national creative thread. Now we have no history. We are not connected to anything other than our families. A little exaggeration here to be sure, but I'm trying to make a point.

Popular psychology tells us that if a significant aspect of our personal history is avoided, denied, or repressed, due to a traumatic event in our life, then it's hard to be fully present and available as a person. The shadow of what is denied will inevitably affect our views and our actions, and will be a limiting factor in our psyche and our outward life. Similarly with nationality, if part of our past is not digested, or is avoided because of its uncomfortableness, then it's hard, if not almost impossible to have any real constructive relation with our national history. Many advances in this country throughout its long history ought to make us proud of our country, without being nationalistic, while fully acknowledging the ills of our past. Of course we wouldn't want to commit any of those past cruelties today, which as we have looked at previously, we have thankfully largely grown out of. A blind adherence to our nation always being right leads to extremism of the BNP variety, which is easy to identify. But more insidious in my opinion, is the more prevalent disconnected sense of identity: indifferent to our history, strangely rootless, and without a healthy national self-sense; the vacuum filled instead with a vague sense of pessimism, declinism and even self-loathing. Why should others respect us when we don't seem able to respect ourselves?

Comedian David Mitchell, writing humorously about the very successful negative marketing of Ryanair and its unfailingly rude CEO, Michael O'Leary, in *The Observer* says, 'In fact, the cynical, self-loathing British public probably respond more positively to companies that show them disdain than those who try and suck up to them.' We need a healthy national self-sense just as we need a healthy personal self-sense, since both are real dimensions of who we are, and give nuance and depth to our psyche and our functioning. Both need embracing in order to be a whole person, or we are denying part of our actual makeup and identity. To reiterate the simple truism: to be informed about our next step, we need to know where we are now; and to know the present, we need to know what has got us here from the past. In this developmental view, time is all important as a continuum. We don't now have any national story or myth to provide a sense of continuity, belonging or identity. Moral philosopher Mary Midgley, in her *The Myths We Live By*, reexamines the importance of myths, asserting that far from popularly being seen as the opposite of science, myths are rather the central part of it: that which decides its significance in our lives. 'Myths are not lies. Nor are they detached stories. They are imaginative patterns, networks of powerful symbols that suggest particular ways of interpreting the world.'

As already mentioned, unlike in the USA where the Declaration of Independence and the myth of the Founding Fathers still resonates for them today, we have no living national myth. For us, it's different. Gone is the sense of destiny of the Enlightenment and the Industrial Revolution; long dead is the triumphalism of Victorian times, the belief in Empire, of God being on our side, and of the manifest destiny of the British as a civilizing influence in the world; gone is our belief in our ascendency; also largely gone or fading, at least on our conscious surface, is our cherished and long held belief in Parliament and law and democracy and our institutions. Dunkirk, the Blitz and the Battle of Britain in the mid twentieth century for a while gave us a condensed collage of what was best about being British. Yet this too has faded into ancient scratchy black and white footage, less real than Xbox for many of the younger generations, and with much inferior visuals; certainly not 3D, or even HD. Many people are understandably just not consciously connected with all this. Yet it is our story, or at least a few strands of that ever living beast of nationality, as Orwell terms it, that is you and me.

Sweet Thames flow Softly

Pondering all this, I took myself down to the river Thames in London for a change of scenery and maybe a different perspective. I find that being by the waterside is always medicinal. I end up sitting at a weathered wooden table in the late afternoon autumn sun by the window in a pub called *The Grapes*. Here I can palpably feel history and the continuum of time. This is a place where people have been sitting and socialising for the best part of half a millennium; generations of seafaring folk and all those who plied their allied ship trades. The pub, a narrow rickety building leaning precariously out over the Thames in London's old docklands locale of Limehouse, is emblematic of London's river life. The sound of the river swishing and lapping against the buttresses in the wake of passing ferries, evokes the sea; as does the ever changing tidal flow which reminds me that the sea reaches right up here into the city. Amazingly this ancient pub has survived the Great Fire, the Blitz and perhaps even more amazingly, the redevelopment of the Docklands. Charles Dickens looks down rather gravely and pensively from his portrait on the maroon wall to the dark wooden panelling below. He was well acquainted with this tavern, already ancient in his day, writing of it in 1820 as, 'A tavern of dropsical appearance... long settled down into a state of hale infirmity. It had outlasted many a sprucer public house.' A complete and well-thumbed set of Dickens sits in the cabinet by my head, acknowledging the connection. It was from directly below this very pub that Sir Walter Raleigh set sail on his third and final voyage to the New World in 1616, on a quest to discover the fabled *El Dorado*; a voyage more equivalent in its time to a contemporary spaceshot to the outer reaches of the

Solar System. How can we even comprehend what such a voyage meant in his day?

The river outside the window, glistening powerfully in the low sunlight, still speaks of movement and adventure, as it glides its way down towards the open sea. The gulls cascading over the waters, ever on the lookout for booty, hearken to the sea. Four or five hundred years have flowed past, yet really just a handful of generations. From Raleigh to Dickens, to us, to me. What those two great figures have done for us would be hard to encompass. We wouldn't be who we are if they hadn't lived and influenced our culture and history so profoundly. They contributed mightily to our creative thread and added new vistas both geographically and culturally. I can feel the living history in my heart, resonating in my being; it still calls out, like the cry of the gulls. Am I just being romantic, like the search to locate our ancestors so popular and beloved of TV shows today? I don't think so. For also that search for ancestors is responding to a need because people are missing genuine connection and continuity. Oral history has long since withered as a means of spanning the generations.

Well-heeled new Dockland immigrants stand at the bar alongside working class descendants of the old dock industries of rope making, shipbuilding and chandlering in once-grimy Limehouse. The London Docks were the greatest docks in the world; and it was only in recent times of course, that all have decamped downstream to container ports in the estuary. There is never a break in history; it is the story of our lives, our struggles and our development, pushing improbably against the entropy of the universe, to create ever more ingeniously, instead of the to-be-expected gradual settling into dissolution. Modern thought breaks up experience and history into discrete events and dates. It's a useful shorthand, but also a fiction. Reality is, and always has been much more of a stream, a process where everything influences everything else, and one 'occurrence' flows into the next in an endless succession of becoming. As writer and philosopher Owen Barfield said,

> We need not pay too much attention to those historians who cautiously refuse to detect any progress in history, because it is difficult to divide into periods, or because the periods are difficult to date precisely. The same objections apply to the process of growth from child to man. We should rather remind them that, if there is no process, there is in fact no such thing as history at all, so that they themselves must be regarded as mere chroniclers and antiquarians—a limitation which I cannot fancy they would relish.

British Values Evaluated

In pursuit of finding out who we are and what we hold dear, I was at Conway Hall in London for the launch of *The United Kingdom Values Survey* in 2013, the latest study by the Barrett Values Centre. They survey different countries focussing on the peoples' values, based on the common sense premise that the values citizens hold represent what is important to them. Successful nations, in their view, are not necessarily those that have the highest per capita income, or the lowest levels of unemployment, they are the nations whose cultures are in alignment with the values and aspirations of the people.

Presenter Phil Clothier had good news and bad news from their survey of the UK. The personal values held by we British and the values we share at a community level turned out to be generally all refreshingly positive. The top ten personal values picked out by those of us surveyed, included caring, family, honesty, humour, fun, friendship, fairness and compassion, and were all positive. Looking at our lives at a community level, we are also relatively content, with our top ten values including quality of life, family, buying local, community services and friendship. At a community level we were also concerned with several less positive issues: uncertainty about the future, crime, violence, drugs and alcohol abuse. But what was striking was the discrepancy when it came to the results from the values that we *perceive in our nation* i.e. what we think about the way Britain as a whole is going and what values we feel that our country expresses. The top ten values here were *all* negative. The list included bureaucracy, crime, violence, uncertainty about the future, corruption, blame and apathy. It's a very different set of values that we see in our nation, and all of them potentially limiting to progress. By measuring the amount of potentially limiting values experienced by the people of a nation, the Barrett Values Centre comes to an unattractive sounding term called the *cultural entropy* of the country. Cultural entropy is an indirect measure of the level of fear, anxiety and unhappiness that people have about being able to meet their needs. And Britain's cultural entropy is currently, according to them, very high. Along with Italy and France, ours is the highest of a number of European countries which they have measured.

At first it seems strange to me that although at an individual and at a local community level, we feel relatively happy and aligned with most of the values operating in our local community, how come at a national level we have such an overwhelmingly negative view of our country's culture? The survey concludes that we are not allowing our collective values to guide our decision making as institutions, organisations and in our society as a whole. And when I reflect on the results, it does make sense of how I am often struck by how many good, honest, caring people I meet in Britain, and yet how there is simultaneously this miasma of national malaise which here is being identified as cultural entropy: a climate where there seems no bigger purpose and where government does not care nor address the values which really concern us. A climate where comedian Russell Brand is mega popular and goes viral for speaking completely uninhibitedly about why none of us should vote in elections because it is irrelevant and changes nothing and in fact only encourages self-serving politicians.

Is there a British Character?

Is there such a thing as a British or English character? For that matter, has there ever been such a thing, or is it more akin to Lewis Carroll's hunting the mythical *Snark*? Well, the character question is not at all an easy question to answer and to do so, it's worth looking at changing perceptions of what being British or English has meant through history. Much has been written on this subject, past and present, and also about the allied though not identical question of British or English *identity*.

Going way back, early national consciousness would tend to have its locus on the figure of the ruler, the King. England had achieved a partial unity as a kingdom in Anglo-Saxon times, and then more fully and permanently with the Norman conquest, so there is a very long continuity in this island kingdom. Great Britain was only created as a nation in 1707 by the Act of Union between England and Scotland. Linda Colley in her *Britons* convincingly traces how this new identity was forged between English, Scottish and Welsh and was very much dependent on the central shared project of the Empire. The Empire was known as the *British* Empire for a good reason, since it combined the British constituent nations; Scots particularly figured very extensively in the Empire. Often the best opportunities for advancement open to young men on the Celtic fringes rather than in richer London and the South, were in seeking their fortune as part of the grand Empire venture. Naturally enough, in far flung foreign lands, Scottish, English, and Welsh would be thrown together and united in identity against a common 'Other'. Also Colley stresses the power of a shared Protestantism against a predominantly Catholic Europe in cementing a common identity. The French served the role of 'dastardly Other' for umpteen years and wars. We've been fighting with them for the best part of a thousand years and certainly this helped to

159

forge a sense of 'Us' against the 'Other.' Yet coming back to present day Britain and the way the world has now changed so greatly, Colley concludes, writing in 1992,

> We can understand the nature of the present crisis only if we recognise that the factors that provided for the forging of a British nation in the past have largely ceased to operate. Protestantism, that once vital cement, has now a limited influence on British culture, as indeed has Christianity itself. Recurrent wars with the states of Continental Europe have in all likelihood come to an end, so different kinds of Britons no longer feel the same compulsion as before to remain united in the face of the enemy from without. And, crucially, both commercial supremacy and imperial hegemony have gone. No more can Britons reassure themselves of their distinct and privileged identity by contrasting themselves with impoverished Europeans (real or imaginary), or by exercising authority over manifestly alien peoples.

Peter Mandler's, *The English National Character*, has to be one of the most detailed and thoroughly researched work on the subject of our character—if there is one, that is. Essentially it is also the history of an idea, which is his subtitle. To understand an idea, you need to understand its history, and the idea of English 'character' clearly has a history, which has ebbed and flowed and gone underground and sprung out again at other times. Mandler shows how the English through time haven't always thought that they had a character or needed one; though not thinking you have or need a character doesn't necessarily equate with not having one. Yet national character is clearly not an immutable constant. This makes sense to me since there is continuity, yet also great flux. Our popular character stereotypes have fluctuated greatly over time from tough 'don't mess with me' John Bull, to the mild and decent 'Little man', beloved of *Daily*

Express cartoonist Sidney Strube, in the years between the World Wars. During the times of change of the great Reform Acts of 1832 and 1867, it's interesting to note that the notion of national character and identity was being driven by Liberal reformers and not by Conservatives, making an appeal to the common identity and shared nature of all the British, both poor and rich. The reformers felt that nationality was more important than class or whether a subject was a labourer or a gentleman. Appeals about the English character today are often associated with nostalgic conservatism, and this can be interpreted as racism by the hard Left. Times certainly do change.

Victorians became fascinated with the Anglo-Saxon roots of English national identity, tracing our common law origins back to the Angles and Saxons; a popular hobby known as Teutonism or Saxonism. Yet this fascination is noteworthy in that it didn't lead to any widespread form of sinister racism such as occurred in Germany, despite what is often believed nowadays. The eugenics movement of attempting to engineer the population to breed in certain desired national attributes, never really took off here, thankfully.

Believing in British Institutions

National character is one way of looking at our identity, yet there is another way which has been important to Britain and still is important and more relevant than ever. And that is a belief in English or British civilisation rather than character. This force has never lost its power and helps to explain why we didn't completely fall for those racial and national myths so popular on the Continent in the 19th century. Being British did not have to mean being proud of your ancestors' blood when there was the alternative of being proud of your ancestors' achievements. And this became a locus for patriotism in Britain more than crude nationalism. The Empire project helped in this regard since being British included the different races of the Scots, Welsh and

English, and clearly this couldn't be thought of as one national bloodline.

This pride in British institutions was solidified in the Enlightenment, yet its roots go back much further. David Hume, the great figure of the (Scottish) Enlightenment published *The History of England* (sic), a vast sweeping study, in the mid eighteenth century. Hume widened the scope of what had been hitherto been thought of as history. Instead of history being concerned only with the standard 'Kings-battles-conquests' story, he included literature and science in his history. Hume was undoubtedly an early cultural historian. He thought that the quest for liberty was the highest standard for judging the past, and he concluded that after much fluctuation, England had achieved at that point, 'The most entire system of liberty that was ever known amongst mankind.' This book was a bestseller and was very influential over the next century, becoming the accepted historical narrative in Britain. Patriotism was becoming more based on pride in British institutions such as the rule of law, Parliamentary government, freedom of speech, personal liberty, habeas corpus, jury trials, secure property rights, the right to act as one pleases unless a law specifically prohibits it, and legal equality for women, rather than on character. And that list is impressive, and hardly matched at that time in most other countries, in spite of its only very partial attainments from today's point of view.

Hume held that, 'Of any people in the universe, the English have the least of a national character.' This Enlightenment view which has maintained its influence ever since the eighteenth century is optimistic and very cosmopolitan. Our laws, institutions and customs have come to define Britain and our identity more than national character. Though of course this identity may well contribute to our character. So it makes it possible for an immigrant to become British if he or she adopts the values and customs of the country, since identity is not based on blood. This contrasts to Germany, where up until only the turn of the millennium in 2000, being German and citizenship was still based on bloodline and not about whether or not you lived in the country. This led to weird situations such as where seven million Turkish 'guest workers' who had lived most of their lives in Germany were not allowed citizenship, nor their children. At the same time, ethnic (meaning blood related) Germans whose families had lived for centuries across Eastern Europe could claim citizenship, though they might never have set foot in Germany.

The counterbalancing role of State and Church over the centuries has also had an important role in shaping our society and our identity. Church and state in Britain are intertwined and can't really be separated. The first native historian would have to be the Venerable Bede. His *The Ecclesiastical History of the English People* completed in AD 731, has earned him the title 'The Father of English History'. Interestingly, it is the first work of history in which the AD system of dating is used. Rowan Williams credits the church as giving the Anglo-Saxons a shared sense of identity to what would otherwise be little barbarian states. Matthew Parker, Archbishop of Canterbury from 1559–75 was an influential theologian who created a whole body of documents to prove that the English church had always been historically independent from Rome. He held that the church in England had its own ancient story and was not just some outpost of Rome, thus solidifying a potent myth that we'd always been different here. For the British, Protestantism has always been as much an expression of national identity as it was about religion, and Protestantism included many dissenting sects and was hardly a uniform church, yet it provided a common language and cultural references. Of course there is a fair dose of Golden Age mythology in some of our romantic looking back to an imagined old England where men were free and laws fair; no such place ever existed. Mythic memories of King Alfred, perhaps, or stretching further back to the legends of King Arthur? Alfred, the only English king known by the epithet 'the Great', (although this epithet was only accorded by later writers in the sixteenth century, not back when he lived in the ninth century), became a symbol of true Englishness for later generations because of his establishment of the rule of law, of promoting education and defeating invaders and barbarians.

Yet institutions like Parliament do have an extraordinarily ancient history. The tradition of some kind of consultative government had long been a part of Anglo-Saxon society, way before the Norman conquest. At least from the seventh century, there was in England the institution known as the *Witenagemot*, an assembly and advisory body to the king to help governance, taxation and jurisprudence (not to be confused with The Wizengamot, from J.K. Rowling's Harry Potter, a somewhat later work). Even on a couple of rare occasions, the Witenagemot is recorded as having dismissed the king as unfit to rule. The new Norman rulers naturally tried to incorporate such embedded traditions for their own ends. This all arose long before anyone thought of writing anything down and so is part of why we have no written constitution, unlike most other countries; just an endless series of precedents to be referred to.

The ceremonial procedures in the Westminster Parliament look medieval precisely because that's what they are: medieval. Britain's unwritten constitution would have to be one of the oldest constitutions in the world, allowing for the fact, I know, that we haven't got a codified one. The English parliament had power not only in more recent enlightened times, but also significantly, way back in medieval times through its control of taxation. No law could come into being without Parliament passing it. Obviously the medieval and later parliaments were certainly very far from being representative, and yet they did reach down further into the social classes than comparable European bodies. For example, after Simon de Montfort, Earl of

Leicester, led the successful rebellion against King Henry III, during the second Barons' War of 1264–5, he called two famous parliaments. The first stripped the King of unlimited authority and the second included ordinary citizens from many towns and boroughs. Commoners were deliberating on matters of high state. As historian Simon Schama remarks about a particular incident at this time, 'So a cloth merchant or a Suffolk knight with a few acres now got to judge the terms on which the son of the king might safely be released from captivity.'

This incremental progress towards a liberal democracy over the centuries in English and British history, has no doubt been exasperatingly slow from the perspective of radicals and reformers. Yet these slow gains for individual rights have been enough to give the population faith in their institutions, the law, and in a certain degree of progress. It is likely connected to why there was no communist revolution in Britain, unlike in some other countries. And more to the point, we had had our own Revolution far earlier on; 150 years before the French one. It's often forgotten that Britain led the way in revolutions, with the first modern Western revolution in the 1640s, known more commonly as the English Civil War. It tends to get lost in the drudgery of received history as one more series of dates and battles. Following this revolution came the Glorious Revolution of 1688, a relatively bloodless one (at least for those times), where the balance of power really decisively shifted from Royal power to parliamentary power. The protestant William of Orange was invited over from Holland to rule in England, and the Catholic King James, ousted. This has often been seen as the beginning of modern English parliamentary democracy. The Bill of Rights of 1689 has become one of the most important documents in the political history of Britain and never since then has the monarch held absolute power or even the balance of power.

The British parliamentary system for all its faults, has proved very robust and has been exported around the world particularly through the many ex-colonies. The late great freedom fighter and liberator of South Africa, Nelson Mandela, who understandably hated Imperialism and British Imperialism, at the same time remained a staunch Anglophile. He sought democracy while many of his comrades and many supporters of the ANC were communists, and neither did he adopt pan-Africanism. To Mandela, the parliamentary system of government did not imply colonialism. At his trial he said, 'I have great respect for British institutions and for (Britain's) system of justice. I regard the British parliament as the most democratic in the world.' While Britain was the architect of the colonial empire in South Africa from which the Afrikaner National Party formed the more extreme apartheid system, there has since then been a strong counterbalancing response in Britain, of a kind which there has often been to injustices and past wrongs. The anti-apartheid movement was very strong here and Mandela himself said that he regarded Britain as the second home to the anti-apartheid movement.

Britain became a constitutional monarchy, though that sounds a little like an oxymoron given we don't have a written constitution. This slow meandering progress has also, I feel, imbued a deep sense of confidence in the inhabitants of the country, although this has now become fairly unconscious. This sense of belonging and confidence has stemmed from a far off past felt to be somehow just and lawful, and of the people; even though it was far from that in actuality. Paul Johnson, in his English history, *The Offshore Islanders*, points to how in order to bring about change and reform in England, the reformer's best tactic has often been to invoke the past; making the claim that the new reform is essential to restore the original spirit of the law, and of the fairness which used to prevail in times gone by. This belief is obviously fanciful, yet it could strike a chord in people in England, because of this felt mythic history. Even though

England and Britain were for most of our history far from democratic, this sense remained, and still remains. Now aimlessness and post imperial gloom may be much more in the foreground, though this is still a more superficial layer. Though having said this, the recent increasing erosion of faith in government, left or right, disconnected from any historical narrative, is in grave danger of leading to an undermining of part of this very positive legacy of ours.

Tolerance—or rather Acceptance

In our search for who we are, there is another deep quality which runs through the British, alongside the belief in fairness, and that is toleration. These days this is sometimes dismissed as merely being indifference, but I don't think that is true. The word 'toleration' is also not quite accurate with its implications of having to put up with something unpleasant, when the quality I am pointing to in the British is more akin to 'acceptance.' Rowan Williams put it well when I asked him about tolerance, and is linked in with an underlying confidence, which I will come back to soon. 'It's a matter of what makes you not feel threatened. At worst it's "whatever", but there is a sense in which real confidence makes you able to cope with change and instability.'

Sir Jonathan Sacks, former British Chief Rabbi, writes movingly about what Britain has represented to Jews. He says that Jews knew tolerance when they saw it in Britain and they recognised that their lives and those of their yet unborn grandchildren, depended on it. 'For Jews, Britain epitomised a deepdown decency, a refusal to let hate be the final word, a residual, understated, yet unshakeable, humanity. For many years I did not know how rare this was and is.' Jonathan Sacks is not blind to anti-semitism and is aware of over romanticisation; he notes the prejudice including the anti-semitism which could be heard at dinner tables or in pubs in Britain, yet he notes that it wasn't heard in public discourse.

Political parties did not win elections by campaigning against immigrants or minorities. England lacked a rhetoric of hate. That was the difference and it was all the difference. Somehow the body politic in England has built up an immunity to the darker forces of human nature. I say this because we are in danger of forgetting it, and what a nation forgets, it loses........ Why, when a whole continent from Paris to Moscow was convulsed by *die Judenfrage*, the Jewish question, was Britain— not quite, but almost, alone—immune?

Sacks suggests a number of reasons and emphasises one in particular: the value placed in Britain on civil society, which in the absence of, can lead in times of crisis, to what J.L. Talmon called 'totalitarian democracy.'

The fact of being an island nation is taken up by Rowan Williams in an essay, *The Scepter'd Isle*, as one reason that we have developed a toleration and even a degree of humility. Wars through the centuries between the island inhabitants as well as invasions by Vikings, Angles and Saxons, often resulted in inconclusive victories. Being on an island together bordered by the sea, the defeated 'Other' couldn't go anywhere. We were forced to find a way to coexist and accommodate each other. The 'Others' are still here and won't go away. Hegel wrote of 'the cunning of reason' whereby intelligent human development somehow finds its way through the chaos of actual history. Williams sees this cunning at work in our island story, whereby defeated cultures have infiltrated and changed the dominant culture.

And in terms of toleration or acceptance in more recent times, it is revealing to note how the extreme right wing (or the extreme Left for that matter) has never managed to gain much traction in Britain. Support for the National Front, and now the BNP or the EDL, is very small, and has never really grown, though the liberal media sensationalises its size and influence. Critics put the lack of growth down to the fact that Britain's first past the post electoral system stops smaller parties gaining seats, which is true, yet this doesn't account for the resounding lack of support for the extreme right wing in Britain. The BNP received a minuscule number of votes in the 2015 general election. UKIP as a growing protest party can only retain its relative popularity by always scrupulously distancing itself from the slightest suspicion of racism.

Just a glance at the level of far right support (extreme right or radical right) in various continental European countries, puts it in perspective. France's National Front under the more appealing (relatively appealing, that is, compared with her father) Marine Le Pen, is a major force in French politics. She polled almost 18 per cent of the vote in the 2012 presidential elections, coming third in the first round. The Austrian far right Freedom Party, even though long without its charismatic leader, Jorg Haider, took one fifth of the votes in the last general election in 2013. Switzerland's People's Party campaigns with racist advertising that would never be tolerated in Britain. Geert Wilder's Freedom Party is mainstream in Holland. Similar parties are far from marginal in Denmark, Norway, Finland and Italy, among others. And when you look eastward in Europe, it gets scarier. There are ultra right parties like Hungary's *Jobbik*, which are unashamedly racist, homophobic, violent, anti-Roma and anti-semitic, with street militia. And more worrying, Jobbik is currently increasing its popularity, winning over 20 per cent of the vote in the Hungarian national election of 2014. John Gray, from whom praise doesn't come easily, highlights in his essay in *Being British*, the unusual character of Britain which contributes much to this tolerance.

With all of its drawbacks, the British state has the overriding virtue that it is not founded on blood, soil, or faith. In their ways, the United States and France are both doctrinal regimes. To be a citizen of those countries is a matter of belief;

it means subscribing to some sort of civil or political religion - in other words a creed, at once highly contentious and claiming to be rationally self-evident. In contrast... no doctrine of faith is required in order to be British. The British state is a cosmopolitan regime—a state to which one can be loyal without having to belong to any particular tribe or hold to any faith. Cosmopolitan regimes have the invaluable feature that they allow identity to be largely elective, and also plural.

He interestingly observes how cosmopolitanism is best realised in countries that are monarchies or are the remains of empire like Canada and Britain; multicultural, multinational places in which different nationalities coexist and mingle, agreeing on a shared practice of peaceful coexistence.

A Long-forged Self-Confidence

The British have a self-confidence, which in spite of all our self-deprecating gloom of late, still has a residual effect. Perhaps because of many centuries of relative stability and security, and lack of invasions in our island home, along with incremental progress towards more justice and freedom, it resulted in a foundation of self-confidence. This self-confidence is mixed in with a large dose of arrogance for sure. I mean, not many people other than Britons would have the gall to remark aloud on a foreign holiday, that the place is full of foreigners. It's akin to the classic British weather report that the European continent is currently cut off by fog. I've often noticed how British expats never assimilate. I mean on one level we certainly can and do assimilate in other countries. But for example, we never lose our accents. Why? Because we don't want to and we don't feel we need to. We are confidently and truculently defiant; an interesting mixture of healthy self-confidence shot through with arrogance. My own brother has lived all his adult life in Switzerland and enjoys the Swiss quality of life but is horrified if

I ask him if he ever contemplates taking Swiss nationality. My English mother-in-law has now spent two thirds of her life in Australia, yet not a trace of an Australian accent has crept in, and she remains steadfastly British in all matters, while being fully engaged in her local community.

We don't feel the need to fit in. When you travel to other countries like the States, you come across foreign quarters: an Italian quarter, or Polish, or Vietnamese. But you never come across a British quarter. We don't feel the need to do that. Each Briton is sufficient unto his or herself, an island of Britishness. Yet many of us live permanently in other countries. An estimated one million Brits live in each of both Australia and Spain with no intention of becoming naturalised. It's hard to find figures, but the best estimates I've found, are of about 12 million Brits living abroad. Think about that; it's a hell of a lot, nearly one in five of us. A 2014 report listed the UK as producing the greatest number of expats in the world after China and India, both countries with massive populations. We often like to live somewhere else, but in our bones we remain British.

I feel the same. I lived and worked in the States for several years and was granted permanent residency, the old style Green Card which had no expiry date and was thus valid for life, and I would have been eligible for US citizenship. Yet when I moved back to Britain, I found it difficult to hand back my Green Card. Well, actually I didn't find it difficult, I only found it difficult to find the official US avenue to hand it in. The US immigration officer who I eventually spoke with in person, couldn't seem to comprehend that I didn't want my Green Card any more. He was affable yet perplexed. I imagined that the subtext of our conversation was that maybe he wanted to help me through my temporary loss of sanity whereby I would lose my chance to live in the best country in the world and the birthplace of democracy. I felt I needed to praise America or he might be hurt. I assured him that America is a wonderful place, and I'd loved living there, (which is true) but I wanted to live in Britain, my home country, and so I wouldn't be needing US residency any longer.

I feel that our self-confidence as a nation, though it runs underground and often would not be admitted, can have positive effects. It adds to our tolerance and acceptance since we don't feel as threatened by immigration as some countries. If you are surer of your identity, you won't be as threatened. These days, such qualities are at serious risk of being undermined by the closer to the surface insecurities about jobs and prosperity of the recent extended years of recession, and by fears of Islamic extremism and unchecked immigration. Yet this underlying confidence gives an emotional strength and grittiness and it hasn't all withered away since the days of the Blitz. In certain circumstances, it can still be seen.

I have an abiding memory of a late summer afternoon in London. It was 7/7, the day of the London bombings, that fateful day in July 2005. I was standing on the normally very busy Essex road in Islington, just outside the most central zone of London, and it was eerily silent. There was no traffic at all, public transport having been completely disrupted and closed down because of the terrible multiple bombings. Yet filling the pavements there was an endless procession of pedestrians, forced to walk out of the central zone to reach to where public transport was still functioning. I was very moved. Thousands of people walking, not hurrying. It was a dignified and mighty throng with no panic, and for the large part silent. This to me was a demonstration of the emotional strength of the British under pressure. People would not be cowed or succumb to irrational fear and nor would they resort to knee jerk hatred of the 'Other'.

In the 1970s and 1980s, during the 'troubles' in Northern Ireland, when the IRA brought their bombing campaign to mainland Britain, the spectre of explosions potentially happening anywhere, resulted in huge security problems and delays, with umpteen false alarms and scares; every 'unattended package', every forgotten carrier bag, a potential bomb. What was striking to me over those twenty-five years from the early 1970s, was how people were not panicked, and found the whole thing a very irritating nuisance. We just went about our business. In London, where many of these occurred, we just grumbled about another Tube delay which usually turned out to be a false alarm. More deeply, it made mainland British less sympathetic to the IRA's justifiable grievances, and produced the opposite; a sense that, 'we are not going to be bombed into submission', and a stubborn digging in of the heels. The IRA eventually realised that this was not the most effective way to gain the political and social changes that they were rightfully fighting for. This approach doesn't work with the British. This grittiness, tenacious obstinacy and emotional strength still runs through the national psyche.

Imagine such a decades long terror campaign being waged in New York, and what the American reaction would be. It would likely be, from our point of view, rather hysterical and portrayed as akin to the end of days. In fact, you don't need to imagine it: after the awful Boston marathon bombing in 2013, a number of American commentators themselves have commented and criticised the vast overreaction to a couple of inept wannabe terrorists. The whole city of Boston was locked down by the actions of two young brothers. Their own uncle dismissed them both by saying that their main motive was 'being losers'. I don't want, in any way to diminish how despicable and utterly awful that horrific attack was, tragically causing loss of human life, great trauma and many injuries, yet my point is that the tremendous degree of public fear and terror whipped up by the media and all concerned, was very questionable. The British media as well as the official reaction to similar incidents on our home turf is in danger of following suit in this trend of lack of perspective and increasing hysteria.

The Contribution of Empiricism

In trying to understand our sense of identity, it's likely that the British philosophical tradition has also helped inculcate a sense of confidence and tolerance and of fair play over the centuries. We may tend to think of continental philosophers when the word 'philosopher' comes up and we don't tend to hold philosophers or intellectuals in high esteem here, unlike in say France, where public intellectuals can be TV celebrity chat show guests. Yet Britain has made a major philosophical contribution to the world and to the development of science, and it has had a distinctive flavour. Empiricism was the practical philosophical movement which arose and flourished mainly in Britain in the seventeenth and eighteenth centuries, with main players John Locke, David Hume and George Berkeley. Holding that all knowledge originates from sense experience and relying on experience and evidence, instead of any notion of innate ideas, empiricism suited the British mind. With England's Protestant breakaway from the deadening weight of orthodoxy of continental Catholicism, there was much more freedom to inquire and experiment. Britain had become a major seafaring nation and adventure and invention was in the air, and was the spirit of the age, as Hegel would have put it. There was much interest in practical things that worked and a pragmatism about ideas which improved lives and trade. The American empiricism and pragmatism is a British legacy.

Empiricism grew out of the environment of experimental science and early modern philosophy in Britain in the seventeenth century. Francis Bacon has rightfully been called the father of empiricism and he, more than any other single person, founded the scientific method: a clear and planned procedure for the investigation of everything natural. Bacon's early practical approach disregarded the hoary 'truths' of unquestioned assumptions and superstitions handed down from antiquity. Instead of looking to the past, Bacon opened the future by changing science from contemplation into a practical inventive endeavour which laid the ground for the dawn of the Industrial Revolution.

> Those who have taken upon them to lay down the law of nature as a thing already searched out and understood, whether they have spoken in simple assurance or professional affectation, have therein done philosophy and the sciences great injury. For as they have been successful in inducing belief, so they have been effective in quenching and stopping inquiry; and have done more harm by spoiling and putting an end to other men's efforts than good by their own.

Thus spake Francis Bacon. Hepworth Dixon, in his biography of Bacon, concluded that the whole of humanity is obliged to him for his enormous influence in the modern world. He states that every man who rides in a train, sends a telegram, follows a steam plough (the biography was written in Victorian times), sits in an easy chair, crosses the channel or the Atlantic, eats a good dinner, enjoys a beautiful garden, or undergoes a painless surgical operation, owes Bacon something. Thomas Jefferson, Third President of the United States and author of the Declaration of Independence, wrote: 'Bacon, Locke and Newton. I consider them as the three greatest men that have ever lived, without any exception, and as having laid the foundation of those superstructures which have been raised in the Physical and Moral sciences'.

Thomas Hobbes, in his early days a young associate of Bacon, is remembered for his later *Leviathan*, written during the English civil war in the 1640s, which called for states to have a strong central authority to prevent the otherwise inevitable mayhem. This led to the phrase of his which we all know; the one about what the state of mankind without such government would be like: 'solitary, poor, nasty, brutish, and short.' (This phrase was also more recently used as an epithet in an altogether different context by comedienne Jo Brand to describe the small of stature, right-wing comedian Jim Davidson.) Many of us don't realise that Hobbes also contributed some of the fundamental principles of British and European liberal thought: the natural equality of all men; the rights of the individual; the insistence that all political power which is legitimate must be based on the consent of the people and be representative. His liberal interpretation of the law is something which we British still hold dear: that people should be free to do whatever the law does not explicitly forbid.

In Chapter 2 I dwelt on the downside of our nation, yet I feel it is more than balanced by various positive national qualities, and positive contributions from our past. I'm not trying to make a case for Britain being especially 'Great' or that it is better than other countries, but instead to come to a more balanced view of ourselves; one which we can be proud of, while acknowledging our limitations, and all the regrettable actions of the past. A kind of national health service for our national psyche, you might say.

At this point, I need to add one caveat, so that what I am saying is not misunderstood. Having concentrated on the importance of our nationality, I don't want to give the impression that our nationality is the most important element of who we are. We are obviously much more than this. I hope we could all come to realise that first and foremost we are human beings on planet earth, and then secondarily we are citizens of a particular country. It's just that many liberals espouse only the 'being human' aspect of our identity, while the nationality part has been relegated to the dustbin of toxic nationalism. And that does us a great disservice as I have attempted to convey here, by cutting us off from the rich stem of the body which has produced us. So I am re-emphasising the nationality side of the picture deliberately. The more conscious we are of the various elements of which we are constituted and which condition our outlook, the more we enable a degree of freedom and disembedding from the unconsciousness of knee jerk reaction and from tripping over our shadows.

Always Becoming

How to conclude this elusive quest for the essence of who we are as Britons? While I can't definitively say who we are, we can get a sense of who we have been in past centuries as a stream with various tributaries feeding into it, leading to who we are today. Being British is too static a term for who we are. It's not a 'thing'. It's an event always in process, a becoming. *Becoming* British is more in line with actuality than statically *being* British. In fact I would preferred to call this book *Becoming British*, but for the likelihood that such a title would look like a kind of guide to achieving citizenship. We are constantly becoming British, whatever that may come to mean. And what it means has changed and will change. What are we becoming? Well, that can certainly be influenced by how conscious we are of what we have and are, and a healthy national self-sense. The flow of the past washing into the choppy seas of our changing world, mixed with all the immigrants who have come, are coming, and will come to our shores, all affects the outcome. No one is unaffected. We are all in a process of becoming, and Britishness is one element. Should we be preserving our British traditions? Yes, but not by being conservative. Conservatism kills rather than conserving. The best way to preserve traditions is by being progressive. Value the past; value what has come before; learn from it, yet without cloying nostalgia. Then traditions can be constantly reinvented, and be relevant for our changing life circumstances. We honour the past in this way by flourishing in the present.

Being British is about embracing the project of being British and our shared values, and joining this adventure. Eddie Izzard called us a mongrel nation, and we are, and we have always been so; that is part of our richness. Not blood, religion, belief, but willingness to join, accept basic principles and values, and coexist, defines being British. Continuity and deep roots in our rich culture and values, and a certain healthy immunity to being so worried by the fact of change, mixed with the fact that we are constantly changing. The positive qualities forged over centuries can serve us well in the melting pot of globalisation. Being both 'local and global' is sometimes quoted as a desirable aim, yet we have to first embrace local in terms of our identity, before we can creatively play our best role globally as a post-colonial country. And paradoxically, the more we can first see ourselves from the global developmental altitude of being first and foremost a human being, the more we can embrace and embody our national identity without it becoming some kind of divisive and petty nationalism. Since being British is not a matter of race or blood, it is a nationality open to new and existing immigrants and not confined in any way to white ethnic Britons. Immigrants can also chose to absorb and embrace these British values I have talked of, which include those of fairness, toleration, acceptance, confidence, humour, as they can embrace the historical and unfolding story of being British and shaping the becoming of Britain. And while there are many difficulties, this absorption is increasingly taking place.

Modernism and science championed the 'category'. It invented the category, a separate pigeon hole for everything, and then everything was to be categorised, ordered, and set apart. Many advances in knowledge and science came through this rigorous way of objectifying and dissecting life. Yet it divided up life in a way which had never before happened in human history. Up to that point, people had always consciously been in some form of active participation with life and their surroundings. Today we need a renewed felt sense of our active participation. It is easily forgotten that this categorisation and dividing up is a map of the terrain; a handy and immensely useful map, but still only a map. The actual territory of life and reality is not a map, it's a constant flow, a process which never stands still and is more defined by 'events' than by discrete 'things'. Everything is not every *thing*, but rather *everything* is a process.

A story better matches this flow of events. We can re-embrace our national story. It never went away; we just rejected it for understandable reasons of confusion and guilt. The nature of life is a stream. There are naturally local and regional strands of this story which add richness and diversity. These can be comfortably nested in the concentric and expanding circles of our personal and national identity. Our new story needs to be a larger one of valuing our past and seeing our lives as part of a developing stream, one in which we can have some degree of agency in helping to shape a better future for us all. It's not history; it's our story. In truth, who we are is a story and yet we British don't have a living story or myth at this point in the story. As I have explained, the old stories of 'great' Britain have been discredited and dropped, for understandable reasons and we are left with no uniting and creative thread—or at least we are barely conscious of such a thread—which amounts to much the same thing. Our story is part of the larger story of Western civilization and shares many commonalities, yet it has its own very distinctive features. It's the story of Britain and the next chapters are as yet unwritten. It's us. It's you. It's me. It's the story of our once and future selves, to paraphrase T. H White's famous rewriting of the myth of King Arthur.

Chapter 9

Patriotism Reloaded

Patriotism has nothing to do with Conservatism. It is actually the
opposite of Conservatism, since it is a devotion to something that is
always changing and yet is felt to be mystically the same.
George Orwell

From our examination of the long forged nature of British
identities, values and culture in the preceding chapter, it should
be clear that we have a considerable amount to feel proud of,
while fully acknowledging our national ills and the great
sufferings and injustices of the past caused to many people both
at home and abroad, and more especially in the Empire. Indeed
it would be very natural for Britons to feel very fortunate to have
been born in this country, or to live here (if they were born
elsewhere), and to have the freedom and opportunities and rights
and culture, which is denied to so many people and countries in
the world; a situation, incidentally, which has prevailed for the
vast majority of people throughout the vast majority of human
history. Yet as we know, feeling fortunate is not generally our
outlook today in Britain; or if it is, it is deeply buried. Think how
hard it is for us to express love of our country or to say, 'I'm
proud to be British!'; a phrase which is more likely to make us
squirm with post-colonial embarrassment. Think back to the
discomfort of my 'flag test' of an earlier chapter.

Re-examining Patriotism

All these uncomfortable feelings coalesce in the notion of *patri-*
otism, which is exactly why I feel it is an important subject to re-
examine. The Oxford English dictionary defines patriotism as
'vigorous support for one's country'. You might think that's not

so exceedingly difficult to swallow, but it seems that for us, it is. Of course, I'm well aware how much horror and bloodshed has been unleashed in its name, and many great thinkers of the twentieth century onwards are fairly unanimous about what they think of patriotism. Namely, not much. 'You will never have a quiet world until you knock the patriotism out of the human race,' said George Bernard Shaw, and in a similar vein from Bertrand Russell: 'Patriotism is the willingness to kill and be killed for trivial reasons.' And understandably so, as we've covered before, given centuries of wars and endless calls to unquestioningly fight for one's country.

I was pondering this very loaded notion of patriotism and took a break for some exercise in the park in East London. It's strange when you are focussed on an issue, how sometimes serendipity really does seem to tumble out in front of you. 'We need people like you and me!' said the athletic young guy watching my worthy attempts at a set of chin-ups on the bar of the open air gym apparatus in my local park. Although I can't do many reps in one set, I diligently work to maintain my level of fitness and strength as I get older, with a daily mixed routine of exercise. The confident young man, who introduced himself to me as a personal trainer, offered helpful tips and demonstrated correct form in pull ups, as he floated upwards to the bar gracefully, seemingly immune to gravity. Sensing my perplexity at his first comment, he continued, 'Yeah, we may have a nuclear deterrent in Britain, but if we are attacked, we'll need fit men to defend our country. And most young guys today in Britain are out of shape and overweight; they'd be useless. You'd be needed, even though you're older.' You might be getting a little leery with this story, wondering where I'm leading; perhaps imagining a far right cadre of nut jobs doing military training in Epping Forest. Yet this young guy was here in the park teaching children how to use bars and ropes and had his own young son along with him. He felt that kids today don't spend enough time climbing and swinging to learn important coordination skills. Oh, and also, I didn't mention that this guy was a black Caribbean Briton. He was simply uninhibitedly expressing his pride in his country.

Unfortunately it's a sad fact today in Britain that expressing pride in your country is often seen as the province of extreme right wing bigots. Yes, I know that many of us do enthusiastically support our national team in the Olympics or Commonwealth Games, yet that is one very circumscribed domain where it is socially acceptable to release the natural feelings of belonging and support for our team which we all have. Outside of this socially acceptable zone it is more or less left to those from immigrant backgrounds to express patriotism for the rest of us. Shahid Malik, who is from a Pakistani British background, made a well-known New Year's speech in a similar vein, while a Labour MP, several years ago.

We must not allow a small group of right-wingers to hijack our flag and steal our identity. I believe that patriotism is one of the most effective weapons in combating the religious and BNP type extremism that we know exists. It saddens me that some people are concerned that their pride in being English may be interpreted as being racist, while others want in particular non-white people to feel like they can't truly be English or British........

We have a rich heritage in this country and our values have helped to shape the world - our sense of fair play, democracy, the rule of law, the welfare state and our system of rights are things which been copied and exported across the world. I do sometimes think we forget just how privileged we are and take our rights for granted. We must never forget that millions died for our rights and with these rights come responsibilities especially towards one another to be neighbourly and to create a zero tolerance attitude to extremism.

A Post-traditional Patriotism which is not Nationalistic

I am firmly of the opinion that we need a new post traditional patriotism as part of our moving towards a national healthy psyche; the NHP, if you like. I could call it a progressive patriotism; a term used by musician and activist Billy Bragg, who is one of the very few on the Left who stands up for patriotism at all these days, as in his autobiographical, *The Progressive Patriot*. Or we could talk of a post-postmodern patriotism, but it's too technical a term and a mouthful. It's important to be clear that I am not calling for a renewed nationalism. Patriotism and nationalism are not necessarily the same thing at all. I can't put the distinction between the two any clearer than by quoting Orwell's brilliantly clear summary:

> Nationalism is not to be confused with patriotism. Both words are normally used in so vague a way that any definition is liable to be challenged, but one must draw a distinction between them, since two different and even opposing ideas are involved. By 'patriotism' I mean devotion to a particular place and a particular way of life, which one believes to be the best in the world but has no wish to force on other people. Patriotism is of its nature defensive, both militarily and culturally. Nationalism, on the other hand, is inseparable from the desire for power. The abiding purpose of every nationalist is to secure more power and more prestige, not for himself but for the nation or other unit in which he has chosen to sink his own individuality.

Of course it's important to note that the term nationalism can and is used in different ways, and there are many nationalists who are not seeking power at the expense of other groups nor have any xenophobic attitude, in the way that Orwell suggested. American columnist Sydney Harris made a helpful clarification between patriotism and nationalism back in the 1950s by saying that, 'the patriot is proud of his country for what it does, and the nationalist is proud of his country no matter what it does; the first attitude creates a feeling of responsibility, but the second a feeling of blind arrogance that leads to war.'

Historian Linda Colley laments how nationalists invoke history only to distort it. So we are not talking about a blind nationalism which supports everything one's country might or might not do. Patriotism doesn't mean you automatically back your country in going to war or in fudgy foreign incursions or policies. It's being proud of your country for what it is worth being proud of, and not being blind to its defects; but rather working to change those too; whereas nationalism can lead to a whitewashing of your own country, and defending the indefensible. As I said before, it is often left to immigrants to express pride in our own country. Similarly in Australia, it has taken an immigrant Australian, Tim Soutphommasane, to write *Reclaiming Patriotism*, bringing a more inclusive and generous sense of national belonging and renewal to the more limited kind of flag waving patriotism still existing in Australia (unlike in Britain, where we are well past that stage, as noted in the 'flag test').

A discussion of patriotism is not merely an academic one, and has an important bearing on often heated debates about immigration and multiculturalism. Our multi-ethnic makeup in Britain today is a fact and is one of the consequences of Empire. It is who we now are. And rightly so. Immigration policy and multiculturalism are vast subjects and this book cannot even begin to cover their multiple facets, and I am not going to attempt to do so. Yet a post traditional patriotism can give a helpful perspective which is neither of the conservative nor liberal variety. A deeper and more integrated conscious sense of our own national identity is invaluable, in my opinion, for being able to wisely negotiate the emotional subject of our attitudes toward immigration and multicultural Britain.

I'm not talking of that backward looking sense of identity and patriotism which abhors change and is fixated on keeping everything as it was (or was imagined to be) in the past. A positive sense of our own national identity can give us the confidence to not react out of post-colonial guilt towards the subject of immigration, feeling that we have no moral right to restrict the influx of immigrants into Britain. We clearly can't have uncontrolled immigration in a small crowded country, yet we can be confident enough in our identity to recognise the great invigoration and economic and cultural benefit continuously brought in by new immigrants. Also, we can have the self-confidence to assert the positive reasons for why we want and need some degree of integration of new immigrants. Knowing being British is not about race or blood but is elective and about hard won shared values gives us positive reason to want and expect a degree of integration without being afraid of being thought of as racist. Because it is not racist. If we as British don't respect ourselves and our nation, then we can't expect new immigrants to respect us either. Lack of self-respect in our British national psyche is much more likely to lead to unhealthy degrees of self-chosen segregation in new immigrants.

There are many parallels to our British predicament in France, another once great colonial power and now doubting its own identity. French intellectual Pascal Bruckner in his *Tyranny of Guilt, An essay on Western Masochism*, speaks devastatingly of his own country:

> Because it is no longer first, France has concluded that it is nothing, and has indulged in self-denigration for the past decade, fixated on its pain like a spoiled child... It is not certain rappers cries of hatred for the Republic that are worrying—it is France's disgust with itself that is a matter of concern.... We dislike ourselves much more than they reject us. A country so unsure of itself is incapable of arousing

enthusiasm in its youth, whether native or immigrant.

Reclaiming Patriotism

We need to rehabilitate patriotism, so that we can again allow ourselves to feel pride in the country we have actually got; the one we are living in and are part of; that inclusive and multicultural Britain; that country which so many have struggled for so long to create its important values, laws and culture. In one way, it is very simple. All I am really talking about is a healthy national sense of self-acceptance; just like as an individual you would ideally want to be able to accept yourself, without hating or feeling embarrassed or guilty or avoiding whole chunks of yourself. And just as in the case of an individual, it's not healthy to indulge in grandiose notions about yourself, but rather to have a more mature self-confidence which doesn't need to prove itself by posturing. Well, the same goes for a healthy national self-sense. Nicholas Beecroft, a psychiatrist himself, takes this approach on very fully with his novel and innovative *Analyze West* which personifies Western civilisation as a very troubled individual who comes to a psychiatrist for help. The psychiatrist treats him or her (called West, naturally) as a patient with various therapies, examining the West's collective psyche and its woes and strengths in this fictional yet incisively accurate account, eventually bringing about an integral transformation in West's often depressed state.

As we have seen, both in Western Europe and Britain, there have been the profound effects of the wars and ideologies of the twentieth century and this and other reasons have led to a great erosion in our faith and belief in our Western Enlightenment project and story. On top of this in Britain, we particularly suffer from declinism, post-colonial ennui and guilt and embarrassment from The Empire; made worse for its being largely unrecognised and unfaced. It's no wonder that the idea of patriotism doesn't exactly light us up, and with our postmodern sensibilities, positively repels us.

Whether that patriotism is towards being British or being English is not what I am particularly concerned with here. Reclaiming and being appropriately proud of an English identity, or a Scottish, Welsh, or Irish one, is a whole subject in itself, and entirely valid. As I have said throughout, although I write about being British, I hold strongly to the view of nested hierarchies of identity and that what is most important is being part of the human family first and foremost. It is just that modern and postmodern voices have largely drowned out the fact that we global village human beings are also embodied and rooted, and need belonging as a healthy part of our being and identity. Being proudly British need not be regressive; it's progressive and is more holistic in its inclusion of more of our total sense of being. This renewed patriotism is not of the Right or of the Left— not that today there is much sense remaining of a leftist patriotism anyway.

Scottish moral and political philosopher Alasdair MacIntyre, in his famous *Is Patriotism a Virtue?* Lindley lecture in 1984, even went so far as stating that patriotism is essential for living a morally good life. He gives an original and powerful defense of contemporary patriotism. In contrast to old Enlightenment approaches of attempting to arrive at a universal answer regarding morality, or the converse, which is what he sees as the completely relativistic views of particularly Nietzsche and Sartre regarding morality, MacIntyre holds that morality is rooted in real communities; in particular villages, cities, nations. Each community has its own history and culture, and that morality needs loyalty to such a community. It's interesting to find a modern philosophical view such as MacIntyre's in his attempting to deal with the complexity of morality and virtue, pointing towards the importance of belonging and acknowledging the fact that we have roots in the countries and communities we come from or live. Again it points me back to the fact that human

beings are part of a story, and any attempt to disembed us intel-
lectually and philosophically, leaves out key parts of our larger
self-sense, which are needed in order to be healthy.

It's not that I think contemporary British people don't possess
any pride or love for their country. In a grave emergency it would
reawaken as it has done in the past, and the British when pushed
can be very stubborn, pugnacious, courageous and full of grit.
This love and pride has now gone underground in our psyche, a
mere trickle of a stream in a drought. But if it continues to be
undermined as it is today, then I am concerned with the long
term effects. It will cut us off from the ground swell and thread
of our history, culture, life, tradition, learning, which has
nurtured us and which has produced us.

To conclude on the subject of patriotism, it was G. K.
Chesterton who, while being an English patriot himself, took the
idea of patriotism further still, expanding it out into a universal
approach to life which he called *cosmic patriotism*. In his fascinating and unorthodox book, *Orthodoxy*, he proposes *cosmic
patriotism* as a kind of primary loyalty to life beyond pessimism
and beyond commonly accepted notions of optimism. Chesterton
felt that the mere pessimist has an inherent problem in not loving
what she criticises; while the problem with the mere optimistic
patriot is that she doesn't think the country or world needs
changing. This kind of optimist, 'will be less inclined to the
reform of things; more inclined to a sort of front-bench official
answer to all attacks, soothing every one with assurances. He will
not wash the world, but whitewash the world.' The only right
kind of optimism for Chesterton was a kind of universal patriotism based on an allegiance to and love for our world and to our
locale, rather than treating our belonging as if it were entirely
optional. In his words:

My acceptance of the universe is not optimism, it is more like
patriotism. It is a matter of primary loyalty. The world is not a

lodging-house at Brighton, which we are to leave because it is miserable. It is the fortress of our family, with the flag flying on the turret, and the more miserable it is the less we should leave it. The point is not that this world is too sad to love or too glad not to love; the point is that when you do love a thing, its gladness is a reason for loving it, and its sadness a reason for loving it more. All optimistic thoughts about England and all pessimistic thoughts about her are alike reasons for the English patriot. Similarly, optimism and pessimism are alike arguments for the cosmic patriot.

Chapter 10

Shared Genius

*In spite of current ads and slogans, the world doesn't change one
person at a time.*

*It changes as networks of relationships form among people who
discover they share a common cause and vision of what's possible.
This is good news for those of us intent on changing the world and
creating a positive future. Rather than worry about critical mass,
our work is to foster critical connections. We don't need to convince
large numbers of people to change; instead, we need to connect with
kindred spirits. Through these relationships, we will develop the new
knowledge, practices, courage, and commitment that lead to broad-
based change.*

Margaret Wheatley

The Village that Changed the World

The village that changed the world is quite easy to miss. Driving
out of the centre of London north-east through Islington along
Essex Road en route to Stoke Newington, you have to negotiate a
roundabout circling a small green fringed by stately, tall London
plane trees like an atoll in the urban ocean. Now swallowed in the
continuum of the metropolis, you are momentarily in what used
to be an agricultural village well beyond the bounds of the city:
Newington Green. If you're driving, blink and you've missed it.

I can understand if my claim for this diminutive spot as the
village that changed the world sounds a little fanciful and over
the top, a kind of exaggeration which I, along with most of my
fellow British, are not fond of. Yet bear with me, for it was right
here throughout much of the eighteenth century where some
momentous creative events took place which made this otherwise
unmemorable place truly earth changing. And just to say, as will

become clearer throughout this chapter, as well as wanting to convey the strong creative thread running through the history of this nation, I want to illuminate the often collective nature of creativity, both now and in the past, which I believe has always been the case. Furthermore, I want to deliberately look at creativity in a much broader sense than only to do with creating objets d'art, music, literature or physical inventions, as will become apparent.

Starting from the late seventeenth and throughout the eighteenth century, freethinkers and religious dissenters, especially Unitarians, came to the village of Newington Green. It was conveniently close to and yet outside the City of London and provided a place where they felt freer to express their views. To give an idea of the restrictions still in place on what you could say in those times, up until 1813, for example, it was still a heresy and strictly illegal to deny the Trinity, a view which is, of course, fundamental to the beliefs of Unitarians, who believe in God as one person and not as the Trinity. And while being burnt at the stake for this heresy had ceased in 1612, denying the Trinity could still be met with civic exclusion and imprisonment.

Dr Richard Price, a libertarian and republican, arrived in the village in 1758, to take up his post of minister at the Unitarian church on the Green and over time gained notoriety for speaking out without fear against the government on all manner of controversial issues such as supporting the American colonies in the War of Independence with Britain, radical approaches towards justice and social reform, and later backing the French Revolution. His house at number 54, The Green (which, incidentally, is still there and interestingly forms part of the oldest surviving row of terraced houses in London) became a centre for gatherings and dinners with a range of radical thinkers and social reformers of many persuasions. And much creativity emerged from the meetings, often over dinner, held at Price's house and also that of his friend, the liberal publisher Joseph

Johnson who lived close by St Paul's Cathedral. To Price's house at The Green came the men who went on to be the founding fathers of the United States, such as Benjamin Franklin, Thomas Jefferson and Tom Paine, as well as the future second US President John Adams. Philosophers David Hume, Adam Smith and William Godwin were visitors as well as prominent British politicians, clergyman-mathematician Thomas Bayes (of Bayes' Theorem fame) and many other agitators, prison reformers and educators, and not forgetting the great radical, polymath, scientist-theologian Joseph Priestley, discoverer of oxygen among his voluminous accomplishments.

Richard Price's pamphlet supporting American independence in 1776, as well as Tom Paine's famous pamphlet *Common Sense*, have been credited with playing a considerable part in bringing the American colonists (actually they were British colonists at that point) to declare independence, and great numbers of these pamphlets were circulated on both sides of the Atlantic. Pamphlets, cheap to print and to buy, were *the* great revolutionary tool of those times to effect change, and their enormous influence is probably hard for us to conceive of today, awash as we are with information, if not sometimes feeling almost drowned in it. *Common Sense*, for example, sold more copies in 1776 to the American colonists in proportion to the population of the colony at that time, than any book ever published up to that point in American history. Written in simple language it is credited with getting a huge number of colonists off the fence as regards to supporting the fight for independence from British rule, at a time when this aim was not supported by the majority of the population.

This small hub in the village became a hotbed of revolutionary new thinking and creative friction, fomenting and cross-fertilising ideas. One of the most fascinating individuals who joined this grouping and came to live on the Green in 1784 was the young feminist Mary Wollstonecraft, who arrived to run a small school in the village and was greatly influenced by these sincere radicals. The much older Price and Johnson were like mentors to her at that time. Later, when the prominent conservative Edmund Burke wrote an attack on Price's support for the French Revolution, both Mary Wollstonecraft and Tom Paine were incensed and sprang to the defence of their friend, penning responses; in Mary's case, *A Vindication of the Rights of Men*. In 1791, Tom Paine published his famous *Rights of Man* and Mary followed in 1792 with her arguably even more groundbreaking, *A Vindication of the Rights of Women*, in which she proposed that women are not inferior to men but only appear to be so because of their lack of education. This is the book she is best remembered for and it stands as a—or much more likely *the*—founding work of feminist philosophy in the world. I will return to this remarkable woman later. Alex Allardyce wrote in *The Village that Changed the World*,

> Several historians credit Price as a huge influence on the American Constitution which is broadly predicted in his *Observations (on the Nature of Civil Liberty)*. Indeed, it is likely that Price's writings inspired Thomas Paine to name the new country as The United States of America.

Studying Price's pamphlet, it is very easy to see clear elements which presage the American Constitution. As a measure of the regard in which he was held (in this case for his expertise in financial theory) Price was invited by the US Congress (though he declined) to come to America and organise the financial administration of the newly formed country.

This is just a taste of what emerged around that small green between a relatively small group of friends and collaborators, with emerging new ideas, values and worldviews which were to affect the very structure of society and government in areas such as social justice, philosophy, reform and feminism, and which still reverberate down the centuries to us.

Creativity in Britain

The Newington Green story is to me an example of what creativity encompasses when seen in a bigger picture. It extends far beyond the narrower and still commonly held view of creativity as only producing beautiful or novel objects, and of single creative souls labouring alone. It includes the oftentimes collective nature of creativity and its significant role in how our history and our future comes to be made. I will return to this theme shortly in more detail.

Creativity is clearly important to all of us and I think that, as a nation, we British have much to be proud of regarding this key quality, both in our past and also very much in evidence today. It's surprising to me how we often don't tend to recognise the value or centrality of creativity in British life; yet if we tend towards a cynical bias, we are more likely to perceive decline wherever we look, and in doing so, miss the presence and ongoing value of our nation's creativity. I'm not suggesting, of course, that the UK has some unique monopoly on creativity compared to any other country. But what I am suggesting is that we often don't appreciate this quality in our national character and, also, I am attempting to look at creativity from a fresh and, I feel, empowering angle. I want to expand the way we think about creativity and show how this drive or force is much more than merely a valuable quality possessed by certain gifted individuals. I feel instead that it is a very central thread at the heart of being able to understand our history and progress and our aspirations for the future.

Before speaking further about any particular British expression of creativity, it might be good to pause for a moment and consider what do we mean by creativity anyway? It's a popular concept and buzzword these days and becoming more creative seems to have more appeal than ever. Broadly we could say that creativity is the originating or inventing of any new thing which has value. The new 'thing' ought to seen very expansively as a product, solution, artwork, idea, way of thinking, worldview, joke, cultural effect, and it is, of course, a moot point about what constitutes being valuable. There are academically no end of definitions of what constitutes creativity, but for clarity I'm happy with Czikszentmihalyi's simple working definition as, 'the process of producing something that is both original and worthwhile'. My only problem with the brilliant work of this psychology professor, famed for his work on the notion of flow, is my embarrassment at attempting to pronounce his name to friends in quoting him. After all, as John Cleese famously said, 'The aim of any good English gentleman is to get safely to his grave without ever having been seriously embarrassed.'

As I said, although we tend not to think so and certainly are reluctant to trumpet our qualities, as a nation we British have been and still are remarkably creative. I've frequently heard it said that after the combined sector of banking, financial services and insurance, the creative sector is the second largest sector in the economy, although I am unable to substantiate this claim. In fact it's difficult to come up with hard facts about a nation's relative creativity. Britain is credited with having one of the largest creative sectors percentage-wise of any country. To get a sense of what is technically meant by the creative industries, this is usually taken to include writing, art, design, theatre, TV, radio, films, marketing, advertising, fashion, product development and certain types of scientific research and development.

The creative industries in Britain were said by the government department responsible for measuring such things, DCMS (the Department of Culture, Media and Sport) to produce 5.6 per cent of GVA (Gross Value Added—which means both profits and wages) in 2010, in comparison to France's 2.8 per cent and USA's 3.3 per cent. In 2011 this figure was adjusted down for Britain to 2.9 per cent by DCMS. What happened in 2011? The consensus is that, no, it wasn't that British inspiration suddenly took a nosedive after we left the noughties. NESTA (National Endowment for Science Technology and the Arts) points out that this doesn't signify that Britain never had a significant lead, or doesn't still have a significant lead, but rather that the figures for other countries need a similar downward adjustment. Hasan Bakhshi and Alan Freeman of NESTA point out that the problem is that there is no single accepted definition of what exactly constitutes the creative industries. For example, France wants to include cookery while Italy wants to include religion.

Today Britain is internationally (even if not always nationally) known for creativity in terms of design, media, fashion, writing, architecture, popular music, theatre, TV programmes, film, especially documentaries, comedy, computer games and the arts generally. British TV formats are licensed and remade for American audiences, and, at the same time, there is a much larger and ever-growing market internationally for finished British TV programming, especially drama and factual, most notably in the USA. Indie companies have proliferated and the BBC is proving uncharacteristically entrepreneurial and, yes, actually earning quite some revenue internationally. From costume dramas like *Downton Abbey* to the laddishness of *Top Gear*, from the nature classics of David Attenborough to the full spectrum of Reality shows, the Brits are in the thick of it. In a report on the phenomenon by CNBC business, Nick Southgate, the head of a British media company, said,

There is a hunger here (in the UK), a desire to create and always lots of ideas, much more so than in the US. They (the US) will need ideas, and the challenge for companies like ours is to exploit that. I don't have the head of Warner Bros on the phone every day telling me what to do; if anything it's the opposite. They're investing in us is because they believe in not having everything homogeneous. They want local creativity.

Danny Boyle's opening show for the London Olympics which I mentioned before, was a spectacular expression of creativity which could only have come out of Britain. A humorous Olympic opening? Sending up your own country? I mean, what other country would dare—or probably more to the point, what other country would even have the outrageous idea occur to them—to do something so humorous and outside the norm, bringing together such disparate, amazing, hilarious, moving and ironic elements, using the national talents of film, theatre, popular music, literature and surreal comedy? And what's more, to make these elements tell a powerful story about Britain's past, present and future so poetically. That's quite an accomplishment. Rather than attempting to match the previous leviathan show of the Chinese, (which would have been impossible anyway) the British did their own thing with quiet aplomb, rewriting the rules of opening ceremonies. In the fashion world, Britain has gone from being a poor cousin of Paris, Milan and New York, to now becoming a leading world player in its own right with fashion now providing as much to the UK's GDP as the combined total of publishing and car manufacturing according to the British Fashion Council, *Value of Fashion* report in 2012. (And in case you're wondering if that statistic means anything, yes, Britain still manufactures a surprisingly whopping number of cars.)

Creativity and invention, of course, played a leading role in Britain's historical development especially with the advent of the Industrial Revolution, which patriotically I feel duty bound to add, was, of course, a British emergence. The Industrial Revolution clearly rapidly changed the history of the world and, arguably played *the* single greatest part in actually creating the modern world as we know it. So when we hear phrases like 'how Britain created the modern world', it's actually not hyperbole. British inventors were hyper-productive in the period from around 1770 to 1850 and were then dominant in the world. The key technologies for power, for cotton spinning and weaving, for iron making, for machine tools, etc., were British. And yet the innovation in Britain spread far beyond these familiar areas, encompassing civil and mechanical engineering, mining, shipbuilding, food processing, paper, glass, etc., etc. Summing this period up, historian and economist Deirdre McCloskey said, 'The Industrial Revolution was neither the age of steam, nor the age of cotton, nor the age of iron. It was the age of progress.' The great period of British material invention, in a way continued right up until about 1950. Manufacturing declined in Britain in the second half of the twentieth century, though, interestingly, since then the current of creativity in the UK could arguably be said to have found other outlets, and flowed through non-manufacturing modern and postmodern expressions, many of which I outlined above.

British scientific inventiveness has a track record of centuries. And it's not just a matter of revelling in the many long-past glories of achievement back in the Industrial Revolution, when British innovation was acknowledged to be world dominant. Nobel prizes have been awarded since 1901, and since then British scientists have won more Nobel prizes than any country in the world apart from the USA. Harry Bingham, who brought my attention to this fact, says in *This Little Britain*,

> It's hard to avoid the feeling that, as with the British literary achievement, there's something about Britishness and science that makes them go happily together. The empirical spirit, so precocious in Newton's England, so notable in the philo-sophical tradition, seems alive and well today, and that Nobel medal table seems to prove it.

Though having said that, Bingham cautions how increasingly British Nobel prize winners are likely to be based in the States, and that national policy these days for nurturing scientists of the future is inadequate.

Talking of our country's literary achievement, a friend said to me that I couldn't write a whole section on British creativity without mentioning Shakespeare; and it's true, I can't. There are so many subjects deserving of much fuller coverage and I can't possibly do them justice or even mention them in a book such as this which is attempting to follow a thread and not get lost in all the rich side avenues and chambers. So I am deliberately highlighting (cherry picking, you may justifiably accuse me of) examples which may be somewhat less well-known in order to cast a fresh light on what we think we already know.

Of course, Shakespeare occupies a unique place in British and world literature. His writing seems devoid of any human short-comings, whether it is lyrical, perceptive, poetic, angry, romantic, evocative, witty, or spiritual. Not only that; Shakespeare changed the way language and literature could be used and thought of ever since. John Carey says of Shakespeare's writing in his *What Good are the Arts?* 'All written texts require interpretation and are, to that extent, indistinct. But with Shakespeare something new happened. An enormous influx of figurative writing transformed his language—an epidemic of metaphor and simile that spread through all its tissues.' This advance by the Bard reverberated through literature henceforth and not just in Britain, but globally. English (for some reason you can't say 'British', though I mean British) literature has given the world the works of Shakespeare, Dickens, Austen, Scott, the Bronte sisters, Conan Doyle, R.L. Stevenson, and a myriad more, continuing into the twentieth century. Just in terms of sheer popularity, the most translated author in the whole world, funnily enough, is Agatha Christie. Harry Bingham comes up with an interesting calculation that of the 41 most translated authors in the world, more than a third of them are British.

One other factor which Steven Johnson points out in his *Where Good Ideas Come From*, is that great innovators tend to have a lot of hobbies. Orwell notes in *The Lion and the Unicorn*, his classic essay on England, that a characteristic of the British, 'which is so much a part of us that we barely notice it,' is, 'the addiction to hobbies and spare-time occupations.' Darwin, for example, had many other interests, such as pigeon fancying, the effects of earthworms on the soil, geology, coral reefs, and, though none of these were directly responsible for his theory of evolution, the knowledge from these hobbies provided associations which fed into his great theory. Many British inventors are similar in their eclectic interests and hobbies; a seemingly general national trait.

Collective Creativity

Creativity is often unquestioningly assumed to be primarily an individual endeavour and certainly there are extraordinary individuals like Isaac Newton who seem to give credence to that view. Yet there is much evidence pointing to the fact that the flowering of creativity is greatly influenced by the milieu and the right company and other factors. Czikszentmihalyi in his, *Creativity, Flow and the Psychology of Discovery* says, 'An idea or product that deserves the label "creative" arises from the energy of many sources and not only from the mind of a single person. It is easier to enhance creativity by changing conditions in the environment than by trying to make people think more creatively'. Textbooks like to make it sound like there was some Eureka moment for each inventor but it is generally not like that. In the Industrial Revolution, for example, there was much collab-oration with many individuals and firms adding refinements and ideas to the inventions. It's simplistic textbook neatness to view, say, James Watt as the sole inventor of the steam engine, when actually he refined a machine which had had input from a number of other innovators for a number of years. Even Darwin's world shattering theory of evolution hinged on proving ideas which had been abroad in scientific circles for a considerable time. The rush to publish *On the Origin of Species* was prompted by the likelihood of fellow scientist Alfred Russell Wallace, who had independently come up with a similar theory, beating him to it.

The Newington Green story is a case study in what can emerge when the right minds come together, between people who cross disciplines and are prepared to take risks and challenge the status quo. Out of the interaction of their ideas and the positive creative friction this generates, new syntheses may manifest which otherwise would not have occurred. And that newness, in the Green example, whether of the rights of the American colonists or the rights and equality of women, is now part of us, part of our shared culture and our very make-up. This is easily taken for granted today, yet it behoves us to recognise the struggles which have made these advances part of our received culture today, so that a child born today in Britain will almost inevitably grow up with a worldview in which, for example, democracy and women's rights are foundational and self-evident. As the classic historical parody, *1066 and All That* would have said, this is a GOOD thing.

I had often pondered on reading about Mary Wollstonecraft as to how on earth could she be apparently so far ahead of other women and men? I mean, just to call her merely ahead of her time would have to be a great understatement. Then when I learned about the supportive environment at the Green where radical and critically thinking men treated her with respect — exceedingly rare in those days — and shared their differing and profound views, it made sense to me. It doesn't take away from her own individual greatness but it does place it in a context and helps to understand how culture and society develop: through small groups of enquiring individuals who each are striving to create a better world in some way or aspect.

Yes, creativity is individual and personal, and yet it is much more than that, in ways we are only beginning to understand and which enable us to look at history (and more interestingly the future) through a more complex lens which can encompass and accommodate more of the subtle and interactive dimensions of how emergence occurs. And I'm deliberately focussing on some of these less well-known, yet in my opinion, significant aspects of our British story. By the term emergence, I'm referring to the way in which complex patterns and systems arise out of a multiplicity of simpler interactions, and which cannot be predicted by analysing the simpler components. Entirely new properties and behaviours emerge without any master plan, it being singularly impossible to foresee the new characteristics from knowledge of the constituent parts alone. Emergence is now recognised as increasingly important in many fields and it is especially relevant to our understanding of the way that cultures and societies develop and as to how creativity takes place. As well as not being possible to predict the outcomes, another very interesting feature is how small the 'seed group' of an epochal shift might be. For instance, it has often been said that the Renaissance, that momentous period which transformed culture and society in Europe and the world in the fifteenth century, was the result of only 500 or 1000 people, a minute number for such a sea change.

Scenius: the Ecology of Creativity

I've always rather admired producer and musician Brian Eno for his unerring ability to create and recreate, and his always managing to be seemingly one step ahead on a cultural edge over a period of decades. Eno has coined the very useful term 'scenius', for this phenomenon of collective creativity as opposed to individual genius. Here's what he said at the Sydney Luminous Festival in 2009, and it's worth quoting at length:

I was an art student and, like all art students, I was encouraged to believe that there were a few great figures like Picasso and Kandinsky, Rembrandt and Giotto and so on who sort of appeared out of nowhere and produced artistic revolution. As I looked at art more and more, I discovered that that wasn't really a true picture. What really happened was that there were sometimes very fertile scenes involving lots and lots of people—some of them artists, some of them collectors, some of them curators, thinkers, theorists, people who were fashionable and knew what the hip things were— all sorts of people who created a kind of ecology of talent. And out of that ecology arose some wonderful work....

So I thought that originally those few individuals who'd survived in history—in the sort of "Great Man" theory of history – they were called "geniuses". But what I thought was interesting was the fact that they all came out of a scene that was very fertile and very intelligent.

So I came up with this word "scenius"—and scenius is the intelligence of a whole... operation or group of people. And I think that's a more useful way to think about culture, actually. I think that—let's forget the idea of "genius" for a little while, let's think about the whole ecology of ideas that give rise to good new thoughts and good new work...

To summarise, here's how the man himself puts it: 'Scenius stands for the intelligence and the intuition of a whole cultural scene. It is the communal form of the concept of the genius.' This view of scenius is a useful shorthand to help us see the advance of culture and values within a whole society. When a conducive cultural greenhouse environment occurs, especially at the point of epochal shift, there is much more likelihood of new ideas, views, discoveries, being able to flourish; and then they may spread if the surrounding life conditions are ready and the new view is seen to demonstrably work better than the old one. As Kevin Kelly, founding executive editor of *Wired* magazine, has pointed out in his support of the concept of scenius, creative people bring out creativity in other creative people, encourage positive peer pressure, support through mutual appreciation what has been discovered, and see the success of the individual as a validation of the whole group.

From this understanding of the context and milieu for creativity, I would like to look at one or two more examples from British history which illustrate this point. And, of course, the Newington Green story can be seen to fit naturally into the 'scenius' genre. Taking this wider view on history affords a very different reading of the story than the old linear approach of memorising a succession of dates, kings and battles, which has bored stiff whole generations of pupils like myself in secondary school.

A Cup of Scenius at a Coffee house

Nowadays dropping in for a latte and a biscotti or maybe an overpriced attempt at a panini in your local Costa coffee or Starbucks sounds pretty ordinary and pedestrian, and it's a bit of a stretch to see visiting there as contributing to advancing the leading edge of culture. Not so in the seventeenth century in London. In 1652 the first coffee house opened in London and the concept spread like wildfire and soon there were many hundreds of coffee houses in the city. And I'm not exaggerating; I mean literally that many. What if I was to say that for the next hundred years the London coffee house was at the revolutionary forefront of cultural, scientific, literary, political and artistic development in Britain? Again, I don't think that's an exaggeration.

Coffee was a new exotic import from the Middle East and the coffeehouse provided an extraordinary social setting which was unique and very far from the drunken atmosphere of the then prevalent ale houses or the extremely exclusive formal gatherings of elite noblemen. For the price of a penny admission for the coffee, anyone who was reasonably dressed could come in, sit down in comfort, smoke a pipe, read the newspapers and pamphlets of the day, and take part in spirited conversation and debate, where quick wit and new ideas were the currency and drunkenness was frowned on. As opposed to the squalor and rowdiness to be expected in the taverns, coffee houses were sober, tastefully decorated establishments with bookshelves, gilt framed pictures and decent furniture. There were rules for patrons of coffee houses and once you stepped through the portal, all men (and of course being those times it was only men) were considered equal and no one had to give up their seat to a 'finer' man. Swearing was punishable with a fine and games of chance were prohibited.

Very quickly, coffee houses began to develop distinct clienteles who shared a particular profession or area of interest and people gravitated to the ones which catered to their interests, with individuals often having several they would frequent. There were coffee houses for political discussion, ones for literary pursuits, others for scientific discussion and even experimentation on the premises, with Isaac Newton and other scientists notably dissecting a dolphin on the table of the Grecian coffee house. Not to be attempted in your local Starbucks or Costa coffee for health and safety reasons. It sounds a far cry from the mind numbing uniformity of our present corporate coffee franchises. There were coffee houses for commerce in the City and those for ship owners and sailors. Runners would carry the latest news and gossip from one coffeehouse to another. People used them as their office, giving their address as that of their favourite establishment rather than their home. As London historian Dr Matthew Green says in an article on the history of London's lost coffee houses,

> Coffeehouses brought people and ideas together; they inspired brilliant ideas and discoveries that would make Britain the envy of the world. The first stocks and shares were traded in Jonathan's coffeehouse by the Royal Exchange; merchants, ship-captains, cartographers, and stockbrokers coalesced into Britain's insurance industry at Lloyd's on

Lombard Street; and the coffeehouses surrounding the Royal
Society galvanized scientific breakthroughs.

Coffee houses were not unique to London, being also popular in
various European countries, but what stood out in London was
the way they entered into and altered the very fabric of society
and its institutions in such a profound way. King Charles II in
1675, recognising the revolutionary threat that these free
thinking, animated networks could pose, especially in the
political arena, attempted to close down the coffee houses, with
an edict banning the sale of this seditious brew, but the outcry
and momentum forward was far too strong and unstoppable, and
the King was forced to give up in dismay. In France, by contrast,
coffee houses were assiduously watched and spied on for any
sign of dissent or treason. As social historian G. M. Trevelyan
said, 'The Universal liberty of speech of the English nation...was
the quintessence of Coffee House life.'

Coffee houses opened up hubs and creative avenues for the
greatly rising number of middle-class men who no longer toiled
at manual labour but were businessmen, clerks and merchants,
engaged in mental work in offices. Coffee houses served as a
popular forum for education and self-improvement as well as for
debate and gained the nickname 'penny universities'. This all
emerged at the beginning of the Enlightenment and coffee houses
provided the means to spread and develop the new spirit of rationalism which characterised the Enlightenment and with it the
unprecedented advances in nearly every domain of human
activity. If our age could be said to run on oil, well, then certainly
in the early days of the Enlightenment, in London it ran on coffee
or at least was lubricated by the strong dark liquid. (Apparently
the brew they drank would be disgustingly unpalatable to us).
The conditions were right for the emergence of a new
consciousness: rational forums, a spirit of equality between
people and a shared eagerness for something better; it created a

potent mix—an Enlightenment incubator for modernity—and the results spoke for themselves. A cup of scenius? Who would think that going to a café for a cup of coffee would help create the modern world?

An Alternative Historical Narrative

As I said, I'm deliberately focussing more on collective expressions of creativity since I feel the way we think of creativity needs to be widened from our more commonly held individual and personal associations. Because we live in the age of the individual, we can tend to have a bias towards looking at everything from an individual point of view and can miss the significance of the larger thread of creative unfolding. Our view still has echoes of the old 'Great Man theory' of the nineteenth century where history is perceived as being largely about stringing together the impacts of outstanding 'great men'. Once you start to look, other examples of collective creativity begin to appear and come into focus from past history and through to the present. And of course, there are powerful stories from all over the British Isles, not just the London of my previous tales. There are so many examples which I would like to include to illustrate this alternative narrative of history and creativity—particularly since it is not the historical story which most of us imbibed at school—but I recognise that I have to pare it down.

The Scottish Enlightenment in the eighteenth century in Edinburgh was one such major and world-influencing example, with its flowering of scientific, literary and philosophical achievements from the likes of philosophers David Hume and Francis Hutcheson, geologist James Hutton, economist Adam Smith and poet Robert Burns, among many others. This small city became the very epicentre of the Enlightenment for decades, with its particular Scottish flavour of an optimistic belief in the human ability to effect betterment in individuals and society guided by the power of reason only. Edinburgh transformed itself from a poor, backward dump of a provincial town in the early eighteenth century, referred to at the time, as 'the sink of abomination', to rise, phoenix-like, to become instead 'the Athens of the North'; the most cosmopolitan centre of learning and culture in Europe. Most fascinating of all to me in relation to the collective creativity which we are examining here, has been highlighted by David Denby writing in the *New Yorker*, about the seemingly unique nature of the relationships between these famous Scottish figures in this small city of only forty thousand people.

> To an astonishing degree, the men supported one another's projects and publications, which they may have debated at a club that included amateurs (say, poetry-writing doctors, or lawyers with an interest in science) or in the fumy back room of some dark Edinburgh tavern. In all, the group seems rather like an erudite version of Dickens's chattering and benevolent Pickwick Club.

Another very interesting and distinctly fruitful gathering, especially in terms of products, inventions and bricks and mortar, no less than ideas, was the Lunar Society of Birmingham. As with most of these examples, generally there was a lack of formality involving membership about such 'societies'. The participants were drawn together by their passion for the shared themes of the particular grouping, and such loose arrangements have, time and again, seemed more than sufficient and a tremendous spur to creativity. Called the Lunar Society because they met on the full moon in order for the extra light to make the journey home by horse carriage easier and safer, the 'Lunarticks' as they cheerfully called themselves, met regularly between 1765 and 1813 and, from their correspondence, it's obvious that they enjoyed themselves and had a lot of fun as well as achieving a staggering amount.

It drew from the whole wide swathe of those in the Midlands who subscribed to Enlightenment values, including prominent industrialists, intellectuals, philosophers and slave trade abolitionists. Leading members included the famous potter and social reformer Josiah Wedgwood, anti-slavery campaigner Thomas Day, Joseph Priestley and James Watt. They were led by the physician and natural philosopher Erasmus Darwin. Between them, the discussions and debates of this informal 'revolutionary committee' of the Industrial Revolution united science, philosophy, social reform, business and the arts, and they didn't just talk; they also managed huge businesses and built canals and factories and changed the face of the whole region. In fact they were the powerhouse behind what has been called the Midlands Enlightenment.

Moving into the twentieth century there were the 'Inklings', a loose literary grouping in Oxford who met for many years, most notably in the venerable Eagle and Child pub in the city to read out loud and discuss their latest unfinished writings, which were usually fantasy and mythological novels. You can still see the cosy little, well-worn wooden nook in the venerable pub today, where the group would cluster together. I recently visited 'The Bird and the Baby', as the Inklings called the pub, out of fascination for the meetings they held here on a Monday or Tuesday lunchtime for years in the forties and fifties especially. This famously included luminaries such as C. S. Lewis, popular among the young again today through the Narnia films, Charles Williams, Owen Barfield and a certain J.R.R. Tolkien who would read aloud from his work in progress, which had the unlikely working title, *Lord of the Rings*.

Moving on to the 1960s, another emergence of collective creativity was the phenomenon which sprang up in London. Initially a relatively tiny core of people, as often seems to be the case in all the examples we've considered, were responsible for a widening cultural vortex which put London at the leading-edge in the 1960s in the fields of fashion, style, design, pop art, photography and popular music. From fashion icon Mary Quant and her miniskirts, to Carnaby Street, to artists like David Hockney, to avant garde stores like *Granny Takes a Trip* on the King's Road, to the trio of photographers, Bailey, Donovan and Duffy, who were arguably the first celebrity photographers, to the expanding explosion of pop and then rock music, it's undeniable that something momentous surely happened in that period.

I can't possibly do justice to that multifaceted creative explosion that was the 1960s in Britain, but just to mention one strand to illustrate it, namely music, since this particular eruption continues unabated to this day. As a lover of pop and rock music, I've been fascinated by the development of popular music from the 1960s onwards, continuing right up to today. If you read accounts from the 1960s, it's striking how, as in all the previous examples, there would often be a relatively tiny core of musicians hanging out together in a small scene of their own, going to each other's performances in clubs in London, and influencing and inspiring each other. Britain continues to be a fomenting cauldron of popular musical innovation and music is a still very much a major British export. I found it interesting to learn that there are only three countries in the world which are currently net exporters of music: USA, Britain and Sweden. I'm surprised how we as a country don't seem to recognise or appreciate this important creative industry of ours. Perhaps because it started as teenage rebellion and anti-establishment, it often seems to have been perceived officially as somehow not part of the 'real' economy, and rather ephemeral and inconsequential.

In many other areas too, creativity continues at the forefront in Britain and it's not a case of looking wistfully backwards at past glories. For example, Silicon Roundabout in East London has now organically matured into the third largest start-up cluster in the world. A rebuilt Kings Cross in London is fast becoming a major creative hub with the firms and institutes taking advantage of the recognised economies of agglomeration. Google is building a vast billion dollar centre at Kings Cross, freely acknowledging that it is attracted to the site by the presence of new neighbours, Central Saint Martin's art school, and the possible interactions with thousands of art students. Other new neighbours on the same site include the Francis Crick Institute biomedical research centre (the largest centre for biomedical research and innovation in Europe) built in an open plan way to encourage interactions between scientists in different research fields. Creative people like being with other creative people and the results have always spoken for themselves.

Chapter 11

The Sun Never Sets on the Creative Impulse

To exist is to change, to change is to mature, to mature is to go on creating oneself endlessly.
Henri Bergson

Far away in the heavenly abode of the great god Indra, there is a wonderful net which has been hung by some cunning artificer in such a manner that it stretches out infinitely in all directions. In accordance with the extravagant tastes of deities, the artificer has hung a single glittering jewel in each "eye" of the net, and since the net itself is infinite in dimension, the jewels are infinite in number. There hang the jewels, glittering like stars in the first magnitude, a wonderful sight to behold. If we now arbitrarily select one of these jewels for inspection and look closely at it, we will discover that in its polished surface there are reflected all the other jewels in the net, infinite in number. Not only that, but each of the jewels reflected in this one jewel is also reflecting all the other jewels, so that there is an infinite reflecting process occurring.
Avatamsaka Sutra

Humour: a Funny link to British Creativity

While looking at factors conducive to creativity, and particularly in relation to Britain, I want to bring in another possible element: humour. An odd connection? Bear with me. The British sense of humour is intrinsic to the national character and has been honed to a fine art and aesthetic. Humour is a highly developed art here, and in one way or another, nearly every British person is a self-styled comedian; you have to be. It's simply part of our upbringing and conditioning, and is a way in which we navigate social intercourse. As well as being needed for social acceptance, it also supports emotional strength. Ironic, subversive, surreal and quizzical, humour here is the great social lubricant: the way pomposity, pretentiousness and authority is cut down to size in low key and backhand ways. British comedy with its trademark understatement, self-deprecation and deadpan delivery is renowned throughout the world from the many British comedy programmes that are exported.

One particular hallmark of the best British humour is its often absurd and surreal nature, seen for example in Monty Python or The Mighty Boosh, with a cultural pedigree owing much to the Goons, and stretching back through Edward Lear and Lewis Carroll. And it is this surreal aspect of British humour which I think could be quite relevant to creativity in this country. There is an interesting link between humour and creativity. I found out that there already exists quite a body of thinking as well as research on the link between these qualities. And if you stop and think for a moment, it's not surprising that there are strong, shared characteristics. Humour, and especially the absurd, surreal British variety, involves juxtaposing seemingly unrelated ideas, seeing things from novel vantage points, and not surprisingly that's also seen as the basis of all creativity. Take this classic one-liner from much loved, eccentric comedian Spike Milligan, in its juxtaposing of unrelated contexts.

Spike: There's only one cure for seasickness
Somebody: What's that?
Spike: Climb a tree

Or Eric Morecambe's, 'My neighbour asked if he could use my lawnmower and I told him of course he could, so long as he didn't take it out of my garden.'

Attempting to explain jokes is not at all funny and best avoided. You either are tickled pink or you're left untouched and perplexed. A lot of British humour is an expression of inventiveness rather than formal jokes. Edward de Bono, the originator of 'lateral thinking' and authority on creative thinking, says in his book, *I am Right, You are Wrong,* 'The significance of humour is precisely that it indicates pattern-forming, pattern asymmetry and pattern-switching. Creativity and lateral thinking have exactly the same basis as humour.' In the same passage he asserts that, 'Humour is by far the most significant behaviour of the human mind. Why has it been so neglected by traditional philosophers, psychologists and information scientists?'

Rational linear thinking has enabled the great advances of modernity that we all continue to benefit from, and yet if it is seen as the only mode of understanding and the only mode of discourse, then we impose an inherent limitation on our comprehension of the world and of life and impose a limitation on creative activity. In Arthur Koestler's *The Act of Creation,* he made the point that,

> The laws of disciplined thinking demand that we should stick to a given frame of reference and not shift from one universe of discourse to another....the creative act, in so far as it depends on unconscious resources, presupposes a relaxing of the controls and a regression to modes of ideation which are indifferent to the rules of verbal logic, unperturbed by contradiction, untouched by the dogmas and taboos of so-called common sense.

Koestler's most interesting statement on this subject to my mind, though, has to be, 'We all know that there is only one step from the sublime to the ridiculous; the more surprising that psychology has not considered the possible gains of reversing that step.' Transcending common sense in the way Koestler describes creativity and humour is one interpretation of what occurs, though I also like the way philosopher and psychologist William James said that common sense and a sense of humour are actually the same thing, the difference being in their speed. He said that a sense of humour is just common sense dancing. I've spent a fair amount of time pondering these words of James and while I can't quite logically explain exactly what he means, I sense the truth of it. Humour does have common sense rules of logic in its own context; it just happens to mix different unrelated contexts together in rapid succession. I think I'd better stop here however before I dig myself into a hole, since it always tends to be somewhat of a futile exercise to try to analyse humour.

Who knows how much the eccentric and surreal humour of the British has been a contributing factor to national creativity? Yet in its anarchic displacing of habitual views and frames of reference, it is surely likely to be one contributing factor. As James Joyce said in Ulysses, 'He laughed to free himself from his mind's bondage.'

Failure to Capitalise on Inventions

Given how creative and inventive I have been saying the British are, it has to be said as a counterbalance, that as a nation we have a woeful record of not capitalising on inventions, whether by lack of funding, lack of vision in the powers-that-be, or lack of entrepreneurship.

A classic case in point is Frank Whittle's invention of the jet engine. Whittle, a young genius of an RAF pilot, put forward his vision in 1928 for an engine to power a plane which would be able to fly at unheard of speed and height. The Air Ministry had little knowledge about this topic and were singularly unimpressed, dismissing his design as 'impracticable', and showed no interest whatsoever in his concepts. A similar lack of response was to come from private industry which Whittle was then free to approach, being as the official Air Ministry saw no use in his plans. Thus it was that for years, Whittle was to receive no support from either government or private industry. Frank Whittle was a daredevil flying instructor in the RAF with a reputation for aerobatics who had destroyed two aircraft in rehearsals for an air force flying team. One of his superiors shouted at him after the second crash, 'Why don't you take all my bloody aeroplanes, make a heap of them in the middle of the aerodrome and set fire to them – it's quicker!'

In 1930, he took out a patent for a design for a turbo-jet engine, pursuing his research and the realisation of his dream on his own. Eventually in 1936, with a few supporters, Whittle started his own company, testing the world's first jet engine in 1937. The German airplane designer Hans von Ohain independently patented a jet engine in 1934, four years after Whittle's patent. The German designer, of course, received copious official support from the Nazi government and was able to fly the first jet plane in 1939, well before Whittle's engine had its maiden flight in 1941.

After this 1941 flight, one of the few long-time supporters of Whittle, Pat Johnson, uttered the classic line, 'Frank, it flies.' Whittle replied, 'Well, that's what it was bloody well designed to do, wasn't it?' Almost immediately, this new jet-powered aircraft was outperforming the best conventional planes. The jet engine was, of course, a gigantic leap forward which immediately relegated all the fastest propeller planes of the day, all the ME 109s and the fabled Spitfires, to antiquity. But the stress and strain for Whittle working almost day and night with few people to help him and almost no money, twice led to his being driven to a nervous breakdown, though fortunately he did recover and the genius of his invention was eventually recognised. The British government very belatedly realised how important Whittle's invention was for the war effort and eventually took over his company Power Jets Ltd in 1944. Whittle received almost nothing after the war for this nationalisation of his company, and this distasteful experience led him to switch from being a committed socialist to becoming a campaigner for the Conservative party. It was only in 1948 that Whittle was finally compensated, when he received an award of £100,000 from the Royal Commission on

Awards to Inventors and he was made a KBE. There has naturally been speculation of the 'what if?' kind around this story. Since air superiority was so crucial in the Second World War, Whittle's jet engine could have been powering Allied fighter planes much sooner than the German version and we can only imagine how radically that might have changed the outcome of the war.

In another 'what if?' reality, could we today be looking at Silicon Valley being synonymous with our own Thames Valley with IT clusters proliferating and with who knows what British household names instead of Intel and Microsoft and Apple? I know there is actually a Thames Valley computer industry concentration, yet it's really rather a pale shadow of the Silicon Valley in California we all know. British innovation in the computer sphere was, in fact, swift out of the blocks. Charles Babbage, Victorian mathematician and engineer, is now commemorated as certainly one of the fathers of computing, with his design for what he called his Analytical Engine. This was a plan for the world's first programmable computer. Like all modern computers, it was designed so that the computer would be potentially infinitely variable with the facility to have different 'programmes' inputted. Babbage conceived this in 1834, even prior to the Victorian age. Clearly a genius, the only ever so slight problem was that he had invented it more than a hundred years too early. It was an electronic age invention designed in the steam powered mechanical age, so unfortunately it couldn't be actualised. (Interestingly, a plan is afoot to build an Analytical Engine in Britain by the time of the 150th anniversary of Babbage's death in 2021).

Nowadays everyone is familiar with the WWII efforts of Bletchley Park in code cracking with the first electronic, digital computer called Colossus. Yet Colossus was kept highly secret right up until the 1970s for some obscure reason and so this extraordinary invention had much less influence on computer development than it might otherwise have had. I have often wondered if this might be a reason why British computing subsequently has lacked the influence of the American computer industry, since Britain was a computing pioneer in the 1940s and 1950s. In fact, the world's first commercially available computer was a British device called the Ferranti Mark I, available from February 1951 and based on a Manchester University machine. Ferranti's first computer salesman, Vivian Bowden, had trouble convincing even the then significant computer expert, Professor Hartree of Cambridge, of the potential market for this new-fangled device. In September 1951 Hartree said to Bowden: 'We have a (digital) computer here at Cambridge; there is one at Manchester and one at the NPL (National Physics Laboratory). I suppose there ought to be one in Scotland, but that's about all.'

Yet it seems that historians don't attribute Britain's subsequent loss of leadership in computing to anything as glamorous as my notion of the Official Secrets Act locking up our national brilliance. The US market for computers was so huge, their resources so much greater, and the Cold War defence industry so big, that computing was far better nurtured than in Britain with the resulting US dominance in computing. It has to be said, though, this represents a familiar pattern in Britain's more recent history: official short sightedness and lack of vision, unwillingness to take risks or provide venture capital in contrast to the more entrepreneurial attitude of the States.

The History of Creativity

Since one theme of this book is about the value of taking an evolutionary view on culture, it's interesting and revealing to look at the history of creativity. How old do you think the word 'creativity' is? The Oxford English Dictionary dates the first usage of the term to 1875. I was really quite astounded to discover that creativity is actually such a relatively new word. And even then, the term was not in general usage for a long time afterwards. It seems that the person who put the word creativity on the map was British philosopher Alfred North Whitehead, with his famous Gifford Lectures at the University of Edinburgh in 1927, using it as a centrepiece of his process philosophy, which I discussed previously.

This evolution of how creativity has been thought of through the ages—allowing for the fact that the actual word wasn't used for most of that time, and other words like 'imagination' were used instead—is instructive. In ancient times, most cultures had no concept of creativity in the way we understand it and art was not thought of as creation. When Plato was asked in *The Republic*, 'Will we say, of a painter, that he makes something?' he answers, 'Certainly not, he merely imitates.'

It is often said that the idea of creativity, at least in Western culture (Eastern cultures had their own myths, such as in India, for example, with Brahma, the creator) had its origins in the Bible with its story of creation in Genesis. Yet the creativity spoken of here is very different from our modern understanding of the term. In the Bible, and hence the Judeo-Christian tradition, creativity was the sole province of God. Creativity was exclusively seen as divine in its origin and so human beings were naturally incapable of ever creating anything new except as being mere tools for expressing God's glory. Both the ancient Greeks and the Romans had a similar view that inspiration came from the Gods and creativity was solely a conduit for the sacred and divine. It hardly needs to be said that this is a very different view to our modern concept of creativity. Yet this was the unassailable view held for many centuries through until the Middle Ages. The particular individuals who toiled and carved the statues, painted the frescoes, designed and built the vast cathedrals—sometimes a process lasting far longer than their own lives—were anonymous and unimportant.

It was only in the Renaissance that it first began to be possible to conceive of human beings as real agents of creation themselves: that there were great gifted people whose works of art stemmed from the individual's skill and abilities and were not solely from God. This marked the beginning of our modern understanding of creativity, yet this was a very gradual shift, for the great Renaissance artists were anything but secular. As Mike King says in his highly original *Secularism*, 'The Renaissance period offers difficulties to the secular mind. It is baffling to find that the "freethinking" of the time was more concerned to think freely about religion rather than against it.' The Florentine Academy of Marsilio Ficino who inspired the likes of Botticelli, Raphael, Michelangelo, Durer and Titian, was a spiritually based community with a Neoplatonist view. An evolving view of humankind and our capabilities is beautifully summed up by a member of Ficino's Academy, Pico Della Mirandola, who published his *Oration on the Dignity of Man* when he was only 23 years old. Speaking in God's voice in this passage he clearly articulates the new emerging optimism about the mutability of humanity.

> We have made you a creature neither of heaven nor of earth, neither mortal nor immortal, in order that you may, as the free and proud shaper of your own being, fashion yourself in the form you may prefer. It will be in your power to descend to the lower brutish forms of life; you will be able, through your own decision, to rise again to the superior orders whose life is divine.

The more modern view of people, and more specifically of individuals, as the sole agents of creativity really only started to come into its own with the advent of the Western Enlightenment in the eighteenth century. The classical view of divine creativity gradually came to be eclipsed and then almost totally replaced in the modern Western mind by the emphasis on great men (and women—though most often men) and their creative abilities.

This has continued into our times with the ever increasing emphasis on the individual and agency. As I have already detailed in various examples, now this exclusively 'individual' model of creativity is expanding and even being replaced in some quarters with an understanding of the importance of the collective nature of creativity and the context in which it arises. Nowadays creativity is a much vaunted term, studied and researched in academic institutions and in business, and everyone would understandably like to be more creative.

Broadly, we've developed historically through different generally accepted views on creativity: from creativity is divine; to creativity is about the individual and there's nothing divine about it at all; to the new idea which is gaining credence that perhaps creativity is more a collective emergence than due solely to an individual's abilities. Then there are different yet important nuances of views about what is responsible for what I am referring to as collective creativity. Malcolm Gladwell in his book *Outliers* attributes success and innovation largely to a combination of circumstances and conditions, rather than just genius or creativity. With his fascinating examples of left-field factors which most of us would never think of, such as the arbitrary birthdate for cohorts of basketball players, and how that affects their becoming employed in basketball teams, he shows the complexity and circumstantial nature of why some people are successful and their creativity recognised, and why some are not.

Matt Ridley in *The Rational Optimist* has a different angle of explanation. He says that at some point in our evolution—and he's referring to cultural evolution of the last 10,000 years—human intelligence became collective and cumulative unlike anything which has happened in any other animal. The key distinguishing factor in Ridley's view is, 'that at some point in human history, ideas began to meet and mate, to have sex with each other.' Ridley is arguing that culture becomes cumulative as human beings began to exchange things with each other and ideas mated with each other; in other words, the cross-fertilisation of ideas. And the sexual connotation is of course very apropos to his point here.

Both views certainly capture quite a degree of the truth, though in my opinion, there is an overly reductionist emphasis to these views, whereby creativity is solely explained by interactions of ideas or genes, or by the total circumstances and milieu of the person or people involved. To me these views of creativity have very considerable validity *and* in addition there's another dimension to the drive to create which I want to introduce. And while I'm talking about different views, just to mention that these days, much of the popular literature and self-help books on the subject of creativity, focus on and extol how we can become more successful in business through thinking more creatively. This is important, though to my mind there does tend to be a somewhat overly utilitarian tone to much of it. Then it is too easily reduced to merely a set of tools to become more productive or successful and again to my mind, it loses an essential part of the picture.

The Creative Impulse

I was on a leadership course out in the genteel Sussex countryside a few years ago. It was early morning and we had been set an exercise the preceding day to come up with 'something creative from our hearts' and for each participant to present their piece to the group in the morning session. I was racking my brains to come up with something original, personal and creative, and, as not infrequently happens at moments like this, feeling clueless and rather inert.

So I went for a stroll in the grounds in the still, chilly, early spring morning, and just let in the beauty of the surroundings. All of a sudden, quite unexpectedly, I had a flash which literally seemed to illuminate everything and I simply perceived what was happening around me differently. I heard the clap of the wood pigeon's wings as it undulated past in flight and the explosion of song of the robin in the apple tree, in the grounds of the rural house where I was walking. But I heard it differently. I somehow sensed the ivy questing up the old brick wall of the outhouses, feeling into every crevice and the new spring shoots of the arum lily forcing through every obstacle to come into the light. I sensed—and more than that—viscerally felt the life force thrusting through them, and, most significantly, I felt the same animating force through myself as well. 'This isn't about me at all. It's about all of us; it's about Life!' I half muttered to myself or intuited; I wasn't clear which.

What I experienced at that time is an example what I have come to call *the creative impulse* in myself. And I'm deliberately calling it the creative impulse rather than saying 'I had a creative inspiration', or something similar, because I intuitively saw that this is not 'my own private, personal creativity'; the drive and force behind it is universal rather than confined to being only exclusively individual and personal. This insight was further confirmed when the morning leadership session commenced. I scribbled down my revelation into a poetic kind of Walt Whitman-esque 'Song of Myself', and when I read it out with a passion that was a natural expression of the experience itself, everyone seemed struck by how moving it was. I was also struck by the very different creative stories and presentations given by all the other participants, yet what struck me most was the commonality of the impetus driving their own passionate renditions. I was perceiving what they were saying through a new lens and all I heard at that moment was the universality of the creative impulse, not a bunch of individuals having their own creative moments.

This sent my thinking in a new direction. This episode was one of a number of experiential moments which has made me realise that there is what could be termed a universal creative impulse and that the driving force behind creativity which, for much of recorded human history has been characterised as divine, is actually real. We may or may not choose to use a label like 'divine' with all its connotations, yet it helps make sense of what is animating the urge to create, which I think is important. To be clear, I don't mean in any way that we are merely channels for some force or drive which is separate from ourselves. Creative expression completely depends on the aptitudes, life experience, degree of development and knowledge of each person, which gives it a unique, developed and tempered expression. Each person's expression will be different and there will be as many expressions as there are people. And yet simultaneously the creative impulse transcends the individual. The implications of this distinction will become apparent as we proceed.

Also, before anyone accuses me of anthropomorphising birds and plants in my revelation above, I obviously don't mean that robins and wood pigeons, let alone ivy plants, are consciously creative. The creative force animating nature, is not in my opinion conscious, at least not in any human sense of the word. It depends on the highly evolved and complex human brain and mind and our uniquely highly developed self-reflective awareness to be consciously creative and to warrant the use of the term 'creative impulse'. So I feel that a very useful term to help explain and understand the depth and significance and multidimensional nature of creativity is the creative impulse. This term has been used in the art world occasionally and is the title of one guide to art, though I was surprised to find that the phrase actually isn't in the dictionary. I don't know its origin, though it is used by Whitehead among others. By creative impulse I am referring to the innate impetus and drive of life itself which is felt by human beings as the urge and passion not only to create but also to enquire, to understand, and to try to create a better world. This creative impulse is felt individually and it is also felt and shared collectively as is apparent in the joy and creative sparking of some of the 'scenius' gatherings which we have looked into. And, most significantly, in the universal nature of this impulse, it also encompasses what was always historically referred to as divine, to give what I feel is a truer, more inclusive picture of what actually occurs in the creative process at all levels.

I feel we are in need of a more integrated synthesis of how we regard creativity which includes the individual and the collective and which also recognises a universal thread or current in the creative process; in other words, it reincorporates something greater. Not as a return to the past but as a greater synthesis. I'm not for going back to anything and, in general, I don't think a retro-romantic idea of any kind of return to a mythical (read rosy and fictional) time will serve us well. Life is moving forward and like it or not, there is no going back.

Abraham Maslow rightly points to the universal nature of creativity which he sees as an innate and precious aspect of being human. 'The key question isn't "What fosters creativity?" But it is why in God's name isn't everyone creative? Where was the human potential lost? How was it crippled? I think therefore a good question might be not why do people create, but why do people not create.' Indeed. And, in a similar vein, to return to Czikszentmihalyi's research on creativity: 'Creativity is a central source of meaning in our lives' he says, giving two main reasons: Firstly, 'Most of the things that are interesting, important, and human are the results of creativity.' And secondly, 'When we are involved in it, we feel that we are living life more fully than during the rest of life.'

What he says is true in my own experience and I imagine everyone else's too. In those moments when we are fully engaged and inspired by a worthwhile activity, idea or project which is close to our hearts, it inherently gives us a sense of meaning and purpose; we don't have to invent meaning to imbue it with meaning. At those moments there is no question of dwelling on existential doubt about life, of the kind, 'What's the point of it all anyway?' or of feeling somewhat alienated. This is not a question of just keeping busy or absorbed in activity so that we're distracted from existential questions. At those moments we know it to be self-evident from our own experience and inspiration right then that we are at the heart of life, on the pulse of life moving forward, and that life has inherent fulfilling meaning and purpose.

I've talked about the development of culture and consciousness through time, through the history of Britain (and of course a similar yet distinctive unique thread could be traced for all countries), as well as through the lives of individuals. In medieval times, God was everything, the individual was unimportant. With the advent of the Enlightenment, the individual was empowered and the creator God went out the window, so to speak. With the pluralism and egalitarianism of recent times, the collective is coming to the fore rather than only privileging the individual. Now I believe it's time to re-include the universal current of the creative impulse while still fully honouring the individual and collective dimensions.

So to put it another way, as I sit here typing this chapter, at certain moments I definitely feel the thrill of the creative impulse animating me as I strive to express something new and I hope worthwhile, that I don't quite know how to phrase. This isn't 'my' own private creative impulse. When I share a fascinating enquiry with my wife, and when she is passionate about the conversation too, (and fortunately for me, she happens to share some of my interests), it's not 'her' personal private creative impulse that she feels coursing through her. We are then collectively experiencing, inspired by, and are animated by *the* creative impulse. I'm suggesting that there is a singularity and universality to the creative drive or impulse. This is not to deny in any way the creative ideas and achievements of an individual, and undoubtedly there have been and are, some outstandingly creative people. Nor does it diminish the importance of individual agency; in fact quite the contrary since it highlights the greater context and responsibility we each have for our actions. Of course we feel things personally, including the creative impulse, and I am just suggesting that there can be a bigger context for our personal experience of creativity. Yet because in our age we rightly cherish our hard won individuation, we tend to overly focus on the individual and not see the current of the creative impulse which is not unique to us, but shared by all. And it takes a developed individual who can hold multiple perspectives, to be able to see both the personal and the collective as part of a larger whole.

In fact, what is a more integrated way of looking at creativity is that it very much includes the individual's unique expression shaped by his or her talents; and at the same time, it includes the universal nature of this urge or drive which can be shared together between people. In fact, it's been my repeated experience over the years from a considerable time spent facilitating group dialogues, that the creative impulse expressed by one person, in the right conditions in a group, is very likely to evoke the same impulse in another or others, if they have a broadly shared interest. This is one important reason why *scenius* is such a powerful phenomenon in contributing to advances in culture and society.

No Universal Panacea

As a realistic idealist, I also think it important not to paint too rosy a picture nor to imply that creativity is some kind of universal panacea. The creative drive is a wild force which can be used for all manner of dubious and even diabolical ends, and in itself is no guarantee of beneficial results nor of ethical behaviour. There is certainly an interface between creativity and insanity, and creativity can easily have a destructive effect on individuals and those around them, unless the person is well grounded. History is peppered with examples of great men and women who were conduits for and driven by an unusually powerful creative force and who produced extraordinary work, yet harmed themselves. Van Gogh is an obvious example as is Arthur Rimbaud. And in our time, a number of the most blazingly creative musicians were like shooting stars, burning out from drugs and crazy over-indulgence. Think Jimi Hendrix, Syd Barrett, Jim Morrison, Keith Moon, Kurt Cobain or Amy Winehouse, just to name a few of the pantheon of the early-departed in the rock arena.

Also artists who create the most sublime, beautiful and even sacred works, may act and live a life bearing little or no relation to the beauty of their creation. Over the years I have learned not to be surprised when a favourite artist turns out to live a life which seems to bear little or no resemblance to the quality of their work. I marvel at the creativity and beauty of the music of Miles Davis who famously is reputed to have single-handedly reinvented jazz music no less than five times in his long career. And then from loving his music, I have read biographies of Miles, and was surprised to find a very opposite and deeply unflattering portrait of my hero.

'Destructive creation' has recently been coined as a play on the economist Joseph Schumpeter's famous term, 'creative destruction', which originally suggested that innovation leads to economic growth. Now it looks clear that, since the recent global financial crisis, some kinds of financial innovation have far more downside than upside and are actually destructive; for example, derivatives and unconventional new types of mortgage, benefitting the few at the expense of the many. Creativity in itself, as I said, doesn't guarantee any ethical behaviour and, more importantly, it is a wild force which has to be tempered by the ethical and moral development of human beings, which we have to bring to the equation. In the past, there was at least a certain grounding of the creative force, as it was associated with the divine, with something bigger and more important than oneself, and it was also held within the framework of religion and the Church. In our times there is more scope for rampant egocentricity, with our emphasis on the primacy of the individual, and nothing to balance out and integrate that force. Having the wherewithal to know the surge of the creative impulse as also an expression of a more universal force, can help us hold a greater and more balanced perspective, with less ego inflation.

A National Creative Thread

Leading edge thinkers in science are also coming to a new view on creativity. I listened to a lecture by one of the world's foremost molecular biologists and complexity theorists, Stuart Kauffman, the author of *Reinventing the Sacred.* He called for a new way of looking at what he terms the 'ceaseless creativity' of the cosmos, marshalling considerable evidence to show how it can never be fully explained or predicted by the natural laws of science. With a kind of ultra-minimalist spirituality, Kauffman states that God can be taken to mean this natural ceaseless creativity and he went on to say that we don't need a creator God, but we do need creativity.

As mentioned before, it was Alfred North Whitehead who popularised the word creativity, and he has had considerable influence even though he remains somewhat obscure. And what is particularly relevant for our discussion here is how Whitehead placed creativity as the ultimate metaphysical principle. As Whitehead poetically puts it in *Adventures of Ideas,* which is the most accessible of his works: 'The creativity of the world is the throbbing emotion of the past hurling itself into a new transcendent fact.' Whitehead felt that God could best be understood as a principle which he famously called, 'the creative advance into novelty', and the potential for novelty, for the new to emerge, is present in every moment and not separate from the process of evolution. He also said that, 'Creativity is without a character of its own..... It is that ultimate notion of the highest generality at the base of actuality.' And this gives me a sense, if I understand Whitehead correctly, of how creativity is not a quality or thing in itself but is that which is the very impulse of this vast unfolding and evolving process which we call Life. And it is us that provide the character.

One reason why Whitehead's work is not better known is that it is so complex and hard to understand, as you've no doubt gathered even from the couple of simple quotes (yes, these really are some of his simplest quotes). He didn't seem to feel the need to simplify his work and also it's difficult because of his radically different way of conceiving reality. I personally have trouble even understanding the various interpreters of his work, and they seem to be always trying to gain a greater grasp of what the master actually meant. Yet his process philosophy is a recognised school of thought and one which I am convinced has much to teach us, most of all because it is more in line with the actuality that the universe and life is a process. It is only in the mid twentieth century that we have learnt about the vast time scale of the universe and how it came into being (at least according to the currently most accepted theory) nearly 14 billion years ago with the Big Bang and has been expanding out from that moment onwards in an unbroken surge. Therefore, we human beings are also inseparably part of this singular process, too. We are that process in motion as we live our lives now. We are much more a process than we are an individual, with the interesting twist that this doesn't deny our individuality, since part of the process has also been to lead to our individuation.

Yet our way of thinking has not at all caught up with what we now know about the universe, the world and thus also ourselves. Our mammalian brain is understandably not wired to conceive this kind of process view as part of our psychology. Being British as a nationality is also part of a process, a development, with an evolving character and a core creative thread which is distinctive. Nothing is ever static. Part of our identity is our national one, and that identity is also evolving over time. Orwell, speculating in the dark days of WWII in 1940 about how England would emerge from the cataclysm, said, 'But England will still be England, an everlasting animal stretching into the future and the past, and, like all living things, having the power to change out of recognition and yet remain the same.' We each are expressions of that creative thread. We have arisen out of that distinctive culture and contribute to it and it itself is developing. It shapes us and we shape it and so it moves on.

As we have seen, there is a strong current of creativity in Britain with its particular flavours, both past and present, and it is a wellspring. The more we recognise and let go of limiting cynical beliefs about what we are not capable of, and what is not possible, the more I am convinced we can be in greater touch with the creative impulse and what may be possible. Recognising the creative impulse as both personal and universal also allows us to more easily sense the creative thread of Britain which constantly seeks for outlet, for expression, tempered and shaped into new cultural flowerings by the qualities and development of people; in other words, us. And while I may have waxed lyrical about the creative impulse, obviously there is no force which is going to create a better world by itself. It does come down to people making intelligent choices and acting on their inspiration. It's individuals and small groups of people who have to enact change for the better. And that's the way it seems to have always worked throughout history, as Margaret Mead famously said, and as the examples previously mentioned, tend to confirm.

In spite of the extraordinary challenges of globalisation, loss of identity, social and financial turmoil, and erosion of faith in our institutions and government, we can find new solutions. We can look for renewal to the stories I've recounted. Being free from the past doesn't mean ignoring it, but being informed yet not bound by it. Otherwise we risk unwittingly acting from knee-jerk responses and creating a merely reactionary future. To be in touch with the creative thread of this country is to see and know the past, its attempts, green shoots, weaknesses, successes and failures. We need to give ourselves permission to let out our passion and conviction and not be stymied in any way by politically correct notions of appearing too certain or one sided—or heaven forbid, too passionate; to feel confident and released to be uninhibitedly creative. The sun never sets on the creative impulse. As Milton said way back in the 1600s,

Lords and Commons of England—Consider what nation it is whereof you are and of which you are the governors: a nation not slow and dull, but of quick, ingenious and piercing spirit; acute to invent, subtle and sinewy to discourse, not beneath the reach of any point that human capacity can soar to.

Chapter 12

A Realistic Idealism

No period of history has ever been great or ever can be that does not act on some sort of high, idealistic motives, and idealism in our time has been shoved aside, and we are paying the penalty for it.
Alfred North Whitehead

An idealist believes the short run doesn't count. A cynic believes the long run doesn't matter. A realist believes that what is done or left undone in the short run determines the long run.
Sydney J Harris

Never before in Human History

It was the twelfth of May, way back, just two weeks after the infamous mutiny on the Bounty. A young member of parliament rose to give a speech in the House, the effects of which still reverberate down through the years to this day. Though there was at that time, no official record of parliamentary speeches, various reporters of the day took extensive notes and pieced together the text. The year was 1789. A short extract will give the flavour:

I march forward with a firmer step in the full assurance that my cause will bear me out, and that I shall be able to justify upon the clearest principles, every resolution in my hand, the avowed end of which is, the total abolition of the slave trade.....I mean not to accuse anyone, but to take the shame upon myself, in common, indeed, with the whole parliament of Great Britain, for having suffered this horrid trade to be carried on under their authority.

We are all guilty—we ought all to plead guilty, and not to exculpate ourselves by throwing the blame on others ....A trade founded in iniquity, and carried on as this was, must be abolished, let the policy be what it might, let the consequences be what they would, I from this time determined that I would never rest till I had effected its abolition.

Three and a half hours later, the young parliamentarian concluded his brilliant oratory and sat down again, after having laid out a devastatingly comprehensive and moving picture of the horrors of the slave trade, by saying, 'Having heard all of this you may choose to look the other way but you can never again say that you did not know.' The speaker was William Wilberforce and he delivered his speech with very little preparation and a mere half page of notes, since he modestly said that he was 'well acquainted with the subject.' It was widely praised as one of the most eloquent speeches ever heard in the House, and was the first ever in Parliament on the issue of abolishing the slave trade. Parliament unfortunately, and yet not at all unexpectedly, didn't heed Wilberforce's speech despite its power and eloquence, for the powers that be were very profitably invested in the continuation of slavery. And besides, in 1789 very few people in Britain or anywhere else for that matter, shared Wilberforce's sensibilities. We tend to forget how much our values and consciousness have developed since the eighteenth century. For example, a majority of the Founding Fathers of the USA, undoubtedly high minded and deeply moral men like George Washington, Thomas Jefferson and Benjamin Franklin, were themselves slaveholders. And this despite the Declaration of Independence with its self-evident truths 'that all men are created equal... and having inalienable rights to Life, Liberty and the pursuit of Happiness.'

So Wilberforce had a very uphill battle on his hands and this was to lead to him spending much of his life dedicated to eradicating the evil of the slave trade, with endless speeches on the same subject until a bill outlawing it was finally passed in 1807. And of course, great step though this was, it did not in itself outlaw slavery, only the transportation of slaves. It wasn't until July 26th 1833 that slavery was abolished throughout the British Empire, right at the end of Wilberforce's life. The plantation owners in the West Indies were compensated to the tune of £20 million for their loss of income. Though the abolitionists felt that compensation was going to the wrong side, it was the only way possible to get the bill passed. Wilberforce said, 'Thank God that I have lived to witness a day in which England is willing to give twenty million sterling for the abolition of slavery.' Just three days later he died.

A great man with a vision of how life could be and how it ought to be. In fact, Rowan Williams, ex-Archbishop of Canterbury, took me by surprise when he told me that, 'When I was invited to name the person who I thought was the most influential in the last thousand years, I said without hesitation, William Wilberforce. The person who made the biggest positive difference to the greatest number of people was probably William Wilberforce.' I don't know who I would choose if asked the same question, but the more I thought about his answer, the more I could see why Rowan Williams had made this choice, for the banning of slavery set a precedent in recorded history. Yet the closer you look at history, as I have said, the great man theory leaves out a tremendous amount, and more true to life in bringing about societal change has often been the role of groups of people rather than only one individual. While Wilberforce is rightly remembered for his great life's work towards the ending of slavery, he was just one of a group of like-minded people who influenced and supported each other and formed a powerful network for this and other advances in society. It's a similar story with the rightful fame of Nelson Mandela in South Africa and his role in abolishing apartheid. Mandela was undoubtedly a monumentally great man and the figurehead of the campaign, yet he would have been the first to acknowledge, as would have Wilberforce in his own group, that he was actually just one of a group of dedicated long term comrades and campaigners.

In recent times, there has been a movement to revise the iconic status of Wilberforce as a great hero, and to generally cut him down to size, all refracted through a postmodern lens. Moira Stuart's *In Search of Wilberforce* documentary in 2007 on the occasion of the 200th anniversary of the abolition of the slave trade, goes out of its way to undermine his status and belittle the passing of that law. While adding fullness and nuance to our understanding, by showing for example, how slave revolts also helped to hasten the end of slavery, and pointing out how abolishing the slave trade didn't in itself stop slavery, on watching this film and on reading some writings in a similar vein, you might wonder if we wouldn't have been better off without Wilberforce. I realise that heroes do tend to be made larger than life and impossibly perfect, which is not helpful since it makes them unattainable as human examples to ordinary mortals. Yet much of the move to downgrade Britain's past, can in my opinion be attributed to the unwitting imposing of our pluralistic post-colonial values of today, retrospectively onto our view of the events of past centuries. I mean, just to take one positive example following the passing of the 1807 law in Britain that I mentioned previously: the Royal Navy created the West Africa Squadron to attempt to stop the slave trade by mounting patrols off the West African coast. It was responsible for freeing about 150,000 slaves and captured 1600 slave ships in the period between 1807 and 1860, with many of the former slaves being resettled in Jamaica and the Bahamas.

The Clapham Sect & Tony Benn

Returning to the subject of idealism, it is the idealistic urge, call or drive in people, whether religious or humanitarian, struggling for greater freedom, dignity and rights, and how it has shaped Britain's story, which I want to examine more closely in this chapter. It's worth looking a little longer at this momentous time and the extraordinary effect of Wilberforce and more particularly his small band of close friends who became known as the Clapham Sect. Not that they ever were a sect, but somehow this peculiar name stuck. As unlikely as Newington Green, Clapham, then still a village some three miles from London, became the home for a group of high minded evangelical Christians who were wealthy businessmen, professionals and politicians. Centred on the church of John Venn, the rector of Clapham, it was only natural that Wilberforce would come and join them to live in Clapham where he became their chief parliamentary voice. Clapham Sect members included Henry Thornton, the financier, James Stephen, the brilliant lawyer who served as the group's legal mind, Zachary Macaulay, one time Governor of Sierra Leone and a number of others. Living for the most part in the same village, they would be in and out of each others' houses and could plan and talk together very easily and informally, each bringing different and complementary expertise to the table. Their singleness of purpose, networking power and influence made them a tremendous independent force in English social and political life.

Historian Stephen Tomkins, author of *The Clapham Sect* describes them as, 'A network of friends and families in England, with William Wilberforce as its centre of gravity, who were powerfully bound together by their shared moral and spiritual values, by their religious mission and social activism, by their love for each other, and by marriage.' They led a decades long struggle to end the slave trade and were involved in numerous other causes to relieve poverty and child exploitation, abolish debt, combat immorality, bring about penal reform, as well as establishing the National Gallery and the RSPCA. They wrote books and articles and did everything they could to help the poor and helpless. The list of what they did and what they attempted to do, is enormous. As always with idealists, not everything turns out for the better, and their well-meaning project for the foundation and funding of Freetown in Sierra Leone as a home for freed slaves, had mixed and at times catastrophic results.

Although they did not reside in Clapham, two other individuals were also extremely important in abolishing the slave trade: Granville Sharp and Thomas Clarkson. Both worked closely with the Clapham sect and are often considered as members. It was Clarkson who tirelessly gathered all the dreadful facts about slavery and lectured throughout the country and provided Wilberforce with the substance of his parliamentary speeches. The 'Claphamites' expressed an extraordinary degree of personal generosity, dedication and integrity. These were wealthy people who often donated a huge proportion of their income for charity. Tomkins concludes his book on the group by saying about these very practical and idealistic Christians, 'Few people can make a more persuasive claim to have been doing the work of God in the world.'

The Clapham sect had an idealistic vision and certainly went a long way towards realising it. Yet in their time, they were often ridiculed, disliked and treated with suspicion. Looking back today, you might think that their vision was so self-evidently a 'good' thing, that surely any reasonable person would have agreed with their cause. But not so at all. And when we come to our present time, and especially in Britain, as we looked into in Chapter 2 in relation to pessimism and cynicism, idealism is often more strongly than ever regarded as naive, unrealistic and even downright dangerous. While this is very understandable given the disasters and horrors visited upon humanity by various supposedly utopian and idealistic projects of the twentieth century, to dismiss all idealism and attempts at progress and to hold a fundamentally pessimistic view of ourselves and our future, will not serve us well in my opinion. I want to examine idealism, utopianism, optimism and realism a bit more closely, since it has an important bearing on our ability to create a better society and culture in this country.

Several years ago I had the good fortune to spend an evening with a well-known figure who was certainly an optimist and idealist, and I have to say that I came away quite inspired and uplifted. I feel privileged to have met this man not long before he passed away. My wife and I were at a charity dinner and being the only vegetarians we were seated on a table of our own with the only other vegetarian, veteran politician Tony Benn. We were fortunate to have the opportunity to spend the whole evening deep in fascinating conversation with him, and what was striking to me was his passion and spirit which remained utterly undimmed (if not increased), though he was in his mid-eighties. More aware than most people of the difficulties in attempting to advance society from his many decades trying to do just that in the dirty trenches of political struggle, his attitude remained unflaggingly and fierily optimistic. 'I get up at 6am and go to bed at midnight and every single day I hope to have learned something new.' I was struck by his youthfulness—not physically, for he was at that point clearly becoming more frail—but of spirit. Harold Wilson once joked that 'Benn immatures with age', yet Tony Benn was certainly not naive and he readily reflected on and tried to learn from the inevitable mistakes he, like everyone else, had made in life. His chosen epitaph: 'Each and every one of us has to be given confidence. If anyone asks me what I hope people will say of me after I have gone, I hope it will be, "Tony Benn - he encouraged us." I would like that written on my gravestone.'

On another occasion, I saw Tony Benn after he had unveiled a plaque to commemorate the Peasants Revolt in 1381 in Highbury, North London, where understandably cheesed off peasants expressed their grievances by burning the stately pile, Highbury Manor, belonging to the loathed poll tax collector, Sir Robert Hales, who was executed by the peasants. A number of people wanted to say hello to Tony Benn afterwards and I chatted with a local man, a Turkish immigrant, who had brought his son along, a youth of about eighteen. 'I don't agree with his (Benn's) politics, but I want my son to meet and shake the hand of a great man, a man of integrity, not like other politicians.' Again and again I have met people from across the political spectrum who held Tony Benn in high esteem. I mean, what politician apart from him could walk on stage to speak at Glastonbury Festival (called the Left Field, of course) and be given a rapturous reception by the crowd rather than enduring a fate something more akin to a modern day version of what happened to the unfortunate Sir Robert Hales. This is the kind of positive effect that someone like Benn could have; a person who has principles and integrity and who sticks to his idealistic vision without pandering to transient popular opinion.

Idealism and Optimism

Clearly though, idealism and utopianism certainly can be very naive and lead to unintended adverse consequences. At its worst, it can be diabolical, as in the cases of Hitler's and Stalin's dreams of ideal societies. These days, idealism, even in a more charitable interpretation, is often seen as hopelessly unrealistic and starry eyed. And yet when we swing towards the opposite pole of pessimism or cynicism, this attitude can also have insidious and long term deleterious effects, for we may as a result of our stance, be disinclined to make any attempt to change our country and world for the better. Philosopher Susan Neiman subtitled her book *Moral Clarity*, as *A Guide for Grown-Up Idealists*, and she calls on the progressive left to renew its lost faith in the Enlightenment project. By 'grown-up idealist' she means someone who recognizes the *equal importance of things as they are and things as they should be.*

Think about what you mean when you tell somebody to be realistic. What you're really saying is, 'Decrease your expectations. Things aren't going to get much better. They'll probably get worse and you've got all your psychological bases covered if you assume actually the worst.' So that's a form of realism that says, 'Well, the way that things are now is the only thing that's real and it's the only thing we should pay attention to.' A grown-up idealist pays attention to both. He says, 'I absolutely can look at things as they are in the face while still guiding my actions by ideals of things as they should be.'

Common sense indicates to me both that some kind of progress is possible and crucially that it is up to us to make it happen. This is reasonable optimism and not irrational hope. Progress is certainly not at all guaranteed and our attempts at progress need to be closely monitored, in part to distinguish what kind of 'progress' is actually worthwhile; a very considerable amount of what is labelled progress is actually very questionable as to whether it is even desirable. Because something may be possible to do or develop doesn't mean we should necessarily head that way. Yet if we believe that some kind of progress is possible in terms of making our world a better place, then we will be far more likely to attempt to do something, for example, about many of the pressing problems we face nationally and globally. If we pessimistically don't believe we can change anything much, then we don't do anything. Which is more realistic?

The realistic idealist doesn't dismiss the concerns of the pessimist. It's important to be cognisant of what may go wrong and to temper that idealism intelligently. So optimism and realism can go hand in hand; in fact that is the desirable condition. Effective leaders are optimists and are more effective in bringing out the best in those around them, because people respond to a vision of a better future and how they have a role in creating it. Anthony Seldon wrote in *The Independent* how he envisages that the politics of optimism will be the defining theme of this century. I certainly hope so, though in the interests of disclosure, I freely admit to being an optimist and a realistic idealist myself, as Seldon clearly is too. Seldon outlines the urgent need for a positive approach in many areas of British public life: calling for example for a 'positive education', which is not about the acrobatics demanded to produce the required set of exam results, but is more focussed on preparing children for meaningful lives; 'positive policing' centering on deterring crime rather than the emphasis on punishment; 'positive transport' whereby the starting point takes into account the reasons we are traveling and then attempts to make it as attractive and environmentally friendly as possible. These all matter because quality of life and general well-being are just as important as GDP, in fact more so, once GDP is sufficient to meet basic needs.

Optimism, being a fellow traveller of idealism, often suffers from the same problems of naivete and being unrealistic. Yet I see room for a sceptical optimism which is aware of the tremendous problems which actually exist, yet looks to possible solutions. There can, in my view, be a subtle optimism stemming from a deep sense that Life and its current and thrust towards greater expression and integration is essentially at its core, inherently positive. This is far from a starry eyed or doctrinaire optimism which is sure everything will turn out well, or proscribes one single way, or sees humanity on the brink of being saved, or some New Age fantasy that we are poised to enter a new Golden Age. It's rather a conviction based on seeing development in action, in oneself, in inspiring individuals, throughout culture and history. It's seeing what could be possible, in spite of so much that is so appalling in the world today, knowing that it will never fully be reached, but that the working towards it is a kind of fulfillment in itself.

Progress: a Mixed Bag

I have previously quoted from popular optimists such as Steven

Pinker and Matt Ridley, who are at great pains to demonstrate with impressive reams of evidence, just how much better life is for us today in almost every possible way than in the past, and why we should be optimists regarding progress. And I agree with much of what they say, as should be evident by my use of their findings. They provide a much needed balance to the pessimism endemic in educated circles about modernity's technological and industrial advances over the last several centuries. Listening to some of these intellectuals, in their highlighting only the pathology of progress, you might think that we would be better off if we had never had the Enlightenment or the Industrial Revolution at all. So people like Matt Ridley with his 'rational optimism' counter this skewed trend very well. Also he convincingly shows up the short-comings of apocalyptic thinking, analysing some of the many past Doomsday scares which never came to pass, showing how their linear thinking projected into the future is a very poor fortune-telling guide; one big reason for that being that people respond innovatively to threats and so they don't come to pass. I remember being very worried as a student back in 1972 on reading *The Limits to Growth*, a book about the computer modelling of exponential economic and population growth coupled with finite resource supplies, produced by The Club of Rome. The predictions were scary. Predictably, in retrospect, the dire predictions didn't come to pass. And while I'm thinking of it, neither did the acid rain disaster scenario destroying the world's vast boreal forests, which is well investigated by Ridley. I'd wondered why we suddenly never heard any more about that impending form of doom, until I read Ridley.

However, there does seem to be another agenda behind the work of Ridley and Pinker, and also Dawkins, in their largely unquestioning and reflex defence of modernity against any criticism. I am grateful for the much needed balance they bring by countering the extremity of those who seem to be against almost any kind of progress. Yet Ridley et al often go further than this by tending to dismiss concern about the very real dangers of unfettered modernity; the ever increasing industrial and technological production at any cost, and its effects on people and the environment. Some people profit mightily, while others, often in developing countries, are exploited and their land degraded in the name of progress. Progress does not necessarily equate with what is good or needed. I believe in progress and I see a kind of directionality throughout all life, and certainly life is at odds with any notion of any steady state. But we do need to respond intelligently and sensitively and monitor and question what we are doing. Unquestioned allegiance to progress such as the belief in allowing society to be determined by a completely unregulated free market is a recipe for disaster for many who happen to find themselves on the wrong side of 'progress'. Modernist aficionados like Ridley can't help but downplay or even dismiss concerns about climate change and other very real problems. Being a pessimist is no solution at all, but we do need an intelligent and sensitive tempered idealism which recognises the very real concerns of the pessimists. Because we do face very real problems which can't be optimistically glossed over.

John Gray always has something interesting and contrarian to say and I find his radically independent view both refreshing and challenging, even though I often find myself disagreeing with him. On the subject of progress, in his *Black Mass, Apocalyptic Religion and the Death of Utopia,* he more or less draws exactly the opposite conclusion from the one I am drawing as one of the themes of this book. Yet we seem to share a conviction in the centrality of a driving thread through human history—his is just a diametrically opposite interpretation from mine. According to Gray, the horrors of Nazism, Soviet Communism and Bush's war on terror are different forms of an essentially utopian impulse which originate from an Enlightenment idea of progress. According to him, this misguided and dangerous belief has its roots in Christianity. The liberal belief in progress is just another expression of this ancient religious drive. He sees this belief as now having morphed, becoming secularised and continuing unabated in politics, directly leading us to more wars and disasters. Gray sees the drive of human beings (at least those of us in the West; he has more time for laissez faire Taoists) as infected by this utopian (read dystopian) impulse. To attempt to improve human beings is impossible, and worse still, it is the cause of all our trouble, as we merrily carry on with the conceit and illusion that we are somehow different from animals.

Powerful bold stuff, but I don't hold with this view at all, as no doubt is evident by now. In spite of all the ways in which the utopian impulse or the creative impulse has undoubtedly been misused for awful ends throughout history, I am convinced that there is abundant evidence to show that the great advances in human emancipation, toleration, dignity and equality have been a result of dedicated individuals and groups who acted on this very same impulse, which I feel is inherent in human beings and did not originate from ancient Christian prejudice. Tempering this innate drive by our own moral development, more just, dignified, and inclusive actions and movements have been initiated by pioneering individuals, bearing in mind that it is of course a very meandering and slow process over centuries. Most scholars now argue that utopian traditions are not specifically Western or Christian and that such traditions have existed in most cultures of the world. I can't resist quoting from *The Telegraph's* review of *Black Mass*, which is actually quoted on the back cover of the book itself. While admittedly not exactly doing justice to his well-argued thesis, it is nevertheless amusing, 'A load of bollocks..... could hardly be more bonkers if it was crawling with lizards.'

A Personal Utopian Experiment
I personally helped create and live out an utopian experiment

way back in my younger days, though I would never have thought of it as such back then. It was only years later that I realised that this was its nature. Not an earth shatteringly large one for sure, but now I look back on it, I see that it was a utopian impulse which inspired me in that venture. It was for me an extraordinary formative learning experience, one that I wouldn't have missed for anything. I realised long afterwards that I was following in the footsteps of countless reformers, idealists, activists, dreamers, both religious and political, flowing down the last centuries.

Disillusioned with the likely predictable groove of my middle-class life ahead after university, I helped found an alternative community based on spiritual principles and a simpler 'back to nature' ethos; what was then called a commune, and which now would be termed by the academics of utopianism, an 'intentional community'. The setting was the unlikely one of a conservative dormitory village in the stockbroker belt of Kent. With idealistic and inclusive principles, we worked the land and meditated, and engaged in social work in the local community. We decided together to always make room for a couple of residents with mental difficulties, on the premise that collectively we could absorb any fractiousness and be of service. And wild though it occasionally was, it actually worked for a while. One valuable rule we made between us all, was that we be self-supporting and no one could be on the dole, since we felt that if we were supposedly trying to demonstrate a different and more sane way of life, then we shouldn't be welfare dependent. It was an immensely thrilling time when I felt that my life was so open ended that anything was possible, and not just for me. I felt a surging conviction that we really could forge a radically different proto-society, sensitive, caring, attuned to spirit and nature without the stultifying power structures of regular society; everything was up for question initially in this new dawn. The liberation, empowerment and creativity released was inspiring and for a short while it seemed that we really could succeed.

My communal experiment was of course just part of the late 1960s and 1970s movement among mainly young people, of rejecting the status quo, and trying to create alternative simpler and more grounded communal ways of life. Like all good things it didn't last: not all of the twenty residents gave equally, creating resentments; disillusionment grew from a perceived lack of integrity in one of the key leaders; we weren't developing the career skills needed for us to actually have more impact. And also, it is exhausting work to tend huge plots of vegetables with no power tools, and to collect and chop wood (no chain saw, on principle) to heat the fireplace, to satisfy our ecological values. I realised later that this is why we had the Industrial Revolution, so that we wouldn't have to be (in our case voluntary) peasants. There's not much time for anything else if you do everything by hand and besides, you feel knackered once the physical work is over for the day. Nevertheless my small experiment lasted four or five years, and in many ways it illustrates some of the pros and cons of utopian experiments. Yet as I said, this was one of the most exciting times of my life, where I felt on the edge in a very healthy way, and really exploring human potential. Utopian movements and idealistic individuals and groups have greatly altered the course of British history and brought about a great deal of all which is most valuable about our culture. The Clapham Sect is but one example. And I think it is important to recognise this contribution, as it gives us perspective on our current more gloomy outlook.

Early British Utopians and Idealists

I find it interesting that there is a whole academic discipline devoted to studying what we are talking about here: utopianism. Probably since the dawn of civilisation, human beings have dreamed of a better life, an improved existence. Whether as an ideal beyond this world, a heavenly existence, or as dreams and visions leading to social experiments here on earth, there have been myriad expressions of this universal impulse to reshape and improve our lives. People hope and dream and this is an intrinsic and precious part of being human. I want to explore utopianism a bit more closely in order to illustrate what a profound effect it has had in shaping Britain. I feel that the subject needs a little rehabilitation in our present time, since the very word has become a synonym for naivety, being unrealistic and even thinking dangerously.

One of the most comprehensive academic studies of the subject, *Utopian Thought in the Western World*, a 900 page tome by husband and wife academic team, the Manuels, covers five millennia from ancient Sumerian myths up to the present. They see the utopian propensity as a universal impulse as fundamental to us as breathing. Our dreaming and wanting a better society is age old and takes different forms organically as society changes, since it is always related or tethered to our actual lives in some way; in other words, it has some basis in reality.

But the first utopia was English. Well, no of course it wasn't, but in one interesting sense it is true. Thomas More coined the word 'utopia' in the sixteenth century in his book of the same name about an imaginary island paradise. The Manuels mark More's work as pivotal since unlike previous utopias which were more otherworldly, in his book *'Utopia'*, his vision is of man rather than God now creating society here on this earth and is not about a heaven to be reached after death; an important juncture in our British history where human agency is now thought capable of bringing utopia into existence right here on earth. I also think that More's work which led to the acknowledgement and *naming* of this propensity in human beings, was perhaps even more important. Now More had created a focus by identifying the common strand in myriad visions, and he initiated a huge genre of literature which still flourishes to this day. 'Dystopia' was a much later addition to our language and our literature and yet at root, is also derived from utopian thinking. More was clearly a brilliantly idealistic and principled man; a Renaissance humanist who cared for his ideals enough to be willing to lose his head by refusing to compromise with Henry VIII by recognising the King's divorce. Thomas More lived at a time when the Western outlook was opening up, with the Americas recently 'discovered' by Europeans, and the arts and literary worlds were beginning to flourish as never before.

Francis Bacon followed in the seventeenth century with another utopian work, *The New Atlantis,* which introduces scientific thinking into society with his technological vision of paradise on earth and his insistence that science has to be governed by higher values. The British utopias were becoming more grounded in changing society, although these individuals were too far ahead of their times to have many people around ready to adopt their ideas, apart from their peers. A multitude of small and large utopian movements sprang up in the following centuries in this country, some short lived, others enduring, and way too many to even list. Chris Coates', *Utopia Britannica* chronicles literally hundreds of examples.

The English Revolution of the 1640s and the dramatic change precipitated by the temporary abolishment of the monarchy opened the door to a dazzling variety of experiments, some whose influence can still be felt in our present times. The revolution unleashed forces in the flow of previously forbidden books and ideas which all the later conservatism couldn't re-cork back in the bottle. Although this particular experiment came to an end and the monarchy was restored, 'the England of 1660 contained the chromosomes of a modern country, the first in the history of the world', as historian Paul Johnson put it. It was a time when talent and ability were now being recognised and rewarded in a similar way to how it had been in the New Model Army of the parliamentarians. This was partly how England's navy rapidly gained its supremacy on the seas, with a new meritocracy applied to naval officers. New learning was flowering, just as Francis Bacon had called for in previous decades; education prospered and new universities were proposed. Great revolutions release such energy and this English revolution was nearly 150 years before those of France and America.

The Putney Debates

One particular event from those times etched itself into my mind ever since I first heard about it and it gave me a glimpse into that revolutionary world and the utopian possibilities which emerged. I never learned about this in history lessons at school. It's an event which, while strangely not widely known today, nevertheless affects each of our lives today. It took place in 1647 in Putney, then a small town outside London, and has become known as the Putney Debates. I recently visited the small fifteenth century church of St Mary the Virgin, nestled on the banks of the Thames in Putney, the scene of this event. The church was badly damaged by fire recently, yet has been well restored to produce an interesting blend of ancient and new; quite fitting really, for what this site is remembered for.

Inscribed large and prominently on a wall inside the church where usually there might be scriptural verse, are these striking words, 'For really I think that the poorest he that is in England hath a life to live, as the greatest he'. Spoken by Colonel Thomas Rainsborough in the mid seventeenth century, these were radical words indeed, and doubly so, coming from a high ranking officer way back then. For it was here in this very church on the 28th October 1647 and for the following two weeks, that a group of men from the New Model Army plus civilian representatives, met together in debate. The choice of venue wasn't significant; the army was camped nearby just outside London, and the church was convenient. Having destroyed the King's armies in England's First Civil War or English Revolution—depending on how you want to look at it—the future was now inconceivably wide open; an opening which had never before existed in history. What kind of England, what kind of society and constitution did they want to see?

The New Model Army was arguably the first army in history to initiate democratic debates which included all its ranks. Fortunately we know about the debates in considerable detail since they were recorded verbatim by the secretary to the General Council of the New Model Army. The forty or so participants in the debates were representative of all classes and included the full spectrum of opinion from right to left. There were distinguished generals like Oliver Cromwell and Henry Ireton; commanders like Colonel Thomas Rainsborough who were of humble birth but had risen in rank through the wars; there were ordinary soldiers such as Edward Sexby and farmers and small tradesmen who had never before had a voice; one attendee is only identified as 'Buff-Coat'. There were civilian political radicals, Levellers, on the radical left, who had come to help the soldiers state their case. Though today levellers would be seen as social democrats, back then they were extreme left radicals. Politics and religion can't be separated in those times and nearly everyone in the debates was a Puritan; a particular strain of Puritan who were known as 'Independents'. They believed in freedom of conscience and in freedom of worship. No one, they felt, should be compelled to attend church or forced to conform to another person's beliefs. Yet we should be mindful that these were very far from secular socialists; everyone was religious in those times and the Puritans were extremely so—if not fundamentalist, in a way that is hard for us to even comprehend from our very secular times.

They had fought wars for a just cause, for high principles, sacrificed much, and eventually after great bloodshed, won. What now was to be the future of England? Why should voting be limited only to property owners as it always had been? What about universal suffrage? Should there even be a King or Lords? Would such radical democratic changes lead to anarchy? This historic gathering tackled these immense issues head on, and for the first time, common people had the opportunity to make their voices heard. Hard though it may be for us to understand today, it was taken for granted in those times that voting should be strictly limited to those who owned property; it seemed as obvious as day that only such property owners could be responsible citizens, those people of means who had a material stake in the kingdom. The grandees such as Cromwell and Ireton could not defend by mere logic, the justness of this ancient order of voting rights based on ownership of property. They could only protest that the changes calling for universal suffrage were too radical and flatly would not be accepted by the general populace; they would result in anarchy and a return to the old monarchy which none of them wanted. The radicals maintained that the concept of the 'freeborn' was more important than the concept of the 'freehold'. At one point the common soldier Edward Sexby famously spoke powerfully and bitterly after hearing the reluctance of the leaders to grant universal suffrage to all men.

Do you not think it were a sad and miserable condition, that we have fought all this time for nothing? All here — both great and small — do think that we fought for something..... I think there are many that have not estates that in honesty have as much right in the freedom of their choice as any that have great estates.......It was the ground that we took up arms on, and it is the ground which we shall maintain.

In the end, a fudgy English kind of compromise was reluctantly agreed upon whereby all those who had helped Parliament and fought in the revolution would have the vote but that it was not yet to be extended to the whole population. Nevertheless, the importance of the Putney debates is that they actually happened and the genie would never again be able to be fully put back in the bottle. This was a very significant advance in British democracy and constitutional reform and paved the way for many of our civil liberties we enjoy today (or we would enjoy if we realised how they had been fought for in the past and what a momentous struggle it had been). As Paul Johnson says of the debates,

> The ideas flung across that communion table—then in all the exciting novelty of their pristine conception—had in the meantime (since the Putney debates) travelled around the world, hurled down thrones and subverted empires, and had become the common, everyday currency of political exchange. They are still with us. Every major political concept known to us today, all the assumptions which underlie the thoughts of men in the White House, or the Kremlin, or Downing Street, or in presidential mansions or senates or parliaments through five continents, were expressed or adumbrated in the little church of St Mary.

Many utopian groups sprang up in those days, often from non-conformist dissenters; and though some were short lived, they laid markers into the future by creating grooves of possibility which they had to some, often small extent, actualised. Once something has occurred, by its very existence it becomes more likely and possible to occur again. For example, the *True Levellers*, started by Gerrard Winstanley in 1649, who called themselves this to distinguish themselves from the Levellers. They were more radical than the Levellers, and they wanted to 'level' property absolutely, believing that land is held in common for all. Becoming known as the *Diggers*, since that's what they did (they occupied and dug and farmed common land), they believed in radical equality and having no personal possessions. Winstanley and his Diggers' utopian experiment, a community on St. George's Hill, Weybridge, Surrey and other Digger colonies he inspired, were not long lasting. They were simply too much of a threat to the existing order and were harried and intimidated out of existence. Yet the seed had been sown and these radical experiments have become famous worldwide and inspired the Left, since the Diggers represent the common people in an egalitarian proto-socialist life.

Manufacturing the History we want to Remember?

When we look back through history, it's important to recognise just how the human struggle for emancipation, towards greater dignity, equality and inclusion in Britain has later been characterised in different ways. And also, the very notion of any kind of inevitable progress has been widely discredited. The Whig view of history, a kind of progressive Protestantism, where everything is seen as marching inexorably towards greater liberty and enlightenment, was for a long time one of the most widely accepted narratives of British history, but has now gone completely out of favour among historians, and the term is now more often used as a pejorative. We often do manufacture the history we want to see. This human struggle or urge for dignity, rights and equality has been variously seen and interpreted as utopian, spiritual, or political, depending on one's viewpoint.

Many of the great idealistic struggles throughout recent centuries which we are looking at in this chapter were motivated by very religious or spiritual people. Some of them were fundamentalists. The socialists and Marxists who rediscovered the revolutionary figures and movements of the 1640s co-opted them into their own pantheon as social reformers, yet often leaving out the religious dimension; explaining away their spirituality by saying that those figures expressed themselves in the idiom of their day, which just so happened to be full of religious references. Jumping further ahead, then we had the political and spiritual side of idealism overtly stated by Christian socialists in the nineteenth and early twentieth centuries. Tony Benn, for example, came from the dissenting Christian socialist tradition, and was perhaps one of the last of this line, with the Left now generally a long way from that spiritually dissenting tradition.

And to take this further: you will likely have noticed some of the similarities between this chapter about idealism, and the preceding chapter about creativity and the creative impulse. This does bring up an interesting point. When we are talking about the utopian impulse or propensity or the creative impulse, or the political struggle for dignity and equality, or the spiritual calling towards creating a better world, are we really talking about quite different things? Or could we be referring to the very same innate impulse or drive, yet interpreted in different contexts and with perhaps different aims? I tend towards the latter view, though this of course is just my opinion, and the issue is very debatable. I see the call and quest towards deeper meaning, for development, and towards beauty, goodness and truth, as a fire in the hearts of individuals throughout the ages. It's just expressed in different ways and means different things to different people in different cultures at different times. Pioneering psychologist and surveyor of the varieties of religious experiences, William James, advised not to get caught up in semantic definitions; he used the term 'religious propensity' lightly, as did the Manuels with their term 'utopian propensity'.

To return to our roughly chronological story of British idealism, at the time of the English revolution in the mid-1600s, there was another radical dissenting religious group which came to prominence. This group, who came to be known as the Quakers, didn't fade away and has come to have huge influence in the last centuries in creating a better society. Today 'Quaker' sounds almost a byword for mildness and lack of threat, but back then they were radicals, centuries ahead of their time, and considered exceedingly dangerous. They stood out by their wearing plain dress, by their pacifism, by refusing to swear oaths, their opposition to slavery, and their teetotalism. Because they refused to swear oaths, believing that Truth is Truth, they wouldn't swear allegiance to the crown and so were debarred from any official positions. They had to create their own innovative businesses themselves and became renowned traders and manufacturers.

Their philanthropic work and creating better conditions for the workers are legendary in Quaker firms such as Cadbury, Rowntree, Fry's, Clarks. They were major players in iron and steelmaking (though by principle, their iron was not for war use) as well as dominating banking and running most country banks. People knew that Quaker businessmen could be trusted, and dynasties of Quaker businesses thrived. Both Lloyds and Barclays banks were Quaker founded, and founded on trust in their word. How they might turn in their graves to see the banking practices today of the firms they started, and which have long since passed out of the hands and control of their descendents. They lived their religion all week, not just on Sundays. An interesting little point is that Quaker shopkeepers always put the price on their merchandise at which they intended to sell it, in contrast to the prevailing custom of haggling over prices. In this way people knew what they were going to pay in a straightforward way. One could speculate on the influence the Quakers may have had in instilling values of honesty and fairness in our society and also in helping embed liberal egalitarian values in the USA as well. A small idealistic group, yet one which has had a disproportionately large effect on the development of this country and particularly on its betterment; giving support to the assertion that utopianism and realism combined together has the best result.

Robert Owen & the Victorians

In this exploration of British idealism, we can't ignore the impact of one pioneering individual, quite ahead of his time, who has had a lasting effect on the culture of this country. In the late eighteenth century, Britain's first 'socialist', and one of the first in the world, long before even the term was invented, was born in 1771 in Wales. Robert Owen, who was later called a utopian socialist by Engels, was a very practical idealist and social reformer whose most important legacy to us today is his enlightened childcare and education policies. He was a mill owner interested in far more than making money. When he took over the cotton mill at New Lanark in Scotland, he gave the workers decent housing, education, healthcare and food at reasonable prices, abolished physical punishment, and shortened the working day—all unheard of at the time. In fact he had to find new like-minded investors since his original ones were so worried by his spending on the workers' welfare rather than making profit. New Lanark became a place of pilgrimage for social reformers and statesmen, and visitors were unanimously impressed by the whole set up and the very good state of the workers. The practical idealism at New Lanark demonstrated how workers were happier and healthier and how productivity improved. New Lanark is now a UNESCO world heritage site, such is its significance. In a speech Owen gave at the opening of his Institute for the Formation of Character in 1816 to the inhabitants of New Lanark, he said,

I know that society may be formed so as to exist without crime, without poverty, with health greatly improved, with little, if any misery, and with intelligence and happiness increased a hundredfold: and no obstacle whatsoever intervenes at this moment except ignorance to prevent such a state of society from becoming universal.

Owen could be said to be the founder of infant care in Britain and a builder of schools as well as being a pioneer in adult education. Another legacy of this great visionary who was born a generation or two before his time, is the co-operative society, of which Owen is regarded as the father. By opening a store where workers could buy good quality goods at a price hardly more than wholesale, he tried to free them from exploitation, passing on the savings made by bulk purchasing to the workers. This is the basis of the co-operative society in Britain.

It's strange how this great national hero of ours is so little known today in Britain, for we all benefit from Robert Owen having lived. Much of Owen's work took place in the early nineteenth century, and predates the Victorian era, an age where Owen would probably have felt more at home. It's interesting that this period, one of the most famous of all periods, is referred to worldwide by this term, taking its name from a British monarch and commencing with the ascension to the throne of Victoria in 1837. The Victorian era, strangely enough, is one of the hardest for us to see clearly. For the average person, 'Victorian' conjures up images of costume dramas of the idle rich, bleak Dickens workhouse tales of the destitute in industrial squalor, and priggish, repressed, pious, uptight values. Think about it: when the adjective 'Victorian' is used, it usually has negative connotations: Victorian attitudes to morality, to women, to sexuality, etc. And the very self-confident architecture has been viewed negatively until recently as fussily ornate and pompous. The grand Midland Hotel at St Pancras in London, now exquisitely restored, was lucky to have been saved from demolition in 1967, while poor Euston station just down the road with its spectacular arches and Great Hall was demolished in the early 1960s to make way for the very dull and uninspiring Euston we know today.

I remember visiting the British Museum a few years back with a largish group of friends, wandering through and admiring the various halls with their treasures and artifacts of different historical periods. Yet when we came to a hall displaying Victorian ornaments, porcelain and silverware, most of my group found it gaudy, unattractive and even distasteful. I too had the same reaction, finding the art sentimental and cloying, and almost annoying me by its existence. In discussion between us afterwards in curiosity about our reactions, it reminded people of their grandparents' living rooms, those rooms which were like miniature mausoleums, with similar looking knickknacks overbearingly crowding the mantelpiece; a room which was only to be entered on special occasions. I realised at that moment that we are still in many ways too close to the Victorians to appreciate the beauty of that period, and more significantly, for us to have a balanced view of that hugely influential time. We are still rebelling against their values—or our perception of their values, to be more accurate.

Yet the Victorians fairly throbbed with high minded causes, and projects similar to Owen's became very widespread and an immense amount of progress for the better occurred throughout Britain between 1840 and 1880, more than had ever occurred before in history. This other side of the Victorian legacy deserves recognition since the advances were huge and they could justly claim to have built the country we live in today. One recent work which goes a long way towards presenting this other side of the Victorians and redressing this imbalance is Simon Heffer's well-researched, *High Minds: The Victorians and the Birth of Modern Britain*. He feels, as I do, that there still remains a climate of prejudice about them. From the chaos, degradation and frankly primitive conditions of the Industrial Revolution for most working people in the 1830s, there arose a Victorian spirit and singularity of purpose, or what Heffer calls 'a mission of benevolence' to transform a 'wealthy country of widespread inhumanity, primitiveness and barbarism into one containing the germs, and in some measures the evidence, of widespread civilisation and democracy'. Heffer sums up his thesis thus,

The greatness of the age was a product of the conjunction of technological revolution, wealth, energy and high minds. It could have resulted in the construction of the greatest temple to Mammon the world has ever seen......That it became more than that was thanks to the mission of benevolence—the pursuit of perfection—that people as diverse as Gladstone, Arnold, Shaftesbury, Mill, Eliot and Dickens took out into the world at this moment when the tectonic plates of society were shifting as never before. If perfection remained elusive, the greater civilisation that they fostered did not. The pursuit of perfection, a minority interest in 1838, had become almost an obligation in 1880.

Alleviating poverty, improving health care, housing, education, extending the franchise, rights for women and for workers were all tackled and improved by a dynamic mixture of reformers, philanthropists, politicians, civil servants, thinkers, writers, scientists and also the church.

The Twentieth Century and Beyond

Utopian literature, which had been invented by Thomas More, continued, and in the late nineteenth and early twentieth centuries, two of the greatest exponents were William Morris and H. G. Wells. Morris' *News from Nowhere* envisaged an integrated future combining utopian socialism with beauty and joy in crafts-manship, rather than seeing work as being a necessary evil. In the book he pictures the Houses of Parliament as then only being used to store manure. H. G. Wells wrote more utopias than anyone else, as he searched to present better ways of organising society, often in the form of novels such as *A Modern Utopia*, and some have dystopian themes such as *The Time Machine*. Founding editor of the journal, *Utopian Studies*, Lyman Tower Sargent, feels that Wells is best described as a pessimistic utopian who always believed it was possible to radically improve human life yet doubted whether people had the will to do so. 'Dystopia' didn't come into general use until well into the twentieth century as a literary form and displaced utopian literature in the last century. Yet on a deeper level, as Fritzie Manuel says that 'At the heart of a dystopia has to be a utopia. You say, "This is awful. This is terrible. We're going in the wrong direction." But you're saying that because you think there's the possibility that it can change. If you didn't think there was that possibility, you wouldn't bother.' Aldous Huxley's dystopian *Brave new World* of 1932 projected into the future, the dire things which he felt might come to pass. But he followed it much later by his utopian work, *Island* in 1962.

One idealistic movement of the twentieth century which is very British and yet which somehow is not widely known at all, is documentary filmmaking. The story is worth expanding on, since this distinctively British development and genre has probably had a subversively positive influence on all of us in Britain. The 'documentary' has been a part of all our lives in this country for such a long time that we take it for granted. We examine the effect of many other influences on our attitudes, yet curiously, very little attention has been given to researching the effect of documentaries in shaping our attitudes in this country.

The documentary as a concept and format, goes further back into our national psyche. Pioneering Scottish film maker John Grierson is credited as the first person to coin the word 'documentary', and he saw the format as the 'creative treatment of actuality'. Grierson drew together a group of young filmmakers, first under the auspices of the EMB (Empire Marketing Board), producing their first film in 1929, a gritty realistic documentary about North Sea herring fishermen and their lives. Grierson believed in the power of exposing the public to the many varied and tough lives endured by their compatriots. He saw film as a way to bring about social reform, and by better mutual understanding to erode class divisions and even provide spiritual uplift too. The filmmakers who gathered around Grierson became known as The Documentary Film Unit, and when funds for the EMB's sponsorship dried up in 1933, Grierson took the whole unit to the GPO, where they made groundbreaking films like *Night Mail* and *Coal Face*. His fellow filmmakers were all liberals and from 1936 onwards, they branched out and dispersed into various production units.

Through the Depression and the WWII, these documentary directors continued to make films fired by their underlying passion and message that showing films about real life could change the world. Films about slums, the Blitz, coal mines, or postmen. Ordinary real lives. They held the fervent belief that if people of all different backgrounds could just see each other on screen, it would inevitably lead to more respect and understanding. One of them wittily quipped that, 'A documentary director must be a gentleman... and a socialist.' Grierson, who saw filmmaking literally as his pulpit, pithily said, 'Documentary outlines the patterns of interdependence.'

Documentaries became part of British culture a long time ago, and this was to continue on with the advent of TV. Taking myself as an example, I grew up watching TV, and must have spent nearly as many hours watching countless hours of TV documentaries, mostly on the BBC, as I spent hours in lessons in school. It has an effect and that's why I feel the documentary has become an integral part of British culture; so embedded, that we can't perceive its influence enough even to be grateful for it. For I contend that it has been a very positive influence starting from a small band of committed idealists who wanted to make a difference. It hardly needs to be said that Britain excels in the field of documentary filmmaking, and it is a considerable national export and success story.

And while on the subject of documentaries, another large and overlooked cultural influence on our national self-sense has to be the BBC. We find it hardest to appreciate that which is ever present in our lives. Attacked by both right and the left, taken for granted, savaged, pilloried, like that other under-appreciated body of ours, the NHS, the BBC is *the* model for Public Service Broadcasting worldwide; and our country is immeasurably richer as a result of it. Could it also have been in its genesis, a British utopian endeavour? Understandably this may sound a bit rich in the light of the extensively covered scandals of inflated severance pay settlements handed out to top BBC executives. Since it's the public's licence fee which funds the BBC, this sounds on a par with the vast bonuses lavished on bank executives whose employers, the banks, we the taxpayers have had to bale out. Yet the British Broadcasting Corporation, established under a Royal Charter, and launched in 1927, was set up with a high minded mission. To represent its values and purpose, the BBC adopted its own coat of arms with the motto, 'Nation shall speak peace unto Nation'. The BBC's most recent Charter states that the mission of the Corporation is to 'inform, educate and entertain' and that it exists to serve the public interest and to promote its public purposes: sustaining citizenship and civil society, promoting education and learning, stimulating creativity and cultural excellence, bringing the UK to the world and the world to the UK. I think that in spite of all its oft pointed out shortcomings, the BBC still serves that purpose at least to some residual degree. When both left and right constantly decry the BBC for its political bias, it must be doing something right.

Since its launch, its cultural influence through radio nationally and through the BBC World Service, as well as through TV, and now the immensely popular BBC online site, has been and continues to be huge. The BBC is both the oldest and largest national broadcasting organisation in the world. I thought it absurdly and lamentably short-sighted when to save a little money, the BBC World Service was cut back in 2011, seriously affecting its status as the world's leading global news broadcaster, which reaches a quarter of a billion people each week. The World Service has been for many decades the epitome of projecting soft power and influence globally for little cost, and peacefully, with a global brand seen as a hallmark of integrity, independence and trust. Former UN Secretary General Kofi Annan once described the BBC World Service as Britain's greatest gift to the world. The BBC is consistently rated as the most trusted and best-known international news provider and its World News is perceived to be more unbiased, objective and higher quality than any other news channel. As staunch defender of the BBC, and 'national treasure' himself, David Attenborough said,

> Public service broadcasting is one of the things that distinguishes this country and makes me want to live here. I have spent all my life in it. I would be very distressed if public service broadcasting was weakened. I have been at the BBC since 1952, and know the BBC is constantly being battered....Yet it is the best bargain that is going.

Another overlooked and—dare I even venture to suggest to call it idealistic—cornerstone of our society is the NHS and the welfare state. Every week there is another shock news story about inadequate care or unacceptably long waiting lists from a hospital or NHS health trust somewhere in the land. The media has us on such a constant and unremitting drip feed of stories of dysfunction, mismanagement and lack of care that it's not surprising that we feel pessimistic about the NHS and perhaps wonder about ditching it for private health care instead. Yet this is a jaundiced view and only part of the picture.

It is a matter of fact that there was a very dramatic change for the better in public health provision, when the NHS was founded soon after the devastation of WWII in 1948. One simple statistic is that people now live on average ten years longer than they did before the birth of the NHS. In fact it's hard for us to even imagine the Britain of the 1930s when access to doctors depended on your ability to pay, and poor people had to sometimes choose between whether they would eat a meal or buy medicine for their children. Universal access to healthcare as a fundamental right purely on the basis of your being a citizen and free of fees or insurance or being tied to a particular job, was radical and idealistic; and this was the one of the first times in the world that it had ever been done. Nye Bevan, the former Welsh coal miner turned Labour Health Minister pushed through the foundation of the NHS in 1948 as part of his dream for a 'new society', a socialist one of course, in his case. Now with a budget of over £100 billion, the NHS is the largest publicly funded healthcare system in the world. Of course the NHS has had many problems and still does, yet it doesn't help that it is routinely used by our statesmen and women as a political football; the two main polarised parties forever imposing their next miracle reorganisational cure on the poor NHS managers who have to implement it, before the opposing party changes it back, or to another politically motivated scheme again several years later.

Being such a gargantuan organisation, no wonder there are problems and abuses and it is right that lack of provision and poor care should be highlighted and dealt with. It's just that such relentless headlines of woe and impending collapse, jades us to the exceedingly un-newsworthy fact that it generally works pretty well. When you chat with ordinary people about their actual experience of NHS care, it can be a surprise how warmly they speak of the doctors and nurses. This is certainly generally my experience too. Our latent allegiance to the NHS only emerges publicly when there appears to be a threat to dismantle it in some way. You may find it surprising that a 2014 in-depth study of the health care systems of eleven of the wealthiest countries in the world by the US based Commonwealth Fund ranked the UK the best overall. The UK's NHS scored especially highly for its efficiency, quality of care and low cost at the point of entry and outperforms all the other countries in the management of chronic illness. Switzerland came overall second, with USA at the bottom. The countries compared in the study were: Australia, Canada, France, Germany, the Netherlands, New Zealand, Norway, Sweden, Switzerland, the United Kingdom, and the United States. If you find this hard to let in, I suggest it is exactly because of this relentless focus in our media on what's wrong with our health system: repeat it enough and it becomes self-evident.

Never Arriving

So where have we come to regarding idealism and the British, after looking at a number of examples through our history? Perhaps the two views below cover the spectrum of our attitudes:

A map of the world that does not include Utopia is not worth even glancing at, for it leaves out the one country at which Humanity is always landing. And when Humanity lands there, it looks out, and, seeing a better country, sets sail. Progress is the realisation of Utopias. Oscar Wilde

An acre in Middlesex is better than a principality in Utopia. The smallest actual good is better than the most magnificent promises of impossibilities.
Thomas B. Macaulay

Coming from that swallowed up and lost county of Middlesex myself, I can appreciate Macaulay's sentiment in a way other than how he originally meant it. Between these two statements we have something of a British practical idealism, tempered and more realistic than high falutin' fantasies of utopia. Take one tablespoon of British empiricism, one of idealism, add a shake of pragmatism, mix well and see what emerges. A tempered British idealism with grounding and vision.

So are utopians and idealists a dying breed today? Superficially it can appear to be the case with our often world-weary attitude, post-Empire. Yet maybe not, when we think about the nature of the problems facing us today and the response that is called for. Some of these problems are bigger than any faced by our forebears, since the issues today involve dealing with global problems which couldn't even have been contemplated or conceived of as being problems in the past. For example, we now seriously need to address the small matter of the survival and health of our planetary biosphere from the effects of human induced climate change. And the form which utopian projects can take are changing radically with myriad more possibilities in social media for digital utopias, bearing in mind that it's the spirit, motive and quality of values which we bring to the virtual table as with any other endeavour, which is crucial in determining the result, rather than the medium. Fritzie Manuel says,

> Utopians in the twenty-first century are those who think we can preserve the world. And it's not one class or society; it's all of humanity. So utopians are no longer simply isolated in little enclaves of their own. Without the whole world to back them, their ideals can't move into a practical phase. We all have to become utopian because we all have to believe we can preserve the world. And if we don't, we should give up right now and go into a cave, or pray, or just think, or spend our time knitting.

The best utopians have always been realists: the ones who focussed the passion of their vision of a better world into practical tangible improvements here on earth. Britain has always produced idealists and we need them more than ever today, with that practical idealism which is part of the national character. Lyman Tower Sargent, sums up the contradictory nature of utopianism and its actual results in human life.

This almost inevitable dialectic of hope, failure or at least partial failure, despondency and the rejection of hope, followed in time by the renewal of hope, seems to be the basic pattern of social change and is, perhaps, the actual logic of utopia, combining, as it does, parts of both previous logics. This dialectic is part of our humanity. Utopia is a tragic vision of a life of hope, but one that is always realised and always fails. We can hope, fail, and hope again. We can live with repeated failure and still improve the societies we build.

Sargent's view certainly mirrors my own experience. I am unabashedly an idealist, though hopefully becoming a considerably more realistic one, the older and more mature I become; being aware that aging and maturity don't necessarily have more than a nodding acquaintance. With the idealistic projects that I have engaged with over the years, I am in turns thrilled, stretched, inspired, brimming with hope; then to varying degrees disappointed, questioning verging on doubting, dejected, 'back to the drawing board', sober learning, revision. And then I resume with renewed hope and find a new avenue. Yet it never extinguishes the fire I feel which emanates from a source unknown; a subtle buoyant optimism which is more fundamental than hope; the passion which I can feel coursing in my veins at peak moments; those times when you know without knowing how you know, that you are smack bang centre in the current of life and your heart beats with life's pulse. It would be easier and less hassle to just not be bothered. And how much more so for those who have taken infinitely more risk than I ever have, often risking their very lives, for the sake of a better society; and for those who felt compelled to create, irrespective of the personal cost.

The utopian propensity or the utopian impulse just doesn't go away, and it will always keep rearing its head and springing anew. We won't 'get over it' as some would wish, such as Gen

X'ers who feel it is merely an idiosyncrasy of the Boomer generation. It is innate to human beings. I personally am convinced that the impulse to aspire towards that which is better or towards goodness, truth and beauty, as it has been phrased by many through the centuries, is one of the most distinctive qualities of healthy human beings, especially those whose survival needs have been met. And our psyche cannot be satisfied solely by healing ourselves or by becoming more integrated as individuals. It's in our nature to create and to aspire.

Utopia can never be reached; we are doomed to failure if that is what we insist on. Perfection, whatever that could possibly mean, is forever unreachable, and besides, no such steady state could ever exist. And if it did, we would hate it anyway; it would almost immediately become boring and deadening. Also the more we become conversant with an evolutionary view, the whole notion of perfection makes no sense whatsoever. We are in process through the millennia, through the centuries and through our own lives. And though there have been and will be dead ends and multiple pathologies amidst the often meandering and sometimes wild ride, there does tend to be a subtle inherent optimism in those who hold a developmental or evolutionary worldview.

As with the investigation of creativity and the creative impulse in the preceding chapter, similarly I feel that expanding our view of the utopian propensity to see it as a universal human dynamic, can help us navigate through and have more perspective on our own feelings. It can help us better contextualise them so that we are less prone to over-personalise everything and to go overboard with megalomaniac notions or to sink into dark despair. We are all intrinsically part, recipient and author of this story we are in together; it's my story, your story, Britain's story and humanity's story, all in one. And this is a new rendition of that age-old story. We want a better society, a better Britain, a better world. It doesn't just happen by itself. I'm fond of integral philosopher, Steve McIntosh's term for the driving force of cultural evolution, which he calls *actual* selection as opposed to *natural* selection. Culture evolves because we actually choose; because people make choices for their lives to be better. And isn't that what idealists have always aimed for? Chris Coates concludes his *Utopia Britannica* with,

Perhaps utopianism has always been a dynamic ongoing participatory process. We just happen to view it through freeze-frame-snapshot-spectacles. If we take a long, wide-angle view of history, not artificially divided into centuries or separated by national boundaries, the sheer scale of wave after wave of utopian experiments looks less like a catalogue of broken dreams and more like a guidebook for the journey to that other place, a better place—the better place that is no-place—utopia.

Chapter 13

The Nature of Nature

When we dote upon the perfections and beauties of some one creature, we do not love that too much, but other things too little. Never was any thing in this world loved too much, but many things have been loved in a false way, and all in too short a measure.

Thomas Traherne, Centuries of Meditation

We discovered 'nature' in the latter part of the eighteenth century, as I only half humorously suggested in Chapter 3. These days 'nature' is incredibly important to the lives of millions of us; whether it's our gardens, a walk in the countryside, on the beach, or a stroll in the green rejuvenation of our local city park. And justifiably so. It would be hard to find many people in this country who don't draw some sustenance and pleasure from nature in at least small measure.

Since it's a theme close to our hearts, in this chapter I'd like to take the subject of 'nature' and our relationship to it and look at it from a different frame of reference. I'd like to take the subject as a good practical example of how a more integrated developmental view of life can both help us relate to nature differently and also help bring a fresh approach to some of the knotty environmental issues with which we are faced. It's just one example, and I could have taken a number of other ones, such as multiculturalism, immigration or religion. I'm convinced that a different attitude where we embrace where we've come from, warts and all, helps inform a more intelligent discussion about where we are headed and what we can or should attempt to do. I hope that taking this 'nature' example can illustrate this point.

I feel that our mindset about nature tends to be unwittingly stuck in well-worn grooves which may not be so helpful today. In my opinion we need a very different conception of, and relationship to nature at this point if we are to navigate the rapidly increasing rate of change in our world, our landscape and our environment in Britain today. I want to show how we are in fact not separate from nature and, radical as it may sound, how we might be better served by dropping the notions of natural and unnatural entirely. In order to explain this different attitude I am suggesting, it's necessary to provide some context, since there is more to this than meets the eye.

Britons as Nature Lovers

That context needs, as a first port of call, to include what nature means to us British today and how it has come to occupy such a cherished and hugely important place in our national culture. The idea of nature has an inordinately strong hold on our psyche. I don't know of any international comparative studies that have attempted to measure the relative importance of such inclinations, but anecdotally the British would have to be in the upper echelons of nature lovers among nations. After all, it's often stereotypically suggested that we are more fond of animals than our fellow humans. Our national bird, the robin, the gardener's friend, which follows us around the vegetable plot waiting for uprooted insects from the spade, has a different character than robins on the Continent. Yes really; this is not taken from a UKIP brochure. Robins are generally shy woodland birds on the Continent and only have their friendly cheeky persona in Britain. The 'British' robin has different behaviour because of our attitude towards wildlife and nature.

Our fascination with animals, gardens, pets, and all things to do with nature is a peculiar and I think, endearing, characteristic of the British. The RSPB is a vast organisation set up for the protection of birds, yet now extended to include the natural world as a whole, since over time of course they realised that you can't just protect certain species; it's the ecosystem which needs protection and conservation. The RSPB is a major landowner and with its rallying cry of 'a million voices for nature' representing a good chunk of middle England, woe betide the government who ignores their weighty lobby. It's the largest wildlife conservation body in Europe. Seabirds on the coast of Britain had their own law passed to protect them from being shot at their breeding cliffs way back in 1869; I don't know of any earlier such legislation anywhere (incidentally, using boys as chimney sweeps was only prohibited in 1875).

There's historically been something quintessentially British about being an amateur naturalist and the country has produced many celebrated naturalists stretching back to Gilbert White and his seminal *Natural History of Selborne* in 1789. White has been credited as being the first ecologist with his concern and respect for nature. Victorians, including a number of clergymen, were often keen naturalists, studying butterflies, beetles or orchids, according to their fancy. These Victorian naturalists often corresponded with each other and one of them amassed a collection of 14,000 letters back and forth about his hobby. This naturalist, a certain Charles Darwin, enjoyed a collaboration with a staggering 2,145 natural history correspondents all over the world, and it clearly bore fruit in his case.

The way parks and green spaces have been preserved and created religiously and passionately in these small islands is visionary and displays an enduring care for the environment and our love and need for living connection with greenery. Even way back in the sixteenth century, Francis Bacon exclaimed, 'God Almighty first planted a garden. And indeed, it is the purest of human pleasures.' In our small crowded islands where true wilderness disappeared thousands of years ago, people cherish their connection with small fragments of the natural world—the local park, their guinea pig, their garden, feeding the birds—as their connection with life. A headline on the BBC website as I write, declares, 'Robin takes up residence in Grantown on Spey shop', with the shop workers no doubt delighted to share their workplace with a wild bird. For years I lived in densely populated Islington in London and my daily walk along the little ribbon of green beside the towpath of the local canal gave me what I can only call spiritual sustenance. The wild ducks and moorhens on the canal were overfed by a charming array of disparate individuals who came to feed them daily. I would chat with some of these characters, and we shared a connection with wildness, with nature; it was obviously important to each one of us, though of course we never talked directly about what it meant to us. It was more, 'Have you seen the heron this week? Did you notice that the nine ducklings are now down to only seven!'

What does this interest in animals and plants say about the British? Eccentric, sentimental, too reserved to express affection for fellow humans? Maybe that's a part of it, yet I believe it is also a positive strand in our conditioning and makeup. Our extraordinary interest in plants and gardens, with gardening often stated as the most popular hobby, is very much part of who we are. Every little garden has a flowerbed, its little Jerusalem. English gardening as high art, with its romantic influence of working with, rather than against nature, has produced classic gardens of such transcendental beauty as to take your breath away. This is artistic expression of the highest order on a par with other great art forms. We don't tend to think of it like that. Many of the best of these works of art are located all over the country in the outdoor living 'galleries' of the National Trust, another vast charity with millions of members and the custodians of English gardens of the highest order. And we can walk amongst and through these works of art.

In more recent decades, this interest in nature and the environment has been inspired and fanned by TV natural history documentaries. It's interesting yet not surprising to me to learn that the world's first natural history documentary film was a

British one, and of course it would have to be about birds. *The Private Life of the Gannet*, directed by eminent biologist Julian Huxley in 1934, was a film about seabirds off the coast of Wales, which actually won an Oscar back then. Since then, wildlife broadcasting has become a key feature of British TV. The person who has done more than anyone to bring the natural world to the living rooms of generations of suburban Britons is of course, David Attenborough. With his unique blend of inspiration, wonder, passion for his subject and scientific knowledge, he has brought concern for the environment to the whole nation. Not by lecturing on the degrading of the environment, but much more effectively by conveying the wonders of the natural world, and his passion for it, he has lit and cultivated that spark of interest in nature for innumerable people, with inestimable effect. Although he has been broadcasting on BBC TV from the early 1950s right up to the present, it was his landmark thirteen part *Life* series in 1979 which really was the tipping point. An estimated 500 million people have watched that series, and it became the benchmark and gold standard for all future productions. Polls show Attenborough to be one of our most loved, and even more significantly, the most trusted person in the nation.

The Attenborough effect has probably shaped some of our attitudes considerably more than we might imagine. Incidentally, we love him not just because he is such a great presenter who transmits his enthusiasm for the natural world. We love him because he represents the best of Britain; the best of ourselves; the best of the high ideal of the BBC to inform intelligently; a cultured voice, yet one not tied to class consciousness. He is our voice, the voice of Britain; a voice inseparable from our sense of the best of ourselves, inseparable from our fascination and love of nature. Walter Cronkite in the States occupied a similar position of trust as anchorman for CBS news for many years, but it is interesting to me, that in Britain, it would have to be a wildlife broadcaster to have such a place in our hearts.

What is Natural or Unnatural?

Nature is especially important to us because we live on a collection of overcrowded small islands where human beings have lived for millennia, and we treasure the greenery still existent. Yet in one sense there is absolutely nothing at all 'natural' remaining, if we mean by that, free of the influence of homo sapiens. All of the land in the British Isles is profoundly altered and shaped by millennia of human habitation. It begs the question, what is natural? It is here that a developmental view can help us. Nature is obviously not static. Darwin put paid to that notion long ago with *The Origin of Species*, showing species themselves to be not fixed categories but snapshots in time in an evolving process. The 'natural' world is not a theme park, a nature reserve or national park. We are inextricably part of nature and the implications of this are profound. There is in reality no nature 'out there'. The world is a developing event where human beings by dint of our sheer numbers and increasing technology are now the largest single determinant of the entire biosphere and its future. What we do or don't do can't be separated from nature.

We love our British landscape: the rolling hills, the distinctive higgledy piggledy patchwork of fields and hedgerows; those picture postcard hamlets with village greens, nestled in little valleys hidden down winding leafy tunnels of lanes; the open moors and millstone grits of the Pennines and the mellow Cotswold limestones. Landscape is a very meaningful term because it combines the totality of the land with its use by humans in a dynamic living synthesis. It's what makes any country distinct from others and helps define our own self-image. Our habit though, is to tend to freeze the landscape image, when of course it has never been static. Our wild and windswept heather moors in the north of England and Scotland are not in any way natural, if by that we mean untouched or altered by human hand or activity.

After the initial clearing of upland trees in ancient times, leading to soil depletion, the poor sour soil was then colonised by heather and since then, stock grazing and rabbits (introduced by the Romans) have prevented tree growth; this being assisted by controlled burning in more recent times to support new growth of heather for game birds like grouse which are then ritually shot at appointed times of the year. It also leads to the beautiful mosaic of different colours and ages of heather spread across the hills. Many villages and towns with the name ending 'ley' such as Henley, Barnsley, Beverley, or simply 'leigh', of which there are quite a number, hark back to a very different woodland landscape. 'Ley' or 'leigh' is a Saxon suffix for a 'woodland clearing' and suggests just how forested parts of our country used to be before it was largely cut down and cleared, leaving it as one of the least forested countries in Europe.

We do need to protect and value our landscape and even more so, our environment, upon which we ultimately depend, and yet also to recognise that change is inevitable and that we are doing a King Canute in attempting to hold back the process. There is often tremendous polarisation between those modernists who want to steamroller ahead, building over anything and everything, extracting natural resources without limit, treating the land as a mere commodity for human use and profit; and on the other side, environmentally concerned sensitive people who feel that nature and the environment is being run roughshod over and must be protected at all costs. Then we have more traditionally minded folk, conservatives with a small 'c', who want to preserve our heritage and protect every aspect of our countryside. Sometimes we have the unlikely alliance of traditional and postmodern groups united against proposed wind farms or fracking.

Landscape is also a matter of aesthetics and our sense of beauty also changes and develops through time. Who wouldn't love a traditional windmill or watermill in their village and yet who wants a wind turbine in their view, even if it's on the horizon? We have of late come to see the beauty and value of canals—an 'artificial' human made industrial transport system predating the steam age—which run through our landscape and we now go to great lengths to preserve canals instead of letting them gradually deteriorate as they ceased to be of use for transport. Medieval castles are rightly preserved, as are ancient tumuli and standing stones of all kinds, yet most of us still struggle to find beauty in the artifacts of the industrial revolution. Who wants a painting of an eighteenth century cotton mill, or its remains, on their living room wall?

Environmentalists and Greens of all description have played a very valuable role in standing up for the environment and highlighting and helping prevent the worst excesses and effects of rampant industrialisation. They have importantly helped to gradually inculcate a more ecological sensibility in all of us to varying degrees; a view which is more systemic and complex and more in accord with the actuality of the world system in which we all live. Only a few decades ago, hardly anyone had even heard of the word 'ecology' outside of its own arcane academic discipline; now every school child grows up learning about ecology and our intricate webs of interdependence. Many of us do our little bit for sustainability by separating the recycling and changing our light bulbs.

Yet like any good thing, it too can become rigid and dug in as a largely oppositional stance against the forces of global business and 'progress'. Being Green in its most strident form can come to mean being *against*: against progress, modernity, capitalism, rather than being 'for' anything practical, except for being 'for' stopping. How can we in reality deal with the fact that we can't just press the pause button on our world and country? I have environmentally conscious friends who abhor cities and are fortunate enough to have the wherewithal to move to the West of England and own smallholdings, reducing their carbon footprint, and feeling more environmentally sound. Fair enough, but it's just not possible for nearly sixty five million of us in Britain to do that. And from my youthful years of attempting going back to nature, it left me with a deep appreciation for the emancipation from backbreaking toil enabled by the Industrial Revolution. Oh, the sheer joy of being able to just turn up the thermostat of the central heating when cold!

Bright Green approaches

I have been interested to see an emerging green movement which is making a realistic attempt to bridge the ideological divide between more traditional greens and the modernists and techno-futurists and to find a constructive way forward. This necessitates dropping any rigid Green-versus-progress attitudes. 'Bright green' environmentalism, a term coined by influential American futurist Alex Steffen in 2003, seeks to actively embrace new technologies, but in a sustainable manner, recognising that no sensitive person feels inspired by the message that we are the problem and should somehow just 'stop'. It goes against the creative human spirit. Extreme green views can make us almost feel guilty for merely existing and using up precious resources, and there are even those who feel we have gone downhill ever since we stopped being hunter gatherers. Bright green or neoenvironmentalism offers constructive and inspiring ways forward which it maintains can simultaneously reduce our carbon footprint. For example, cities with their greater density of living paradoxically use far fewer resources per person than living in the suburbs or countryside, and we can now create much more livable green environments in our cities and large towns at a fraction of the ecological cost of anywhere else in the country.

Living in a city myself, I have been gradually weaned off my very petrol-headed upbringing by forsaking ownership of a car. It's the transport service I want rather than the possession, and so I use a convenient car club for a car whenever I need one. I

realised that I don't need the trouble or expense of being responsible for a ton of metal and assorted synthetics sitting deterio-
rating at the side of the road, for the sake of it being 'mine' and
having exclusive use of this hunk on the couple of times a week I
use it. Besides it gives our town and city streets the clogging
equivalent of arteriosclerosis. It's well nigh impossible if we all
tried to park at once in British cities given the very finite amount
of kerbside space; not to mention the traffic congestion caused by
the sheer number of vehicles. Of course this example wouldn't
work if you live in the countryside but it's an example of a
different way of relating to things; being more interested in the
service provided rather than possessing the 'thing' itself. Alex
Steffen says,

> In its simplest form, bright green environmentalism is a belief
> that sustainable innovation is the best path to lasting
> prosperity, and that any vision of sustainability which does
> not offer prosperity and well-being will not succeed. In short,
> it's the belief that for the future to be green, it must also be
> bright. Bright green environmentalism is a call to use
> innovation, design, urban revitalization and entrepreneurial
> zeal to transform the systems that support our lives.

In a similar vein, the team of architect William McDonough and
chemist Michael Braungart don't subscribe to the belief that
human industry must inevitably damage the natural world and
have taken nature itself as the design model. Guided by the
principle that 'waste equals food', they help companies design
products which, after their useful lifespan, will become nutrients
for further new products. Their *Cradle to Cradle: Remaking the Way
We Make Things* is a bible for this new environmental design
mindset, in stark contrast to what could be called the one way
'cradle to grave' model which has been the norm for manufacturing ever since the Industrial Revolution. In their radical

environmental redesigning, they make the important point, 'Here's where redesign begins in earnest, where we stop trying to be less bad and we start figuring out how to be good.'

Polarised and Emotive Environmental Issues

We can't avoid the fact that there are very pressing environmental issues to deal with and they are more crucial than ever when climate change is also being considered. How do we power our country and meet our energy needs and with what effects? Ever more fossil fuel usage leading to increasing carbon dioxide in the atmosphere, or nuclear power, which helps on the climate change front but leaves nuclear waste to have to be somehow stored safely for umpteen thousands of years? Or fracking? Many pros and many cons too. Alternative power, yes of course, but it won't be able to meet our energy needs for many years unless we invest vastly more into its development, very quickly. It has been estimated that if Britain were to meet its energy requirements solely through wind power, then we would need a wind farm occupying an area equivalent to the size of the home counties to do so. What do we do in the meantime? Difficult questions indeed yet we can only come to the best solution if we don't adopt prior dogmatic conclusions of the 'over my dead body' variety.

Then there is the GM food question which again is often a very polarised issue of for, or absolutely against. Either it's perfectly safe and it is therefore criminally luddite to try to prevent beneficial advances, or it is 'frankenfood' which must be prevented at all costs, even occasionally going as far as to illegally destroy GM crops. It's an important issue but the polarisation works against the coming to safe and constructive solutions. In contrast, the bright green attitude towards such difficulties is positive in its actively seeking solutions. From Steffen again: 'What's really radical is being willing to look right at the magnitude and difficulty of the problems we face and still insist that we can solve those problems. Nothing about a stubborn commitment to solving problems and a faith in our ability to do so needs to be naive.'

Unlike Steffen's view, the environmental debates I've mentioned above are often not entirely rational, and sometimes not even remotely rational, because there are agendas beneath the waterline which may be hidden to the protagonists that drive the emotional charge behind the issues. It's more a clash of world-views between modernists for whom science, business and progress is best for all, and sensitive postmodernists who are extremely cautious about the effects of unfettered scientific progress and tampering with the 'natural' environment. And to complicate the mix there are retro-romantics wedded to a view that whatever is old or ancient is inherently best, and tradition-alists who abhor change and want to preserve everything as it was; frozen at some period in the recent past which unfortunately has usually already vanished.

Then there are also sincere and thoughtful people like Paul Kingsnorth, founder of the *Dark Mountain Project* who believe that we are already in the middle of unstoppable global ecocide, and feel that the only true response is for us to first let that fact in and to grieve for our loss. Kingsnorth had previously devoted much of the last two decades of his life to hands on environ-mental campaigning in Britain before leaving the movement in despair at its ineffectiveness. He and others feel that it is too late for naive 'hope' because we have already fallen over the cliff of ecological catastrophe. Kingsnorth says 'Whenever I hear the word "hope" these days, I reach for my whisky bottle. It seems to me to be such a futile thing. What does it mean? What are we hoping for? And why are we reduced to something so desperate? Surely we only hope when we are powerless?'

I sympathize with his sincere sentiments and he is at pains to point out that he is not a nihilist. It is clear from his writing and his deeds that he really does care, yet his vision is certainly a dystopian one; a view which is striking a chord for increasing numbers of disillusioned green activists. And certainly their concerns can't be just dismissed. All the above views are part of the confusing mix currently at play in Britain.

We are Nature

I implied at the beginning of the chapter that something of a context setting journey would be necessary in order to illuminate a different view on nature, and it includes a philosophical and cosmological element too. With a sensitive developmental view, the whole notion of nature and what is natural is profoundly changed, and while sharing the inclusiveness of the bright green approach, it is actually more radical. Since humanity and all of life and creation is part of one unfolding deep time process, it doesn't make any sense to imagine rigid distinctions between what is natural and what is unnatural or man-made. We are all part of nature. In fact we are nature. It's difficult to think like this, because we are all profoundly conditioned to see ourselves as separate from nature, by an ingraining which stretches back to the Cartesian dualism of the Enlightenment. As Woody Allen nicely sums it up, 'I am two with nature.'

Yet even rationally, our habitual and 'rational' way of seeing doesn't hold water because how on earth could we somehow miraculously be separate from the whole world process of nature which has produced us? Even when I try to think in this different way, I often find myself inadvertently distancing myself from the implications. It's as if I were sitting in a planetarium. You know, you sit there looking at the roof of the dome at images of the night sky or cosmos, being wowed, hearing all those extraordinary facts about the scale of the universe and untold light years and gazillion galaxies. Yet at a deeper level, even then, usually we don't feel part of it—it's 'out there', like a diagram on the wall and we are the 'objective' observer. This distancing of ourselves from our world and universe is a pervasive habit. Yet when I do let in this—what can be referred to as a 'process' way of seeing—even for a moment, it tends to dissipate that vague sense of alienation which so many of us feel today; that peculiar sense of not really being 'at home' in the world.

A shift of outlook doesn't of course in itself change the environment, but it can certainly encourage fresh and less polarised thinking, and be a valuable foundation for more constructive action. Here's an extremely brief history of the universe which is clearly simplistic yet has an important truth to it. Cosmologist Brian Swimme sums up the whole story so far: 'It's really simple. Here's the whole story in one line. This is the greatest discovery of the scientific enterprise: You take hydrogen gas, and you leave it alone, and it turns into rose bushes, giraffes, and humans.'

It's easy to get the wrong idea about what I am suggesting here. By saying that we are part of nature I am not at all subscribing to a more extreme reductionism of the neo-Darwinian ilk: the kind that endeavours to prove that there is nothing at all different or special about us, and that all human behaviour can be adequately explained by unearthing more and more natural selection advantages. Far from it. I think that evolution is much more interesting and mysterious than that. The extraordinary fact that we human beings are not only completely part of a process but are also becoming conscious that we are that process, is an extraordinary emergence of nature itself. For the first time in the deep time history of this planet, we can arguably say that the process of evolution is becoming conscious of itself through us. And paradoxically, this development in consciousness depends on our being individuated enough from the process itself to be able to reflect on the process which has produced us; otherwise we would be just be 'in it' but wouldn't be able to be cognisant of that fact. Personally I find engaging with this way of thinking to be quite mind scrambling yet also exhilarating. It's impossible to comprehend the implications and

yet it can't be discounted because somehow I find that it mysteriously rings true. As Julian Huxley put it, 'Evolution is a
process, of which we are products, and in which we are active
agents.'

Just to be clear—and another necessary digression here: I am
also not speaking of transhumanism, a burgeoning field of
futurism, the term itself incidentally coined by Huxley in the
fifties, although developed and modified since his times.
Transhumanists believe that we can tremendously enhance our
human physical, psychological and intellectual capacities by
means of our exponentially advancing technologies. Scifi books
and movies love speculating on these themes. While a number of
their predictions might well come true—and some, like artificial
replacement human body parts, are already happening—
similarly to neo-Darwinism, transhumanism or techno futurism
can often have a materialistic and reductionistic flavour. Having
said that though, the transcendent element is also a strong strand
in the transhumanist sub culture, where immortality through
science and technology has become a goal for many transhumanists. By popping a prodigious number of pills and supplements, inventor and futurist Ray Kurzweil is famously trying to
stay alive just long enough to reach the point where technology
will allow him to board the anticipated immortality train. Who
knows? Some futurists propose other means to achieve our
immortality, such as uploading ourselves—our mind or
consciousness, that is—onto a silicon chip. Moral philosopher
Mary Midgley is highly critical of such ideas which she calls
'quasi-scientific dreams and prophecies' and sees them as being
driven by a fear of mortality to transcend and escape from the
body.

What I am pointing to is rather different and I feel better
encompasses and honours our multidimensional nature as
human beings. An integral evolutionary perspective sees us as
inseparable from the process, from 'nature', but by no means

necessarily implies a mechanistic and utilitarian view of humanity. On the contrary, as well as the visible exteriors of life, such a view includes the extraordinary development of what could be called the interior dimensions of the process, a view introduced by Whitehead with process philosophy. Just as the exteriors have developed and complexified astonishingly over time (just taking the example of the change in forms from hydrogen gas to rose bushes, giraffes and humans) so there has been a corresponding interior development and complexification: by which I mean the progressive complexification, deepening and integration over time of our capacities for consciousness, culture, values, worldviews, empathy, beauty, ethics, and spirituality. I know there are those who say, 'How do you know that humans have a more developed culture or consciousness than rose bushes or giraffes?' But I'm not even going to attempt to address that one. I've been accused of being specist before, though in my defence, I would say that I've been an unashamed animal lover all my life. We are nature contemplating nature, and by our emergence as self-aware beings, we add a unique value to what I am calling the interior of the process, and the richness of life.

Romanticism and Beauty

This leads me to the importance of beauty and romanticism in our examination of what nature means to us. As we have discussed, by and large most of us in Britain do care about nature in some way. Even in small ways when we tend to our little green patch of garden, or even our window box, there is a life affirming quality to it which nourishes us on a deeper level. Recent studies in Britain keep showing the value of a walk in the greenery of a park for physical and mental health, seemingly often more effective than therapy. There is a deep unarticulated sense that life has value, that this delicate and infinitely complex web of our ecosystem is precious and has intrinsic value, not just to be valued by how it serves our ends. We value beauty, and life would lose so much of its meaning without it.

If this sounds romantic then it's probably because it is romantic. I have to confess to being a romantic and I would be willing to bet that many of you reading this are also romantics, although you may not realise it or relate to that term. Don't be concerned though; you don't have to get over it. I don't mean that you read Barbara Cartland novels or that you are a *New Romantic* with its echoes of that short lived pop musical scene epitomised by the likes of Duran Duran at the end of the 1970s; nor that you necessarily have tree-hugging or New Age tendencies either. The Romantics discovered nature in the latter part of the eighteenth century and although very inspiring to read about their times, I am not suggesting a nostalgic re-embrace of that age. Nor am I suggesting a revival of any Romantic predilection for nostalgically looking backwards, drawn towards crumbling ruins and melancholic ruminations.

Yet the Romantic movement still continues in our present times since it represents for us a crucial connection to the interior dimensions of meaning, beauty, creativity and spirit. The Romantic spirit contains vital elements without which our humanity would be lessened or impoverished. When William Wordsworth stated in the Preface to his *Lyrical Ballads* in 1802, that poetry should be 'the spontaneous overflow of powerful feelings', this was not just a new understanding of poetry but also a different expression of consciousness and self-sense. Romanticism validated the power of the imagination and intense emotion as authentic aesthetic expressions. There were different expressions and flavours of classic Romanticism in various countries; the British variety had little to do with nationalism, unlike its counterpart in Germany, for example. Here its spirit of radicalism, liberalism, idealism, love of nature, and its valuing of imagination, strong emotion and independent creativity could also be recognised again in the 1960s. The 1960s were a modern revisitation of Romanticism. Wordsworth and Coleridge could be interpreted as the first hippies, 'getting their head together in the country'. It is also no accident that Romantics such as William Blake were so enthusiastically embraced in the romantic 1960s, while before then, Blake was surprisingly little known to the wider public.

Today, Romanticism's stock doesn't at first sight look too good when a modern dictionary definition of romantic is 'the quality or state of being impractical or unrealistic'. And if you search on the web for the qualities of being a romantic, you come up with many gooey lists of the 'five (ten, twenty, etc.) sure signs you are a hopeless romantic' type. But looking more deeply, the romantic sensibility has permeated and opened our consciousness to include more and reach deeper, and the Romanticism of today can be said to have moved on from that of the eighteenth century and to have become more integrated into our mindset. Many of the qualities from the classic Romantic period are recognisable today such as our valuing and need for greenery and nature, of the importance to us of the imagination and of intense emotion as authentic aesthetic expressions; the valuing of following one's intuition towards creativity and avoiding imitation of others; and how spontaneity has now become for us a desirable character-istic. Johan Lyall Aitken in *The Educational Legacy of Romanticism* believes it likely that 'the continuing legacy of the Romantics, made new, is keeping divine discontent alive... The lure of suburbia, the call of the country cottage are not only the dislo-cation of the classical and biblical myths to return to the garden, they are Romantic in their origins and language.'

American educationalist Jeff Carreira compiled an updated list of the qualities of a Romantic today. While these are not exactly what a classic Romantic would have said, the through line can however be traced. This list includes: having a consciousness that appreciates both the indivisible wholeness of life and the irreplaceable uniqueness of the individual; not believing that the universe is totally understandable, accepting that life is infinite and some aspects of it will always remain beyond our mind's ability to understand; and a suspicion about the use of power to manipulate and control, seeking instead to find a more natural flow with the life process and surrendering into what wants to happen rather than forcing things into being.

All these are quite familiar today to many more open minded liberals. Interestingly, even possessing a sense of style and our valuing of choices made on aesthetic factors is very much a legacy of the eighteenth century Romantics. And not to forget the now common attractiveness of breaking conventions and making your own rules. This was radical and bohemian in the 18th century, revitalised as rebellion in the counterculture of the 1960s, and is now common or garden individualism today. Reading these, you may rightly conclude that you are a romantic too. And why not? In my opinion a romantic sensibility is a healthy and necessary part of a mature sensitive consciousness today; not in its naive impractical sense, but in a consciousness which includes aesthetic considerations as a vital quality of life and has an open ended and non-dogmatic attitude towards our knowledge and the essential mystery of life which will likely never be 'solved' or 'cracked'.

A Nature walk through the thicket of Categories

Getting back to our theme of nature, the terms natural and unnatural may now not look quite as distinct as before and similarly with our view of what is nature. As a practical way to illustrate, let me take you on a nature walk which highlights this theme of natural or unnatural. This was a stroll I took through an unprepossessing stretch of landscape on the eastern industrial borderlands of London. The ancient marshy flatlands of the Thames floodplain where people (wisely, considering the trouble with flooding these days) didn't choose to build houses, where damp grazing later became a dumping ground for sprawling and polluting industry, and in this case, an old military firing range. It's called Rainham marshes: one of my favourite places very near London where you can find Big Sky and vistas; just past Dagenham and the car works. On a winter's day it can't be beaten for head clearing invigoration and this is what I wrote in my diary about a walk I took there.

The swirl of the wide flock of lapwings against the infinite pale blue of the winter sky takes my breath away. Like a single organism, sensitive and skittish, they circle and then land with one mind on the grassy clumps of the marshes; all facing the same direction, their iridescent green plumage and extravagant head plumes flash strangely exotic. I walk through the head high reed beds, their pale beige at this season imbuing them with an unbounded depth and stillness in the calm air. Nothing stirs in the emptiness which at first seem deserted and then every so often a powerful invisible burst of song erupts from the reeds; unseen Cetti's warblers the very essence of the mid-winter reeds.

I stand silent in the reeds when suddenly, with a low thunder rising within seconds to a roar, there's a gleaming flash and the Eurostar has passed and the noise has vanished as swiftly as it arose; just like the warblers' explosion of song. Then another rumble and the gleaming navy blue flash of HS1 hurtles past in the opposite direction, the shiny and aptly named 'Javelin', the high speed train to the channel coast.

The lapwings and warblers seem oblivious to Eurostar and HS1. Rainham marshes has been sensitively nurtured by the RSPB as a nature reserve on the Thames estuary. Marshes have been seen in the past as barren places of miasma only suitable for draining, fly tipping, or unpalatable industry which was unwelcome elsewhere, and maybe for building new airports? Yet we now know that these marginal areas between zones are the richest for biodiversity and are also crucial feeding stage oases for migrating wildfowl and waders.

Electricity pylons straddle the marshes like spindly Ents and the low hum of traffic from the M25, a constant distant background like the drone in Indian music. Being used as a firing range by the army in the past, saved it from development; the rusty metal targets left on the marsh are now seen as the archaeological heritage of the site and provide a good lookout for perching kestrels.

Is this nature? Or denatured industrial wasteland? A vast landfill site borders the reserve on one side, the dump trucks ceaselessly coming and going, a low background murmur; an old vehicle breakers graveyard on another side. At first I'm a little taken aback by the high speed trains passing so close to the reed beds. I hadn't realised that not just Eurostar but also HS1, the high speed rail link to the coast passed quite so very close. But then I ease into a larger appreciation of the whole palette. The wildlife is unfazed by it all. This is a beautiful mind expanding place; a place that ultra urban Londoners like myself especially need. I'm used to stunted horizons of barely a few yards. My spirit expands with the endless flat vista only amplified by flocks of ducks and waders flying in and out all the time.

And curiously these marshes are actually ancient. The water meadows are strewn with strange humps like moguls on a ski slope, betraying their history; the lumpy grassy tussocks being the result of the industry of ants protecting their homes from the ever threatening water, creating these ant conurbations over centuries. Ant nest islands rising from the mire. Are the earthen mounds lining the banks of the Thames here to prevent floods so very different from the ants' mounds keeping their cities free from flooding?

Landscape constantly evolves, mutates, a combination of all the influences shaping it. Our capacity to appreciate landscape has to develop and move on too. What a beautiful expression of nature is Rainham Marshes and it lies almost within sight of Canary Wharf. In the azure sky, a plane glints silver as it turns silently high up, leaving a gossamer trail drifting aimlessly in the heavens. On the marshes stepping elegantly through the ditches is a stately little egret, a recent species to our shores from warmer climes, (a likely courtesy of global warming), impossibly snow white against the grassy hummocks. I am transfixed. We truly are nature appreciating nature.

I hope this diary entry gives a sense of the Britain we live in, like it or not, if we don't mentally airbrush out the offending elements. This is increasingly the sort of borderland regions which of necessity will typify more of our countryside. I'm not praising the trash and flotsam of derelict industry as if it were somehow cool. As we care more and more for our surroundings, that care will translate in making our environment more attractive. There is nothing inherently ugly per se about industrial building; it just depends how it's done. Care and attention creates a different result. It's pointless for us to try to insist on an idealised primeval past unaffected by humankind. And being such a huge presence on this planet means we humans play a considerable, if not the major part in shaping the unfolding of nature at this point. Yes, certainly we have unwittingly damaged and polluted our precious planet, and have to do everything we can to remedy this degradation, not least because this is our home too.

As nature led to the evolution of human beings, we developed the capacity to self-reflect on the very process that we are integrally part of—an extraordinary emergent quality in itself. So now we have the capacity to reflect on nature and its process and appreciate the beauty. Before that capacity flowered we were immersed and embedded in nature, but did not know it. Then we consciously separated ourselves from nature with the advent of the Western Enlightenment and became individuals in the modern sense, and we advanced so much, with incalculable positive benefits. Yet our spirit was impoverished, which led to many sensitive people romantically embracing nature again. At the same time, the more green hearted we became, the more ambivalent we became about being here; even seeing ourselves as spoilers and interlopers on pristine nature. Now again I feel we need to embrace the totality of all that we are and have created, as nature. That doesn't mean that everything is okay and that a change of view alone where we see beauty in wastelands will magically do anything at all to stop us destroying our precious environment. We should actively resist a lot of thoughtless, ugly, despoiling developments in our environment, where little attention or care has been given to harmful consequences.

I'm not advocating some technologically sterile transhumanism, which worships technology as our future, and would have us live in an antiseptic environment akin to a dentist's surgery. This is equally extreme in its futuristic modernism in the opposite direction. At the same time, it doesn't help to look backwards wishing for a pristine environmental Golden age (which never existed anyway) but to go forward, embracing change and technological advance with our capacities for empathy and appreciation of beauty inseparable. And this is a romantic outlook, albeit one considerably upgraded from the eighteenth century.

I'm sure all of us can find beauty in the swallows and swifts circling effortlessly on a summer evening; defying gravity as they swirl and swoop catching insects in the infinite sky. Can we at the same time appreciate the beauty of the jet plane glinting golden as it catches the evening sun high in the heavens? In our direct unmediated perception, the plane is a sliver of light trailing a mysterious thread of vapour, like tracks on sand. I find it a sight of beauty watching high flying planes as they seem to rise almost vertically, only emphasising the mysterious immensity of the firmament. This is the summer evening sky in our times. And I know in the next moment that I can also start worrying about the depletion of the ozone layer when I gaze at planes in the sky, and that's part of the complex picture too.

One provocative writer who has gone a long way in questioning our attitude to nature is Timothy Morton, an English literature professor specialising in the romantic period who has a lot to say about philosophy as well. He advocates ditching the concept of 'nature' entirely. I am sympathetic as to why he advocates this. In *Ecology without Nature: Rethinking Environmental Aesthetics*, Morton argues that we need a new way of thinking whereby we drop the whole idea of there being any bifurcation between nature and civilisation: this sense of ours that nature sustains us but somehow exists separate from us. Even for us to think of ourselves as being embedded in nature, implies our separation from it. In his words,

> Ecological writing keeps insisting that we are "embedded" in nature. Nature is a surrounding medium that sustains our being......Putting something called Nature on a pedestal and admiring it from afar does for the environment what patriarchy does for the figure of Woman. It is a paradoxical act of sadistic admiration.

In Morton's view, in order for us to really have an ecological view, we have to drop the notion of nature. This has similarities with a process view of the environment where we also can see the illogical notion of there being any separation between society and nature. Ironically it was the Romantics themselves who championed nature and its aesthetic appreciation, inadvertently separating us from the object of our adoration. Nature became a cherished object of our gaze—something 'out there'. Yet a new romantic sensibility can very much coexist with an evolutionary perspective, by extending our aesthetic considerations wider still, rather than seeing environmental beauty as somehow being confined to dwindling fragments of pristine 'nature'.

Speaking of irony, contrary to what you might think, romantic irony has always been a key feature of the romantic aesthetic. Morton emphasises this point and it is another part of the romantic sensibility which can help us nowadays. Classically with romantic irony in a novel or poem, the narrator of the story may suddenly realise that he or she is actually a character in the story, or a character in the story may realise that she is the narrator. And isn't that just the kind of ironic situation that we are waking up to today, not just in a novel, but in a stupendous sense? We are beginning to realise that here we are in the Anthropocene age (that increasingly used term recognising that the effect of human activity on the earth's ecosystems now constitutes its own geological epoch) where the story we are in is about an accelerating reality and everything is going dangerously fast with the biosphere at increasing risk. We are simultaneously narrator and character in this story too, and we are definitely and curiously on the inside of the story too. Julian Huxley well describes our ironic rude awakening:

> It is as if man had been suddenly appointed managing director of the biggest business of all, the business of evolution — appointed without being asked if he wanted it, and without proper warning and preparation. What is more, he can't refuse the job. Whether he wants to or not, whether he is conscious of what he is doing or not, he is in point of fact determining the future direction of evolution on this earth. That is his inescapable destiny, and the sooner he realizes it and starts believing in it, the better for all concerned.

Feeling at Home in our World

Perhaps you, like me, have had flashes of illumination or momentarily seeing from a different angle, where your surroundings come alive, lit up so you see them freshly. Everything looms strange though intriguingly attractive, because you are not seeing through the dullness of habit. In these moments everything is perceived to have inherent value and beauty. Yet rather than calling this an altered perception or a peak experience, I sense that this is just seeing more fully than I usually do. I find that this can occur to me not that infrequently, and the urban environment where I live is then not seen to be mere inanimate matter or 'things'.

All of creation is seen in those moments as in a sense 'alive' without the vast majority of 'it' being dismissed as mere 'objects,' not worthy of inclusion as of value. Morton talks of elevating all 'things' to beings, where there is not this exclusion of 'things' having no value. To me, this represents an intuition of a different way of relating to 'things' where there isn't the same distance or alienation because it is self-evident that we are all part of a singular though messy reality and process which in a certain sense is alive. It helps us see and appreciate material existence in a very different way from the reductive materialist. It could be called a re-sacralization of the world, so eviscerated by modern mindsets which often only see surfaces and measures value by utility.

Richard Jefferies, one of my favourite nature writers and an unconventional mystic, wrote beautifully of his wanderings in the English countryside in the Victorian period. In his autobiography *The Story of My Heart* Jefferies interestingly turns the tables on our habitual vantage point, writing of his 'at homeness' with consciousness and being, while finding 'matter' in contrast thoroughly mysterious and 'supernatural'.

Why this clod of earth I hold in my hand? Why this water which drops sparkling from my fingers dipped in the brook? Why are they at all? When? How? What for? Matter is beyond understanding, mysterious, impenetrable; I touch it easily, comprehend it, no. Soul, mind—the thought, the idea—is easily understood.......The supernatural miscalled, the natural in truth, is the real. To me everything is supernatural.

In case you are wondering, I'm not advocating some kind of magical animism or pantheism such as enjoyed by pre-modern hunter gatherers. While their at homeness and identity with their environment is beautiful, and the envy of retro-romantics, we can never return to such an innocence; we are so far down the journey of individuation as to make their world more or less unreachable for us. What I mean instead is a more complex and integrated re-identification with our world which is only made possible because of our great degree of individuation, or disembedding from our environment; an evaporation of separation which is soul nourishing while simultaneously no inhibition at all to our increasing individuality.

And such sentiments are not only the province of nature mystics. Pioneering complexity theorist and biologist Stuart Kauffman in *Reinventing the Sacred*, describes how complex systems self-organise into entities which are much more than the sum of their parts. Complexity science in Kaufmann's view points to a unified culture where 'God' or the divine can be understood as the natural ceaseless creativity of the universe and of human beings. Though he comes from a very different starting point from Jefferies, what Kaufmann proposes also leads in his view to a greater sense of our being at home in the world along with a heightened sense of wonder and deeper meaning.

The great paleontologist and pioneer evolutionary priest, Teilhard de Chardin, took some of these ideas even further by penning his famous *Hymn to Matter*. Yes really, a hymn to matter. At first sight it does sound pretty far-fetched; to some, perhaps even idolatrous. Worshipping the concrete pavement or an Ikea 'Billy' bookshelf? Well, obviously not his point. Teilhard was one of the finest minds of his times, and his influence has steadily grown since his death in the 1950s. Rather, I think that in this passionate outpouring, he is pointing to a reintegration of how we regard the so called 'material' world and the intangible world of spirit and values. Here's a taste from Teilhard,

I bless you, matter, and you I acclaim: not as the pontiffs of science or the moralizing preachers depict you, debased, disfigured — a mass of brute forces and base appetites — but as you reveal yourself to me today, *in your totality and your true nature*.....

Blessed be you, mighty matter, irresistible march of evolution, reality ever newborn; you who, by constantly shattering our mental categories, force us to go ever further and further in our pursuit of the truth.

If this looks rather panentheistic, (Greek: 'all-in-God', meaning the divine interpenetrates all of nature, while timelessly extending beyond) well, so be it, since I feel we have excluded valuable elements of our humanity in our more conventional and acceptable worldviews today, especially reductive materialistic ones. To honour our multidimensional nature and not be a flatland character, we need to include our intuition, imagination, passion, personal experience, spiritual intimations, creativity and love.

Alfred North Whitehead saw a deep time directionalism in the ongoing unfolding of the world, while being acutely aware of the immense problems and struggles of civilization. He took aesthetic values to a new level with this startling and much quoted statement of his: 'The teleology of the universe is directed to the production of Beauty'. It's difficult to try to encapsulate in writing, emerging currents of understanding like the above, that are more intuited than perceived, and which do not fit in with accepted categories. Even the very language we use is inadequate, language having been formed as an expression of the culture and worldview of its time, although language too is also of course ever changing and developing. And this is not the place for an in depth investigation of such topics as the teleology of the universe or beauty.

Beyond Polarities

So before bringing this chapter to its conclusion, let me just briefly sum up what we have covered and where we have come to so far in this, of necessity, meandering journey into a new story about nature and our relationship with it. We started with our British love of nature, gardens, greenery and its importance in our lives. We examined the British landscape and its 'unnaturalness' and how it is always changing and can't be frozen in time. Investigating the sometimes intractable polarisation of views between environmentalists and that of modernist developers only concerned with 'progress', we saw how the debate is often far from rational. The Bright Green synthesis of intelligent and sensitive development was touched on as a possible helpful depolariser.

On introducing a process perspective informed by process philosophy, the divisions between natural and unnatural could be even more plainly seen not to make sense any more, and I distinguished what I meant from the sometimes more materialistic versions of transhumanism and neo-Darwinism. Also the picture was nuanced by seeing the process of unfolding development as having both exterior and interior dimensions, rather than being simply a cosmology of complexification of matter.

Rather than only attempting to preserve nature as pristine relics, as in nature reserves, we looked at nature today in this country as being inextricably intermeshed with human activity and construction; and touched on how we might more sensitively develop this process. Delving briefly into cosmology we then examined Romanticism and its modern expressions, and why it is a healthy component of our makeup today with its important aesthetics and valuing of nature. We looked at perhaps even abandoning the term 'nature' altogether, given the implications of our separation from it. Lastly we looked at a radically different view of matter and 'things'—a revaluing and re-sacralization of the world—where we are not fundamentally separate, but may be able to find a new 'at homeness' in the world. We can think of all this as an unfolding story that we are inseparable participants in; at once characters in and narrators of, this new story.

The journey in this chapter interweaving various subjects has been taken for one reason: I have been taking the 'nature' theme as one example to illustrate how a more inclusive evolutionary perspective can reframe many of our difficult issues and offer constructive directions forward. As I said at the beginning, I could have just as easily have taken one of several other themes like the EU, multiculturalism, immigration or religion, for example. A developmental view is quite relevant to our situation as a venerable country and culture, or rather mix of cultures, and is of far more than abstract semantic and philosophical interest. We need a new understanding of 'natural' whereby beauty can be appreciated, conserved and developed in our increasingly urbanised environment without attempting to freeze it or turn back the clock. It's infinitely complex and nonlinear, and there are no easy answers, yet we are talking about an ecological *mesh* rather than a mess.

Perhaps the most important and general point is that an inclusive developmental view can take us beyond trying to balance or negotiate the old polarities of man/nature, traditional/progressive, romantic/realistic, preservation/progress, liberal/conservative; techno futurism/green environmentalism; Left/Right, etc. We can begin to distinguish a sensitive ecological future-embracing view which values aesthetics, our rich formative history, tradition and technology, ecology and progress as a single movement.

All this, when it comes down to it, can make a very practical difference as to how we relate to many aspects of our British life, our culture and environment, and open up a renewed appreciation for our natural heritage. We can value our traditions without being at all backwards looking or retro-romantic. The biggest single difference such a view can make though, is to place us right in the middle of a new story; one where we are able to feel at home again, belonging to the world and land which gave us birth; a lost state many of us may wistfully have longed for, connected with tradition, inseparable from our environment. And that's no small thing.

Chapter 14

The Future is Unwritten

I live my life in widening circles
That reach out across the world.
I may not ever complete the last one,
But I give myself to it.
Rainer Maria Rilke

Rediscovering Belonging & Continuity

This story of Britain has been for me a journey of rediscovering belonging: of being part of something wider and anciently rooted. It's recognising I am part of a story, a continuum, a tale that has weaved its way through generations and centuries, uncovering a living connection with ancestors and the past; there's a thread of creativity, of life which flows through the years, the people, the landscape, the culture, to make me and to make you.

I realise that I've come full circle. Born into a post WWII Britain which still possessed lingering greater certainties, where the sense of belonging still remaining from that war wasn't articulated; it didn't need to be; it was just who I was, who we were. Then swiftly followed the rejection and jettison of all this in the 1960s and 1970s; seeing through seeming illusory and superficial ties and bonds. For those of us who came of age back then, we saw many of these certainties as hollow, built on historical prejudice and privilege. Now authenticity was rebellion, deconstruction, tearing down. We were global human beings with no nationality—post-national internationalists—casting out this divisive entangled dross as the ashes of our painful past. As a young adult I felt rightfully alienated from my country, my culture, its traditions, throwing out all binding allegiances to be, as I thought, more true, more free, more myself, in the burgeoning individualism of the times.

And that movement had and still very much has its value. But I realise there is more, and coming full circle is to re-embrace my origins, our shared past and tradition, but in a different way. To rediscover connection, continuity, rootedness again; coming full circle yet in a higher octave. This is not blind retro-nationalism. It's embracing our story from a foundation of realising we are global humans or global villageists, first and foremost. Yet as post-traditional individuals, nationality is still a key element in our makeup and in the totality of our being, with its riches, achievements and horrors to be integrated, if for no other than the simple reason that it *is* us. We can't get away from it; it would be like trying to run away from one's shadow and one's body and being. Embedded in cultures as we are, the past informs but needn't dictate; there is creative potential in making different choices, and more especially if we are becoming conscious of our make up and our past. Many British people of a certain age will likely have a similar experience as myself, and many younger Britons may see all this as just harping on a dead past. Yet the past dictates to us until it is made conscious and owned in the present, when it can instead inform the future. Knowing the past, whatever one's age, can help to understand and even liberate the present.

So where have we arrived at? Examining our received and largely unspoken national narrative of declinism, post-colonial embarrassment, shame and pessimism, all muddied by collective amnesia, another narrative is coming into focus. Seeing the developmental nature of human culture and consciousness can afford us a greater perspective and much more empathy for how on earth we got here. The future is not predetermined by the past; rather the past contain the seeds for multiple possible futures. The endemic creativity, humour, spirit, stubbornness and a certain down to earth strain of idealism of the British can fashion a better future in spite of the enormous challenges ahead. As Andrew Marr concludes in his, *A History of Modern Britain*, 'The threats facing the British are large ones. But in the years since 1945, having escaped nuclear devastation, tyranny and economic collapse, we British have no reason to despair, or emigrate. In global terms, to be born British remains a wonderful stroke of luck.'

Owning our past, finding belonging, can do much in my opinion to open the sluice gates of our national psyche and spirit, letting it flow and connecting with a new story of our times. We will then more easily discover our organic and effective role in the world. Jeremy Paxman in his *Empire* points to the effect that our disconnection from the past has on our own psyches.

Instead of trying to grapple with the implications of the story of empire, the British seem to have decided just to ignore it. It is perhaps possible that this collective amnesia has nothing whatever to do with the country's lamentable failure to find a comfortable role for itself in the world. But it is unlikely. The most corrosive part of this amnesia is a sense that because the nation is not what it was, it can never be anything again. If only the British would bring a measure of clarity to what was done in their country's name, they might find it easier to play a more useful and effective role in the world.

Healthy Citizenship Building

The recognition and reconnection with our national story and creative thread is the main avenue which I have been advocating as a healthy way forward for our national psyche. Yet there are many practical initiatives which could help this process and I will outline several of these. The initial and almost comical problems with the UK citizen test which I mentioned at the beginning of the book have now resulted in the creation of a bona fide citizenship test and ritual to become a British citizen, complete with accompanying flag and pledge of allegiance. A friend of mine who recently became a British citizen, told me that the ceremony was actually far more moving than she would have imagined. And citizenship is a simpler way to encourage and foster belonging than trying to mould people's identity.

David Goodhart in the *The British Dream*, identifies one major reason as to why Britain didn't reinvent itself, say back in the 1970s, with routes to citizenship laid out for new arrivals and why it didn't become more a citizen nation in the way that Canada and America had done.

Perhaps above all Britain did not reinvent itself as a nation because it wasn't a nation in the first place, it was an empire. Many people, especially among the politically liberal and the highly educated, seemed to slide from an imperial idea of the country to a post-national one without passing through a 'normal' national phase.

As Linda Colley has suggested, we could go further and update the citizen ceremony to make the oath of allegiance to the majesty of the people rather than to a monarch. Similarly this should be done with Parliament also formally swearing an oath of service to the majesty of the people. Colley's famous millennium lecture in December 1999 at Downing Street, to then Prime Minister Blair and assorted dignitaries was entitled *Britishness in the Twenty-first Century*, and much of it is still very relevant. She envisages a reinvigorated sense of citizenship as a way for Britain's now diverse population to be better connected with the nation's past. Commemoration and ritual is an effective way to do so and one which I feel would better resonate with the country.

Scotland, Wales, Northern Ireland and England have in some respects different visions of the past, but not entirely so. We could all, surely, agree to commemorate the abolition of the slave trade back in 1806, something which all these islands, and black Britons as well as whites, took part in. We could all commemorate the Reform Act of 1832, the first step towards achieving universal suffrage here. We could all, now, commemorate the Catholic Emancipation Act of 1829, or the end of Jewish Disabilities in the 1850s, or Votes for Women in 1918. And why shouldn't we commemorate independence for India in 1947, since it's part of our history too?'

Many of these events are hazy or little known to many of us today and yet promoting such commemorations would help foster a valid cohesion for all Britons of whatever background. We could add the signing of Magna Carta in 1215, with its recent 800 year anniversary in 2015 to these markers in the progress of greater human dignity and rights. We need to connect the new to the old and to connect the minority with the majority; connecting that part of our radical and reforming past with what it means to be a British citizen now. The groundbreaking Putney debates of the seventeenth century described in a previous chapter remain very fringe knowledge despite being so extremely formative and pertinent to the whole history of democracy. The Suffragette movement is a little more recognised (though barely), while the original pioneering feminist, Mary Wollstonecraft, is generally hardly known. There is as yet, no monument to her, for example, though there is now a group campaigning to rectify this. Designers of coins, stamps and banknotes could all take this view more into account; a formative history which is relevant to men and women here of all ethnic backgrounds.

To know how we arrived at the present from the past is important, and one institution which deserves to be created is a National Museum of British History. The USA has such a national museum in Washington while Germany has its own museum dedicated to national history in Berlin. But not Britain. We need to connect history— *his*-story—to become *our* story; and going forward: our project. Similarly, we are lacking a national day, unlike other countries; a day to celebrate what it means to be British. Where's our July the 4th? John O'Farrell has handily suggested one simple step of converting the already existing celebration of November 5th into our national day. After all, we celebrate it already with fireworks, and it does mark the day that Parliament was saved. It wouldn't have any anti-Catholic residue since no one today has the association of burning Catholics when the 'Guy' is put on the bonfire; though it's possible there are those who might resonate more with the film *V for Vendetta's* climax of blowing up Parliament in the name of freedom.

The overly centralised nature of government administration in England (which is at a far greater level than that of other similar Western democracies) tends to work against our felt sense of democratic participation. In WWII, and following those years of emergency, there was a deliberate centralisation of bureaucracy and administration which effectively ended the great ages of previous local government. We unfortunately never went back to our local and voluntaristic roots as a country. Greater devolution for England would go a long way towards increasing a sense of citizen participation.

We also should make more gestures towards honouring the sacrifices made in both world wars by all those men and women of the British Empire, who fought and suffered or died, and who have not been adequately recognised. After all, where would Britain have been in WWII without the enormous contribution by the Empire soldiers from India to West Africa, who fought on the side of this country? Contrary to how it is popularly portrayed, Britain didn't really ever have to stand alone.

As Colley went on to say in her talk already quoted above, 'The idea, which one so often hears canvassed, that the British past is nothing but an embarrassing saga of sluggish tradition and imperial oppression is absurd. We have a perfectly usable, innovative, collective past, if we only look for and select it.' This doesn't mean that we should avoid our past national oppressions; far from it. It's very important that these should also be taught, so that the shadow can be better faced and absorbed. We have a moral obligation to open up all the restricted files about the colonial period still held in our national archives. But history should be taught in such a way that views it as part of a developing stream of humanity with its empires and attendant dominations and horrors, and not just as a uniquely European aberration of the last several centuries. The shameful episodes in the history of Empire such as the Opium Wars with China and the Bengal famine which was discussed in relation to Churchill, should be taught. John Newsinger in his, *The Blood Never Dried: A People's History of the British Empire,* sets a useful rule of thumb test as a measure of avoidance in any history of the British Empire, by looking to see whether the Bengal famine of 1943–4 is acknowledged or not.

Education is key and I've already mentioned the current paucity and disjointed nature of the teaching of history in British schools. This teaching could be better angled to include such events and to also include the many smaller significant events in local history that are in a similar direction; once you start delving, these can open up in almost any locale. An interest in how on earth we got to where we are today, when followed up locally, soon starts to reveal clues and connections. History could become less the Great Man theory of history referred to previously, and become more a collective history, honouring and remembering those many small gatherings of men and women who struggled to advance rights and dignity, as well as advancing arts and innovation.

To put it in a fresher way, you could say that I am proposing a more inclusive history of 'we', to distinguish it from a 'people's' history, which tends to be more angled to the left wing, and thus can be unattractive to those on the right. A history of 'we' emphasises the collective dynamics of creativity and progress between groups of people in particular milieus, the 'scenius' that was explored in chapter 10, which is often a more accurate portrayal of how culture and consciousness develops, than solely by lone independent geniuses. Also it more accurately depicts the relational nature of our national story. I find it interesting that the process approach to thinking which I have been advocating as a valuable shift in our outlook, is often, these days, known as process-relational thinking, for the simple yet profound reason that the process of history and life that we are part of, is inherently and inescapably completely relational. We are made of everything that has gone before.

Immigration Revisited

The practical examples described above for encouraging citizenship can all be helpful in fostering a better grounding in our collective story. However, there is no simple shopping list of initiatives, which in and of themselves will make the change I've been suggesting. We need to think of ourselves and our place in our country and world in a different way. History is a story which is always in the making and being retold and reformulated. As I've said before, it's our story; it's how we became who we are now. It's the connecting thread between past and present stretching back into antiquity.

I took the example of 'nature' in the previous chapter, and explored in detail as to how an evolutionary view can affect the very way we look and relate to our world. Just to briefly touch on another of those issues which could fruitfully be looked at in a similar way, consider the charged subject of immigration. It would, of course, need a full chapter to do it justice, more especially since it is frequently such a polarised topic between liberals, postmodernists and conservatives, traditionalists, and between left and right. At one end of the spectrum is the belief that anyone should be able to come to Britain, that we have no moral right to restrict people's freedom to migrate. This post-traditional view asserts that nationality is outdated, and that it is restrictive of migrants' freedom by asking for any degree of integration into the host culture. This view has often been criticised as being particularly held by affluent middle-class liberals who themselves don't live in the inner city areas where greater levels of immigration have the most impact. Then there are economic liberals, believers first and foremost in the free market economy, who tend to be in favour of immigration for their own reasons: it tends to help the economy, keeping costs down by providing more workers who are prepared to work for less.

At the other traditional and also more conservative end of the spectrum is the view that Britain is already too crowded and we should severely limit if not stop immigration altogether, fearing that immigrants will take away British jobs and abuse the welfare system, or harm our British way of life; this view is often underpinned by a perceived threat from all the rapid change and increasing mix of different cultures and races. This is felt by those who hold traditional values, whether they be working class left wing or right wing conservatives.

Yet stepping back, Britain like most countries, has always been somewhat of a mongrel nation, with additions from invasions and also waves of immigration over the centuries, such as the Huguenots and then the Jews fleeing from persecution and pogroms, or more recently, Ugandan Asians and Vietnamese boat people. Certainly the numbers of immigrants have increased tremendously in the last fifty years, and the rapid change can feel threatening to quite a number of native Britons. This mixing — and dare I say, enrichment — is one of the legacies of The Empire and has helped made Britain the tolerant and relatively accepting country that it is, with a sense of Britishness being elective and not based on blood or race. You could say that it's a good sign that former subjects of the Empire have wanted to settle here despite the past iniquities of colonialism. Of course, often in the past they were encouraged to come here in times when Britain was short of labour.

At the same time, we need to be confident enough in ourselves not to feel we are being racist in any way, by asserting that controls on the amount of immigration are necessary. A postmodern Briton will likely feel twinges of guilt in calling for any controls, unless he has faced to some degree, the dark side of our colonial history, and has a longer term view on our stream of history. Controls on the level of immigration are vital for preserving the social cohesion which underpins our society, since towns and neighbourhoods simply can't cope with or integrate too rapid or large an influx of new immigrants. This is compounded by the fact that poorer new immigrants are not of course spread evenly throughout the country. They under-standably tend to join others of their own culture in those neigh-bourhoods of towns and cities where poorer white working-class people also tend to live. If the rate of influx is too fast, this can easily create tension, separation between communities, a perceived competition for scarce resources like social housing, and a general overstretching of services. Egalitarian liberals can too easily dismiss the concerns and misgivings of particularly ethnic white working-class Britons about immigration, as being racist, without listening to their experience. It's important that we also listen to the voices of their lived experience of immigration.

We need to listen to all sides in order to find the best way forward. And immigration is a charged subject, with mainstream politicians afraid to tackle it in any comprehensive manner, apart from UKIP, which plays on the concerns and fear of some people. Oxford professor, Paul Collier, author of a major work on immigration, makes the point that 'ever since Enoch Powell's "rivers of blood" speech in 1968, serious discussion of migration has been taboo in British social science.' Social cohesion is a precious commodity which we need to safeguard and nurture. Yet it's fragile and once lost, is hard to regain. We should value our historically long forged social cohesion and take it into account. Narrowly imposing an egalitarian ethos about immigration and not expecting any degree of integration from immigrants into the host society—which can be part of a more prescriptive multiculturalism—can easily hinder integration, creating more separation in communities and damaging that cohesion.

I remember attending a debate on immigration at Cambridge University's Festival of Ideas. The speakers presented good arguments as to how beneficial immigration is and has been for Britain and dismissed the 'immigration mania' created by the media. And I think the case for the overall benefit to the country from immigration is very true and hard to deny. One academic political philosopher who spoke at the debate gave an intriguing presentation questioning whether nation states have the moral right to control the entry and settlement of non-citizens in their territories. It struck me how in an ideal world such a policy might make perfect sense, but away from the cloisters of academia, instituting any such policy would likely create turmoil in our inner cities as great numbers of poorer people from developing countries choose to emigrate. It must be remembered that most poor countries are quite hostile to permanent emigration, because they desperately need to retain the skills of their educated citizens who they have struggled at great expense to educate: these being the people most likely to emigrate. Surveys suggest that something in the region of 40 per cent of poor people would emigrate if they were able to.

Immigration is an emotive subject and easily becomes overlaid with projections of our worries. It would surprise many people to learn that a recent migrant to Britain is more typically a young graduate from Western or Eastern Europe working in the financial, technical or creative industries, according to a University College London study. The director of the UCL Centre for Research and Analysis of Migration stated, based on their studies: 'Immigration to the UK since 2000 has been of substantial net fiscal benefit, with immigrants contributing more than they have received in benefits and transfers. This is true for immigrants from Central and Eastern Europe as well as the rest of the EU.'

Aside from the general consideration of immigration, however, the plight of refugees and asylum seekers escaping war and death is another matter altogether. Britain seems to be forgetting its past tradition of serving as a shelter from the storm for refugees, as it was for Jews in WWII. Pandering to small minded fears of being swamped by asylum seekers and refugees, the media and the government have made many people feel that we can't take in many refugees. The whole furore around refugees trying to reach Britain from Calais has been vastly exaggerated. The numbers who have tried to get to Britain from Calais have been miniscule compared to those entering continental Europe. These people, many from war-torn Syria, Afghanistan and other failing states, are desperate and incredibly motivated and courageous to make it this far. Many have died on route and it is absurd to suggest they are risking their lives on the perilous journey to Britain just so that they can claim welfare benefits. Compared to many countries in the EU, we now accept relatively few asylum seekers and refugees, and far less than countries like Germany and Sweden. Our responsibility to asylum seekers is a different though related question from the general issue of immigration.

Depending on the differing sets of values held by traditional, modern and postmodern Britons, there will likely be conflicting conclusions about the right or most sensible approach to immigration. The subject of immigration, like many others we face, is complex and there are multiple factors to take in and to hold. A developmental view can help negotiate the charged subject of immigration by taking into account the validity of all these points of view without defaulting to any extremes. It includes listening non-judgmentally to the experience of ordinary people who are affected by immigration and not taking up a polarised position either for or against; and most importantly it means not shying away from dealing with this difficult subject. We need to think about the development of the whole system, which includes the conditions in the source immigration countries as well as our own country. This can help us in not getting bogged down in the polarities of old habitual mindsets which can become obstructive by their failure to include significant elements of the picture. Taking a longer term developmental view of ourselves and our nation can help us include and integrate more of the overall picture and to hopefully find constructive ways forward.

How might we synthesise all these contrasting elements practically? To me, this points to the need for a bold willingness to face the issue on a governmental level. We're used to independent committees being set up to deal with historic events where things have gone wrong. Why couldn't we initiate a committee of inquiry into future policy on difficult subjects like immigration? It could be the hallmark of a new era of consensus politics which, unlike the present approach, isn't based on the ideals and foibles of whoever forms the latest government. Such committees could similarly formulate long-term plans to deal with such challenging issues as education, climate change and the NHS. It would need a long term outlook aided by a good degree of independence from the government of the moment. We have become all too used to the kind of government policy which spins like a weather cock with each changing breeze of public opinion. I realise this may sound fanciful and a long way off, but we don't have to accept the same old approaches which clearly aren't working any more. This could point to a new model of decision making.

What Role, if any, for Britain Today?

That brings us to Britain's role today. What role, if any, should we now be having in the world, in Europe? Does even the idea of discussing a role for us in the world sound too Whiggish, imagining history as an inevitable progression towards ever greater liberty? Although I believe in sustainable progress and development, I've been careful to distinguish that a considerable amount of what goes under the banner of progress may not be at all beneficial for the whole. Francis Fukuyama famously wrote about the *ending of history* following the collapse of the Soviet empire at the end of the 1980s. It seemed to him that the Western liberal model of democracy was becoming inevitable. Yet it is now looking like Western liberal democracy isn't going to sweep the world and be the only game in town. I heard Fukuyama speaking at the RSA in London in 2014 and he has also now backed away from that view. Historical inevitability is not something to be banked on, in spite of whatever Hegel said. Having said that though, it is valuable to look at where we have come to, what we have learned, and how we can best develop and contribute in the world, approaching life with a mature realistic strain of idealism but remaining open and adjusting to what is actually happening.

This once great global power, now only a middling size power in the world, is just a smallish collection of islands. Eclipsed and becoming eclipsed by much larger rising countries like China and India, as the axis of economic power starts to shift from the West to the East, can make us feel confirmed in our declinist pessimism. Yet as we have seen, Britain is actually doing much better than our image of ourselves would suggest, and we could just as easily take it as flattery that many countries have copied and adopted so much of the modern world which this country did more than any other to initiate and set in motion. It could be seen as a sign of success, and it is only natural that a geographically small country is going to become relatively less important. A number of British values such as fairness, tolerance, acceptance, rule of law, have now, naturally enough, just become absorbed in modern universal values so that we may feel that there is nothing special about them.

And before moving on, is the nation state as a locus of power and identity, on its way out, past its useful sell by date? Funnily enough, for all the talk of globalisation and all power migrating to multinational corporations and unelected global financial bodies, the nation state is actually not dying out. Nation states are still the main unit of larger organisation and Britain is no exception. In fact, in the wider world there are still nations fighting to achieve their own nation states. And in spite of all our air travel, the vast majority of people still return to their home country and have a strong sense of rootedness.

US Secretary of State, Dean Acheson is remembered for his famous observation, 'Britain has lost an empire and not yet found a role,' a state of affairs which is arguably almost as true now as when he spoke those words in 1962 at a conference on American affairs at West Point Military Academy. His remarks caused great offence in Britain at the time, although he did not at all mean to criticise, being himself a staunch Anglophile. But what is often forgotten, is what he then went on to say, referring to Britain's application for membership of the Common Market, the forerunner of the EU:

> The attempt to play a separate role, that is a role apart from Europe, a role based on a Special Relationship with the United States, a role based on being the head of the Commonwealth, which has no political structure or unity or strength......this role is about to be played out........ Her Majesty's Government is now attempting, wisely in my opinion, to re-enter Europe.

Just as an aside, Acheson's mentioning The Commonwealth, reminded me of the 2014 Commonwealth games held in Glasgow. The superlative sports performances kept me riveted to the TV coverage and it struck me at one moment—admittedly it was a blindingly obvious realisation, yet fresh nevertheless—that these seventy or so nations competing, were the old British Empire, but now proud independent countries of course. I found myself momentarily amazed and also happy that they would choose to compete and be part of this 'Commonwealth', even though the body does indeed lack strength and power, as Acheson observed.

I think that Acheson's fuller statement is prescient and I cannot but see Britain as an intrinsic part of Europe. This europhile sentiment is currently unpopular, with not so many people here seeming to have a good word to say about Europe or the EU, with all our economic ills often conveniently blamed on that institution. Curiously there is very little rational or reasoned debate about this subject, with UKIP spreading emotional scare stories about the hordes of Europeans who (theoretically) might all decide to decamp to Britain. The Conservatives, not wanting to be outflanked by this UKIP populism, make similar noises, while Labour, who you would think would be more internationalist, largely stay silent on the issue, fearing to lose the popular vote. Interestingly the business community, while also not making much noise, are revealed in surveys to be clearly pro-Britain being in the EU, for the simple fact that that is where the largest share of our trade takes place. Matthew Norman, writing in *The Independent* about our lack of having a proper debate about the pros and cons of EU membership, hits the nail on the head.

This debate, if it deserves so grand a title, has nothing to do with reason, and everything to do with the ongoing confusion about our place in the world......for six decades Britain has been riven by the crisis of self-identity that inevitably afflicts a traumatised post-imperial nation.

Many of those Brits who do espouse patriotic views are particularly anti-EU, but to me there needn't be a contradiction. Can't we be confident enough about our identity that we don't fear being totally subsumed in a pan-European union? Most of the other European countries in the EU don't seem to be paranoid with fear of losing their sovereignty. Of course, after the trauma of WWII, continental Europeans naturally tended to look to bind together in the European project as a way forward, while Britain with its different history of empire and also being offshore islands, tended to look to the wider world or USA, or global bodies for involvement outside the nation.

Clearly the EU needs much improvement and reform, and its current financial crisis with the South-North economic health divide, naturally colours our view, yet we forget what an extraordinary achievement its creation has been. Nowadays, many would scoff at the optimism of American social thinker Jeremy Rifkin's 2004 book, *The European Dream: How Europe's Vision of the Future Is Quietly Eclipsing the American Dream*. Yet stepping back, it's amazing that the EU has got as far as it has in making an attempt to shape our global future with soft power. You certainly couldn't conceive of any other bloc of countries in the world being willing to attempt anything remotely as collaborative. Just try picturing the USA entering into something similarly collaborative with Canada and Mexico? Diplomat Robert Cooper, writing in the *New Statesman*, values the EU and our place as part of it:

> The EU (with its twin, Nato) is, for all its faults, a kind of political miracle: the most successful collaboration among sovereign states ever achieved. In spite of the mess of the euro, it is still admired and imitated on other continents. This is the best Europe we have ever had; and Britain, as an influential member, has been a force for good in it. Both altruism and self-interest tell us to remain.

The Economist of course, admittedly rather predictably as a supporter of liberal trade, is all in favour of embracing openness rather than comfortable isolation in a piece entitled *Little England or Great Britain?*

> The shrinking of Britain is not preordained. In a more optimistic scenario, Britain sticks together and stays in Europe, where it fights for competitiveness and against unnecessary red tape. British pressure gradually cracks open services markets, both in the EU and elsewhere........Britain once ran the world. Since the collapse of its empire, it has occasionally wanted to curl up and hide. It can now do neither of those things. Its brightest future is as an open, liberal, trading nation, engaged with the world.

Yet these are rather isolated voices which took some trawling to find. We should have more confidence in ourselves not to withdraw. EU countries like Germany are eager to keep Britain in the EU as a counterweight to their own membership and for the distinctive nature of our contribution. Most EU countries would like Britain to remain in the EU although some are understandably frustrated by our embarrassingly blinkered self-interest which makes European cooperation more difficult. Real discussion of all the pros and cons is needed, and not just a discussion dominated by populist scare stories of the 'what Brussels will try to impose on us next' type. We need real debate about the longer term future and what part we might play in the continent which we are actually a part of, geographically. Our thinking has become so short-term these days. We would do well to take a page from the *Long Now Foundation,* whose avowed aim is 'to provide a counterpoint to today's accelerating culture and help make long-term thinking more common....to creatively foster responsibility in the framework of the next 10,000 years'.

Understanding our embedded reluctance to be a full part of our own continent, due to our being offshore islanders and from our history of looking to a world-wide empire and the Anglo-sphere as our domain, can help smooth down our sense of exceptionalism and make us feel more a part of Europe.

Admittedly, it is hard for us in Britain to have a strong sense of European identity, but that is natural, and Britishness, or other national identity such as Scottishness, will remain far far stronger as an identity for the conceivable future than any sense of being European. As I have said before, the fact that we feel ourselves to have a nested sense of identities with different weightings, like a Russian doll, is only natural. There is still a strong need for the nation state in spite of what post-nation internationalists would have us believe. Liberal intellectuals make the argument that the nation state is too big for local issues and too small for global issues, and hence outmoded, yet this is an intellectual argument which ignores the reality of the average person's experience of a fairly strong identity with the country, leaving aside whether British, English or Scottish, etc. The nation state is still the best way to think about, collaborate and deal with many issues of health, education and anywhere where cooperation and organisation is needed. And yes, much more devolution for England and for the regions and cities could help as well to strengthen the poor level of involvement and feeling of irrelevance that many people currently feel about the political arena.

The Scottish referendum of September 2014 provoked much criticism about Britain as a whole from the natives of these islands, (various other countries being more perplexed, amazed and frankly horrified that we would allow such a thing as a vote on the matter) but not much was said about how the whole exercise was conducted in a remarkably civil and equitable manner. How many countries would even let a section of their population have a vote to secede from the main country? No threat of breakaway states or military coups or martial order, much less threats of retribution or ethnic cleansing. Sounds ridiculous, doesn't it? But that's because we take our stability and order in Britain so much for granted that we have little or no appreciation for it. We are the only country in the world where the police are still not armed, bar a couple of tiny places like Iceland and New Zealand. The Scottish referendum was a model of robust democracy in action.

You could draw the conclusion that perhaps this could all happen because today there is not much sense remaining of even feeling part of the UK, of being British. But I would say that there is a latent shared confidence and sense of belonging, which allows us to accept the differences between us. Though I want to point out that we are now in danger of seriously undermining and dissipating our shared heritage of culture and values and cohesion, if we continue as we are now, in being so removed from our national stream, and from any living story. We need to actively reinvigorate that story.

What, if any, should Britain's role be in the wider world today? Are we just clinging onto old imperial illusions of power, trying to punch above our weight? Clearly we have had to adjust to no longer being a preeminent world power, now downgraded to merely a medium size power, although still with influence, with a permanent seat on the UN Security Council, a member of the G8, as well as being a nuclear power. It's important that we don't have pretensions of our being more influential or powerful than we actually are. That is part of coming to a healthy national self-acceptance of just being Britain, and not a Great Power or empire; and conversely, also not to turn against ourselves with self-loathing, feeling that because we are no longer first, then we must be nothing, with the corrosive declinism that is often part and parcel of that attitude.

We could take the route of opting to be less involved globally and become more like a Sweden or even a Switzerland, and not get overly involved internationally with world problems, especially not militarily. This can seem very attractive for us to stop meddling in faraway foreign conflicts following our unfortunate recent incursions in Iraq, Afghanistan and Libya which have severely tarnished the prospect of any future missions. Yet I think that we have a certain global responsibility based on centuries of involvement around the world. Not that we should automatically follow the USA into every conflict in a knee jerk manner, but our involvement and connection with so many countries, many of which were former colonies, does mean we have connection as well as responsibility. We created many of the national boundaries in former colonies in often unwitting and ignorant ways, creating in some cases, countries which were not viable. Some of the consequences are still being painfully worked out.

The centuries-long British experience in the world and our mixing with other peoples should help in our being involved internationally, but obviously not in an old imperialistic way. There is a crying need for international aid, help, and even military help, but it needs to be done with more understanding of what is actually likely to help. This is needed rather than imposing our Western solutions, such as quick fix 'democratic elections' which might make us feel good, but that may turn out to be fairly irrelevant or worse still, lead to inflaming the situation. Imposing regime change isn't very helpful, as we've found out so painfully. A sensitive developmental view which takes into account the overriding importance of local tradition, societal structure and values, should guide our approach to our getting involved in any foreign interventions. Having an understanding of the very different worldviews sincerely held throughout the world, and how they relate to each other, can help us in not imposing our version of a solution with sometimes disastrous effect. Being sensitive to the developmental nature of cultures and also of religions, would go a long way in helping us not to exacerbate conflicts, but instead to foster ways forward.

It is beyond the scope of this book to show how an evolutionary view can help in negotiating religious conflicts in the world, and most particularly at the moment, Islamic extremism. Yet this perspective can shed light on developmental factors in different cultures which contribute to conflicts which on the surface may seem to be purely religious ones. Our lack of cultural understanding and historical knowledge of Islam have made it much more difficult to counter the real threat of Islamic extremism. Just to take one example, in the West, we have no sense of the negative effect that globalising modernity has on traditional Islamic culture, and the militant reaction against the West that this provokes in some radical Islamists. The ever spreading Western modernity can be perceived in traditional Islamic societies as being identical with secularism, and an attempt to negate their religion—a threat which must be fiercely countered in the eyes of radicals. There is obviously much much more to be discussed on this subject.

Britain is one of the largest donors of international aid in the world, second only in absolute amount to the USA, a far larger country. The Organisation for Economic Co-operation and Development also lists countries by the amount of money they give as a percentage of their gross national income. By this measure Britain gives more than any other medium or large country, being committed to giving 0.7 per cent of national income in foreign aid. The only other countries which give this much are several small Scandinavian countries. This 0.7 per cent target was reached by Britain in 2013, the first country in the G8 to meet this decades-long goal and promise which was set as a common goal at the UN way back in 1970, and endorsed numerous times in conferences since then. Even in times of austerity, with all the cuts made by the Tories, David Cameron told the UN that it was a moral obligation for better-off countries to help poverty in a world where more than one billion people live on less than a dollar a day. The foreign aid budget here has remained ring-fenced. This says something about Britain's commitment to world engagement.

A Rebalanced and more Integrated sense of Ourselves

Throughout this book I haven't wanted in any way to give the impression that I'm saying that the British are better or superior than any other nation or people. The emphasis throughout has been more toward the positive, simply because the negative case about the country has already been fully made; it's the default and unwitting view of many of us. My aim has been to rebalance that view to give a fuller and longer time picture of ourselves. This British journey has taken us from initial more superficial downsides of our society such as lackadaisical moaning, jadedness and pessimism, to reveal the iceberg below the waterline of all our shared unexamined past: to see how much more we are the product of our time and milieu and our past, rather than the completely free thinking independent individuals that we like to think we are.

By taking a developmental view of ourselves and of our history and culture, I do believe that the deeper traits of declinism and cynicism which we have examined can be both acknowledged and integrated into our national psyche. The Empire cast a long shadow in our psyche as the unacknowledged elephant in the room. It was compounded for us by our country's reduced status, the psychological effect of which has been interestingly, considerably larger than the actual objective decline. Since having been an Empire, it's been hard for us to adjust to being a country or nation. Together with our avoidance of our illiberal past, it has left us estranged from our creative past and the struggle for progress, dignity and rights, with no metanarrative or clear sense of who we are, nor any larger purpose. We find ourselves floating rather aimlessly, washed by avoidance and embarrassment at our heritage, in the process tending towards cutting ourselves off from the stream of our belonging and the wellspring of creativity.

The sun has certainly long set on the Empire yet it need never set on the creative impulse, as I've termed the drive and propensity towards creativity. Connecting with this creative thread more unabashedly can reinvigorate many possibilities as it has done through the centuries in this pragmatic and empirical country. This is a creative country and a milieu which encourages creativity is by far the most conducive for untrammelled expression of that creative thread, both individually and collectively. The great world historian Arnold Toynbee, regrettably out of favour these days, put the dangers of not doing so, thus: 'The nature of the breakdowns of civilizations can be summed up in three points: a failure of creative power in the minority, an answering withdrawal of mimesis on the part of the majority, and a consequent loss of social unity in the society as a whole.'

The good news of our exceedingly long and slow incremental progress in dignity and rights through many centuries has given us a very solid basis for character, identity, acceptance of difference and a means for newcomers to be included as citizens too. We are all profoundly formed and influenced by our national origins, which is definitely by no means all bad news, and we need to embrace a more healthy national self-sense; a citizenship not primarily based on race, blood or religion but rather on our values, shared experiences and institutions, long forged and still showing surprisingly stability, in spite of our recent unmooring from our roots. Having said that though, as I have been saying, the challenge is to stop undermining ourselves, our shared culture. This needs active engagement and education and a more expansive view. While it could be seen as objectionable to mould citizens in any particular way, all I am talking about is a rebalancing of the way we are already deeply moulding ourselves into a partial and rootless vision of ourselves, disconnected from the reality of the story which we are part of and which has produced us. We need to support cohesion in these times of increased disruption, immigration and globalisation. This is not a starry eyed utopian project but needs that tempered idealism which the British bring to the equation, a quality that I referred to as realistic idealism.

Neither avoiding our past nor obsessing with post-colonial guilt and shame, will serve us well. We need to embrace a story which can speak to the majority in the country and to affirm that there is such a thing as society and rootedness, and that it is our story. Danny Boyle in his opening show at the London Olympics struck that chord and channelled that sentiment in such a way that nearly everyone in the country could identify with, even if it completely mystified some foreign commentators. Whatever your ethnic background, you could feel part of that specialness which is Britain; and special is quite distinct from superior, just as your pet Labrador is special yet obviously not superior to all other dogs. The Olympic phenomenon allowed us Britons to glimpse a wholly different aspect of our character and fed self-esteem and taking pride in a positive rather than a jingoistic attitude.

As a nation perhaps we could begin to find a new creative way to contribute in the face of the ambivalence that has descended on us and most other Western European nations. There could be the discovery of a truly positive, even rightful role for Britain in European and global society, free to contribute everything we are good at, with all our global experience available for the common good instead of being used for trying to prove we are a global power or being influenced by our avoidance of our past. Can we find a new way, not trundling along the well-worn grooves of the polarities of Britain versus Europe, Left versus Right, special relationship with the USA or not, or global versus local? A longer term developmental perspective on ourselves and our country can help reconfigure many of the knotty issues which we face today. We could come to a new sense of self, a new sense of nationhood, a more integrated sense of identity. Britain could play a valuable role at the crossroads of global culture. We already are seeing London in some respects as *the* premier global city spanning East and West, more than any other city in the world. Though there are no guarantees, there is no reason that our future cannot indeed be more creative and dynamic than our past. As Danny Boyle's Olympic ceremony in London announced in the programme,

> We hope, too, that through all the noise and excitement you'll glimpse a single golden thread of purpose—the idea of Jerusalem—of the better world, the world of real freedom and true equality, a world that can be built through the prosperity of industry, through the caring notion that built the welfare state, through the joyous energy of popular culture, through the dream of universal communication. A belief that we can build Jerusalem. And that it will be for everyone.

Acknowledgements

I have talked with and learned from so many people in this quest of mine to better understand the British, our culture and who we are today. I want to thank my many colleagues, friends and contacts in my network who all added important elements to this story of Britishness. I am especially grateful to former Archbishop of Canterbury, Rowan Williams, for sharing his deep insights into the interwoven narrative of British spirit and history; Professor George Bernstein for his help and counterintuitive American view on the myth of British decline; Mags Blackwell for her rare ability to evoke the creative impulse in whomever she works with. And I want to thank the John Hunt Publishing team.

Most of all, I want to thank my good friend and colleague Steve Jackson for his unflagging passion and encouragement to me during the long gestation of this, at times, meandering project. He graciously served as my trusted sounding board for many a discussion over a period of years, as well as being editor for several drafts of the manuscript. Steve has helped me unendingly with his well-considered suggestions. This work would very likely never have seen the light of day without his unfailing support. He has given me a great gift.

Lastly I would like to also thank my wife, Kyrsten, who always believed in this project and encouraged me throughout. She listened patiently as I would read her each chapter of successive drafts, wisely recognising that rather than a critique, what I needed was a good listener and to be able to hear my own words aloud.

Bibliography

Abolition Project. *Handbill produced by James Wright of Haverhill regarding slave produced sugar.* Available from: http://abo lition.e2bn.org/source_33.html (Accessed 30th September 2015)

—-. *Suppressing the Trade.* Available from: http://abo lition.e2bn.org/slavery_155.html (Accessed 1st October 2015)

Acheson, Dean (1962) Quoted in 'Britain's Role in World' *The Guardian* 6th December

Allardyce, Alex (2008) *The Village that Changed the World,* London: Newington Green Action Group

Bacon, Francis (2010) *The New Atlantis,* CreateSpace Independent Publishing Platform

Barfield, Owen (2011) *Saving the Appearances: A Study in Idolatry,* Oxford: Barfield Press

Barrett R. and Clothier P. (2013) Barrett Values Centre, *UK National Values Assessment.* Available from: https://www. valuescentre.com/mapping-values/culture/sector-industry-examples/nations/uk-national-values-assessment (Accessed 29th September 2015)

Bartlett, Robert (2010) *The Medieval World Complete,* London: Thames and Hudson

BBC News Magazine (2007) *Your 1970s: Strikes and blackouts.* Available from: http://news.bbc.co.uk/1/hi/magazine/6729683 .stm (Accessed 30th September 2015)

BCS, The Chartered Institute for IT. *A brief history of British computers: the first 25 years (1948-1973).* http://www.bcs .org/content/conWebDoc/24070 (Accessed 1st October 2015)

Beck, Don and Cowan, Christopher (2005) *Spiral Dynamics: Mastering Values, Leadership and Change,* Hoboken NJ: Wiley-Blackwell

Bede, Venerable (1990) *The Ecclesiastical History of the English*

People, London: Penguin

Beecroft, Nicholas (2014) *Analyse West*, CreateSpace Independent Publishing

—-. (2014) *The Future of Western Civilisation Series*, CreateSpace Independent Publishing

Bernstein, George (2004) *The Myth of Decline: The Rise of Britain since 1945*, London: Pimlico

Berry Thomas (1978) *The New Story*, Teilhard Studies No.1. Available from: http://static1.1.sqspcdn.com/static/f/558814/15 477548/1323199778867/The_New_Story.pdf?token=7W4eiIVtG q8R6%2Fp%2Ftsp%2B84yPNCg%3D_(Accessed 1st October 2015)

Bingham, Harry (2009) *This Little Britain*, London: Fourth Estate

Bragg, Billy (2007) *The Progressive Patriot*, London: Black Swan

Braungart M. and McDonough W. (2008) *Cradle to Cradle: Remaking the Way We Make Things*, London: Jonathan Cape

Brendon, Piers (2007) 'A Moral Audit of the British Empire,' *History Today*, Volume 57, 10 October

Bridle, Susan (2009) 'An Interview with Brian Swimme', *What is Enlightenment?*, Issue 19

British Fashion Council (2012) *The Value of the UK Fashion industry*, Available from: http://www.fashion-manufacturing.com/wp-content/uploads/2012/04/BFC-The-Value-of-The-Fashion-Industry.pdf_(Accessed 29th September 2015)

Bruckner, Pascal (2012) *Tyranny of Guilt: An essay on Western Masochism*, Princeton NJ: Princeton University Press

Capital Punishment UK, *History of judicial hanging in Britain 1735–1964*. Available from: http://www.capitalpunish-mentuk.org/hanging1.html_(Accessed 1st October 2015)

Carey, John (2006) *What Good are the Arts?*, London: Faber and Faber

Chesterton, G. K. (2012) *Orthodoxy*, Simon and Brown

Coates, Chris (2001) *Utopia Britannica*, London: Diggers and Dreamers Publications

Coffee Houses: 'The Internet in a Cup' (2003) *The Economist* 18th December

Colley, Linda (1999) *Britishness in the 21st century*, Millennium lecture, Downing St. London. Available from: http://www.centreforcitizenship.org/docs/britishness.pdf (Accessed 1st October 2015)

—-. (2009) *Britons: Forging the Nation 1707–1837*, New Haven CT: Yale University Press

—-. (2003) *Captives: Britain, Empire and the World 1600–1850*, London: Pimlico

Collier, Paul (2013) 'The New Exodus' *New Statesman* 21st November

Combs, A. (2013) 'Transcend and Include: Ken Wilber's Contribution to Transpersonal Psychology,' in The Wiley-Blackwell Handbook of Transpersonal Psychology (eds H. L. Friedman and G. Hartelius), Chichester: John Wiley

Commonwealth Fund (2014) *Mirror, Mirror on the Wall, 2014 Update: How the U.S. Health Care System Compares Internationally* http://www.commonwealthfund.org/publications/fund reports/2014/jun/mirror-mirror (Accessed 28th September 2015)

Cooper, Robert (2014) 'The EU has provided us with the best Europe we've ever had' *New Statesman* 16th January

Czikszentmihalyi, Mihaly (2013) *Creativity: The Psychology of Discovery and Invention*, New York: Harper Perennial

Davis, L. and Huttenback, R. (2009) *Mammon and the Pursuit of Empire: The Economics of British Imperialism*, Cambridge: Cambridge University Press

Dawkins, Richard (2007) *The God Delusion*, London: Black Swan

De Bono, Edward (2009) *I am Right, You are Wrong*, London: Penguin

De Chardin, Teilhard (1976) *Hymn of the Universe*, New York: Harper Perennial

—-. (2008) *The Phenomenon of Man*, New York: Harper

Perennial

Denby, David (2004) *The New Yorker*, 'Northern Lights: How modern life emerged from eighteenth-century Edinburgh.' 11th October

Department of Transport (2013) *British Social Attitudes Survey*, Available from: https://www.gov.uk/government/statistics/british-social-attitudes-survey-2013_(Accessed 1st October 2015)

Diamond, Jared (2013) *The World Until Yesterday*, London: Penguin

Eagleton, Terry (2009) 'The liberal supremacists,' The Guardian, 25th April

—-. (2008) *The Meaning of Life*, Oxford: Oxford University Press

Elias, Norbert (2000) *The Civilising Process*, Hoboken NJ: Wiley-Blackwell

Emerson, Ralph Waldo (2003) *Nature and Selected Essays*, London: Penguin

Eno, Brian (2009) Synthtopia, *Brian Eno On Genius and "Scenius,"* Available from: http://www.synthtopia.com/content/2009/07/09/brian-eno-on-genius-and-scenius/ (Accessed 28th September 2015)

Ferguson, Niall (2004) *Empire: How Britain Made the Modern World*, London: Penguin

Finaccord (2014) *Global Expatriates: Size, Segmentation and Forecast for the Worldwide Market*. Available from: http://www.finaccord.com/press-release_2014_global-expatriates_-size-segmentation-and-forecast-for-the-worldwide-market.htm (Accessed 28th September 2015)

Gebser, Jean (1986) *The Ever-present Origin*, Athens OH: Ohio University Press

Gladwell, Malcolm (2009) *Outliers:The Story of Success*, London: Penguin

Golley, John (2010) *Jet: Frank Whittle and the Invention of the Jet*

Engine, Datum Publishing

Goodhart, David (2013) *The British Dream,* London: Atlantic books

Gray, John (2007) *Black Mass, Apocalyptic Religion and the Death of Utopia,* London: Allen Lane

—-. (2004) *Heresies: Against Progress and Other Illusions,* London: Granta Books

—-. (2009) 'A Mini Version of the Hapsburg Empire.' In (ed) D'Ancona, M., *Being British: The Search for the Values that Bind the Nation,* Edinburgh: Mainstream pp.115-20

Green, Matthew (2013) *The Lost World of the London Coffeehouse,* London: Idler Books

Heffer, Simon (2013) *High Minds: The Victorians and the Birth of Modern Britain,* London: Random House

Herman, Arthur (2008) *The Idea of Decline in Western History,* New York: Simon and Schuster

Hume David (1778) *The History of England,* 6 volumes, Online Library of Liberty. Available from: http://oll.libertyfund.org /titles/1868_(Accessed 1st October 2015)

Huxley, Julian (1957) *Transhumanism,* London: Chatto & Windus

INSEAD (2014) *The Global Innovation Index: The Human Factor in Innovation.* Available from: http://global-indices.insead.edu/ gii/documents/GII2014report.pdf (Accessed 29th September 2015)

Jaynes, Julian (2000) *The Origin of Consciousness in the Breakdown of the Bicameral Mind,* Boston: Houghton Mifflin

Jefferies, Richard (2002) *The Story of my Heart,* Cambridge: Green Books

John Ruskin (2010) *Selections From the Works of John Ruskin,* Qontro Classic Books

Johnson, Paul (1995) *The Offshore Islanders: A History of the English People,* London: Orion

Johnson, Samuel and Boswell, James (1984) *A Journey to the Western Islands of Scotland and The Journal of a Tour to the*

Hebrides, London: Penguin

Johnson, Steven (2011) *Where Good Ideas Come From*, London: Penguin

Kauffman, Stuart (2008) *Reinventing the Sacred*, New York: Basic Books

Kelly, Kevin (2008) *Scenius, or Communal Genius*, Available from: http://kk.org/thetechnium/scenius-or-comm/ (Accessed 1st October 2015)

King, Mike (2014) *Quakernomics: An Ethical Capitalism*, London: Anthem Press

—-. (2007) *Secularism: The Hidden Origins of Disbelief*, Cambridge: James Clarke

Kingsnorth, Paul (2014) 'It's the End of the World as We Know It . . . and He Feels Fine' *New York Times* 17th April

Koestler, Arthur (1989) *The Act of Creation*, London: Arkana

Lachman, Gary (2003) *A Secret History of Consciousness*, Great Barrington MA: Lindisfarne Books

Legatum Insitute (2011) *Legatum Prosperity Index: An Inquiry into Global Weallth and Wellbeing*, Available from: http://media.prosperity.com/2011/pdf/publications/PI2011_Brochure_Final _Web.pdf (Accessed 30th September 2015)

—-. (2014) *Legatum Prosperity Index*, Available from: http://media.prosperity.com/2014/pdf/publications/PI2014Brochure _WEB.pdf (Accessed 30th September 2015)

'Little England or Great Britain?'(2013) *The Economist* 9th November

Loach, Ken (2013) Dir. *The Spirit of 45*, Dogwoof. Film

Long Now Foundation (1996) *About Long Now*, Available from: http://longnow.org/about/ (Accessed 29th September 2015)

Lowe, Steve and McArthur, Alan (2005) *Is It Just Me or Is Everything Shit?*, New York: Time Warner

MacIntyre, Alasdair (1984) 'Is Patriotism a Virtue?' Lindley lecture, University of Kansas 26th March

Macmillan, Harold (1960) *Harold Macmillan's "Wind of Change"*

Speech. 3rd February. Available from: http://african history.about.com/od/eraindependence/p/wind_of_change2.h tm_(Accessed 30th September 2015)

Malik, Shahid (2008) *"Be proud to be English" says local MP*, 21st January. Available from: http://www.shahidmalikmp.org.uk/ news/press/news.aspx?p=102235 (Accessed 30th September 2015)

Mandler, Peter (2006) *The English National Character,* New Haven CT: Yale University Press

Manuel, F.E and F.P. (1979) *Utopian Thought in the Western World,* Cambridge MA: Harvard University Press

Mark's Musings (2012) *Danny Boyle's Olympic Programme Notes – full text.* Available from: http://www.markgoodge.com/2012 /07/danny-boyles-olympic-programme-notes-full-text/ (Accessed 1st October 2015)

Marr, Andrew (2007) *A History of Modern Britain,* London: Macmillan

Mary Midgley (2011) *The Myths We Live By,* London: Routledge

McIntosh, Steve (2012) *Evolution's Purpose,* New York: SelectBooks

Mesle, C. Robert (2008) *Process-Relational Philosophy: An Introduction to Alfred North Whitehead,* West Conshohocken, PA: Templeton Press

Midgley, Mary (1992) *Science as Salvation: A Modern Myth and Its Meaning,* London: Routledge

Mirandola, Giovanni Pico della (1996) *Oration on the Dignity of Man* Washington DC: Regnery Publishing

Mitchell, David (2013) 'It's Michael O'Leary's biggest PR gaffe – he wants us to like him.' *The Observer,*10th November

More, Thomas (2004) *Utopia,* London: Penguin Classics

Morris, William (1993) *News from Nowhere,* London: Penguin Classics

Morton, Timothy (2009) *Ecology without Nature: Rethinking Environmental Aesthetics,* Cambridge MA: Harvard University

Press

Mukerjee, Madhusree (2011) *Churchill's Secret War*, New York: Basic Books

Neiman, Susan (2009) *Moral Clarity: A Guide for Grown-Up Idealists* London: Bodley Head

Newsinger, John (2006) *The Blood Never Dried: A People's History of the British Empire*, London: Bookmarks

O'Farrell, John (2009) 'A Day of Britishness.' *Being British; The Search for the Values that Bind the Nation*, In (ed.) D'Ancona M, Edinburgh: Mainstream pp.175–77

OECD (2014) *UK should keep foreign aid at commendable 0.7%* Peer review of UK. Available from: http://www.oecd.org/news room/uk-should-keep-foreign-aid-at-commendable-07-level.htm (Accessed 29th September 2015)

Ofsted Report (2011) *History for all: strengths and weaknesses of school history teaching*. Available from: https://www.gov.uk /government/publications/history-for-all-strengthes-and-weaknesses-of-school-history-teaching_(Accessed 1st October 2015)

Orwell, George (1982) *The Lion and the Unicorn: Socialism and the English Genius*, London: Penguin

Paine, Thomas (2010) *Common Sense*, Seaside OR: Watchmaker Publishing

Paxman, Jeremy (2012) *Empire*, London: Viking

—-. (2007) *The English: A Portrait of a People* London: Penguin

Phillips, Trevor (2009) 'Fair play: It's what we're about.' In (ed) D'Ancona, M. *Being British: The Search for the Values that Bind the Nation*, Edinburgh: Mainstream pp. 247–53

Phipps, Carter (2012) *Evolutionaries*, New York: Harper Perennial

Pinker, Steven (2012) *The Better Angels of our Nature*, London: Penguin

Private Life of the Gannets,The (1934) Producer Julian Huxley, BFI. Film

Putney Debates (2012) *The Putney Debates of 1647*. Available from:

http://www.theputneydebates.co.uk/beginners-guide-putney-debates/ (Accessed 30th September 2015)

Ray, Paul and Anderson, Sherry Ruth (2001) *The Cultural Creatives: How 50 Million People are Changing the World*, New York: Three Rivers Press

Ridley, Matt (2011) *The Rational Optimist*, London: Fourth Estate

Rifkin, Jeremy (2004) *The European Dream*, Cambridge: Polity Press

Roemischer, Jessica (2002) 'Interview with Dr Don Beck: The Never-Ending Upward Quest' *What is Enlightenment?* Issue 22, Fall/Winter

Sacks, Jonathan (2009) 'Covenant and the Remaking of a National Identity.' In (ed) D'Ancona, M., *Being British: The Search for the Values that Bind the Nation*, Edinburgh: Mainstream pp.165-73

Sandbrook, Dominic (2012) *Why does the 1970s get painted as such a bad decade?* BBC News Magazine 16th April. Available from: http://www.bbc.co.uk/news/magazine-17703483 (Accessed 1st October 2015)

Sargent, Lyman Tower (2010) *Utopianism: A Very Short Introduction*, Oxford: Oxford University Press

Schama, Simon (2009) *A History of Britain - Volume 1*, London: Bodley Head

—-.(2010) 'My Vision for History in Schools,' *The Guardian*, 9th November

Seldon, Anthony (2010) 'The politics of optimism will be the defining theme of our century' *The Independent* 2nd October

Sigman, Aric (2009) *The Spoilt Generation: Why Restoring Authority Will Make Our Children and Society Happier*, London: Piatkus

Simone Weil (1998) *The Way of Justice as Compassion*, Lanham MD: Rowman & Littlefield

Singh, Manmohan (2005) 'Of Oxford, economics, empire, and freedom,' *The Hindu*, 10th July

Sleutels, Jan (2013) 'The Flintstone Fallacy,' *Dialogue and*

Universalism, No. 1

Smith, A.W. (2013) 'Hollande, Cameron and how not to be a leader,' *The Independent*, 13th March

Soutphommasane, Tim (2009) *Reclaiming Patriotism*, Cambridge: Cambridge University Press

Steffen, Alex (2009) *Bright Green, Light Green, Dark Green, Gray: The New Environmental Spectrum*, Worldchanging. Available from: http://www.worldchanging.com/archives/009499.html (Accessed 1st October 2015)

Stuart, Moira (2007) *In Search of Wilberforce*, BBC TV. Film

Tharoor, Shashi, *Verbatim Transcript of Dr. Shashi Tharoor's Speech at the Oxford Union Debate*. Available from: http://www.sha shitharoor.in/speeches-details.php?id=335 (Accessed 29th September 2015)

Tombs, Richard (2014) *The English and their History*, London: Allen Lane

Tomkins, Stephen (2010) *The Clapham Sect*, Oxford: Lion Hudson

Toynbee, Arnold (1934–61) *A Study of History*, Vol. 4 (1948), part B, Oxford: Oxford University Press

UCL Centre for Research and Analysis of Migration (2014) *Economic impact of UK immigration from the European Union: new evidence*. Available from: https://www.ucl.ac.uk/news/news-articles/1114/051114-economic-impact-EU-immigration# sthash.x6Riqma6.dpuf_(Accessed 30th September 2015)

Whitehead, Alfred North (1967) *Adventures of Ideas*, New York: Free Press

—-. (1979) *Process and Reality* New York: Free Press

Wilberforce, William (1789) *Wilberforce's Abolition Speech text*, My Learning, Available from: http://www.mylearning.org/lear ning/williamwilberforce/wilberforces%20Speech.pdf (Accessed 28th September 2015)

Williams, Rowan (2009) 'The Scepter'd Isle' In (ed) D'Ancona, M., *Being British: The Search for the Values that Bind the Nation*, Edinburgh: Mainstream pp. 145-53

Wollstonecraft, Mary (2010) *A Vindication of the Rights of Women*, CreateSpace Independent Publishing

Wordsworth, William and Coleridge, Samuel (2006) *Lyrical Ballads*, London: Penguin

World Values Survey (2014) *Findings and Insights*. Available from: http://www.worldvaluessurvey.org/WVSContents.jsp (Accessed 30th September 2015)

Zephaniah, Benjamin (2003), 'Me? I thought, OBE me? Up yours, I thought.' *The Guardian* 27th November

Zinn, Howard (2005) *A People's History of the United States*, New York: Harper Perennial

Chronos Books is a historical non-fiction imprint. Chronos publishes real history for real people; bringing to life historical people, places and events in an imaginative, easy-to-digest and accessible way. We want writers of historical books, from ancient times to the Second World War, that will add to our understanding of people and events rather than being a dry textbook; history that passes on its stories to a generation of new readers.